REVIEWS OF THE DEAD

25 ZOMBIE MOVIES TO DIE FOR

OTHER LIVING DEAD PRESS BOOKS

MONSTER PARTY * BOOK OF HORROR VOL. 2
MISADVENTURES OF THE DEAD
THE TURNING: A STORY OF THE LIVING DEAD
THE DEAD OF SPACE BOOK 1 AND 2
PLAYING GOD: A ZOMBIE NOVEL * THE JUNKYARD
PLANET OF THE DEAD * THE HAUNTED THEATRE
ZOMBIES IN OUR HOMETOWN
NIGHT OF THE WOLF: A WEREWOLF ANTHOLOGY
JUST BEFORE NIGHT: A ZOMBIE ANTHOLOGY
THE BOOK OF HORROR* KNIGHT SYNDROME
THE WAR AGAINST THEM: A ZOMBIE NOVEL
CHILDREN OF THE VOID * DARK DREAMS
BLOOD RAGE & DEAD RAGE (BOOK 1& 2 OF THE RAGE VIRUS SERIES)
DEAD MOURNING: A ZOMBIE HORROR STORY
BOOK OF THE DEAD: A ZOMBIE ANTHOLOGY VOLUME 1-6
LOVE IS DEAD: A ZOMBIE ANTHOLOGY
ETERNAL NIGHT: A VAMPIRE ANTHOLOGY
END OF DAYS: AN APOCALYPTIC ANTHOLOGY VOLUME 1-5
DEAD HOUSE: A ZOMBIE GHOST STORY
THE ZOMBIE IN THE BASEMENT (FOR ALL AGES)
THE LAZARUS CULTURE: A ZOMBIE NOVEL
DEAD WORLDS: UNDEAD STORIES VOLUMES 1-7
FAMILY OF THE DEAD, REVOLUTION OF THE DEAD
RANDY AND WALTER: PORTRAIT OF TWO KILLERS
KINGDOM OF THE DEAD * DEAD HISTORY
THE MONSTER UNDER THE BED * DEAD THINGS
DEAD TALES: SHORT STORIES TO DIE FOR
ROAD KILL: A ZOMBIE TALE * DEADFREEZE * DEADFALL
SOUL EATER * THE DARK * RISE OF THE DEAD
DEAD END: A ZOMBIE NOVEL * VISIONS OF THE DEAD
THE CHRONICLES OF JACK PRIMUS
INSIDE THE PERIMETER: SCAVENGERS OF THE DEAD
BOOK OF CANNIBALS VOLUME 2
CHRISTMAS IS DEAD…AGAIN
EMAILS OF THE DEAD
ZOMBIES AND POWER TOOLS
THE BABYLONIAN CURSE
THE DEADWATER SERIES
DEADWATER
DEADWATER: Expanded Edition
DEADRAIN * DEADCITY * DEADWAVE * DEAD HARVEST
DEAD UNION * DEAD VALLEY * DEAD TOWN
DEAD GRAVE
DEAD SALVATION
DEAD ARMY (Book 10) coming in 2011

REVIEWS OF THE DEAD

25 ZOMBIE MOVIES TO DIE FOR

TONY SCHAAB
ANTHONY GIANGREGORIO

REVIEWS OF THE DEAD: 25 ZOMBIE MOVIES TO DIE FOR
Copyright © 2011 Tony Schaab, Anthony Giangregorio and Living Dead Press

All photos and motion pictures are copyright of their respective production companies. No infringement is intended; all images are used for review purposes only.

ISBN Softcover ISBN 13: 978-1-935458-96-8 ISBN 10: 1-935458-96-5

All rights reserved. No part of this book may be reproduced or transmitted in any form or by any means, electronic or mechanical, including photocopying, recording, or by any information storage and retrieval system, without permission in writing from the copyright owner.
This is a work of fiction. Names, characters, places and incidents either are the product of the author's imagination or are used fictitiously, and any resemblance to any actual persons, living or dead, events, or locales is entirely coincidental. This book was printed in the United States of America.

For more info on obtaining additional copies of this book, contact:
www.livingdeadpress.com

Table of Contents

FOREWORD	1
28 DAYS LATER	5
28 WEEKS LATER	13
THE BEYOND	21
CEMETERY MAN (DELLAMORTE DELLAMORE)	29
CITY OF THE LIVING DEAD	38
DAWN OF THE DEAD	46
DAY OF THE DEAD	58
DEAD ALIVE (BRAIN DEAD)	67
DEAD AND BREAKFAST	76
DIARY OF THE DEAD	83
FIDO	93
HELL OF THE LIVING DEAD	101
LAND OF THE DEAD	109
THE LIVING DEAD AT THE MANCHESTER MORGUE	117
NIGHT OF THE LIVING DEAD (1968)	125
PLANET TERROR	134
RE-ANIMATOR	143
RESIDENT EVIL	151
RETURN OF THE LIVING DEAD	158
SHAUN OF THE DEAD	166
SLITHER	175
STACY	183
SURVIVAL OF THE DEAD	190
ZOMBIE	198
ZOMBIELAND	206
ABOUT THE WRITERS	215

EDITOR'S NOTE

Before each review, there are the words **TAKE ONE** or **TAKE TWO**, followed by initials. This is the way this book identifies each reviewer.

T.S: Tony Schaab
A.G: Anthony Giangregorio

FOREWORD

TAKE ONE: TONY SCHAAB

When I first agreed to take on this project, I had no idea how much hard work could actually go into watching movies.

Now, don't get me wrong; writing this book has been a blast, and I sincerely hope you will enjoy reading it as much as I enjoyed writing it. But believe me when I say that a lot more effort went into this volume's creation than me simply sitting on the couch in front of the TV with a notebook and a glass of my trusty Mountain Dew. I analyzed, I researched, I dug deep for detailed information, I reached out to many of the films' cast and crew members in an attempt to bring together the best possible mix of information for you, my dear reader.

And part of the process was, of course, watching the actual films, which I did multiple times, to ensure I could catch anything and everything noteworthy. These were the viewings I did alone, because nobody wants to watch a movie with a guy who pauses the DVD every thirty seconds to furiously jot down a thought or an idea. So, sometimes, yes: I sat on the couch in front of the TV with a glass of my trusty Mountain Dew. But I used a netbook instead of a notebook, for the record.

For all the hours that went it to making this book a reality, I did it all with a smile on my face, as not only is viewing these films a passion of mine, but so is sharing with other people the important and exciting information about these stories that I uncovered. Readers who may have read any reviews I have written for my review site, TheGOREScore.com and its accompanying book series, will no doubt be familiar with my borderline-obsessive penchant for proudly displaying my passion and wearing my reviewing-heart on my sleeve. I go all-out for every item I review, be it good or not-so-good. I truly don't know how to do this type of thing halfway, it's just not in me to do so.

Way back when this project was first taking shape, the tremendously talented Anthony Giangregorio and I sat down and created a list of what we believed to be some of the top movies in the zombie genre. Now, it's important to note that I said, "*Some* of the top movies." Let me be perfectly clear with this next sentence. *The list of movies we chose to review is in no way a definitive list of the best movies in the genre that ever were, are, or will be.* No one can create an *absolute* grouping of the "best movies," because films mean different things to different people, and the ability for each viewer to have their own opinion is what makes the open discussion about these stories so wonderful.

I even went so far as to say that one of these 25 films we reviewed is "so bad it's good" (I won't spoil it for you, I'll let you read through the book and discover which one it is). I don't expect everyone to agree with everything I say within these pages, but I simply hope you can see merit of the ideas presented, and maybe my words will help you see or think about something in a new light.

We picked the movies on our list for a variety of reasons. Perhaps it was the movie's contribution to the genre at the time of its release. Perhaps it was the unique back story behind the making of the movie. Perhaps it was the singular insight into another culture the film's story gave us. Perhaps it was because the experience of watching the film is such a one-of-a-kind event. Perhaps it was just because the film was so damn entertaining. Whatever the reason, these movies are here, written about in loving detail so you might discover a hidden gem or enjoy reconnecting with an old favorite.

I certainly didn't go through this endeavor alone, and there are a few people that I need to thank for their help in making this book a reality. First and foremost is my favorite undead author and partner in crime on this project, Anthony Giangregorio. Not only would this book not exist without him, he has been a tremendous inspiration and mentor to me since the day I decided to start a professional writing career. "Mr. G" was the editor of the anthology in which my first printed work appeared (Living Dead Press' "End of Days, Vol. 2," for the record), and I can vividly recall his phone call to me to talk about the project. The passion and excitement in his voice, coupled with the fact that he preferred the personal touch of talking on the phone versus shooting e-mails back and forth, made me immediately realize he was a one-of-a-kind individual—and one hell of a writer.

I also want to thank my ladies, my wife Bryrony and my daughter Amelia. Bryrony put up with many a night of my retreating to the Zombatorium (also known as our basement) after dinner, where I remained entrenched for hours, watching these films and furiously writing various drafts of the finished content you hold in your hands. I would come crawling into bed long after she had gone to sleep, and she was always gracious enough to never lock me out of the bedroom or "accidentally" sleep-smack me too much. She was mostly understanding (mostly...), and I'm very appreciative. I also thank Amelia for being such a good baby and routinely sleeping through the entire night, so I could focus hard on this project. I wrote my portions of this book when she was between six and eleven months old, so it was quite a feat for the baby monitor to stay so routinely quiet. I look forward to the decade-and-a-half from now when I may actually feel comfortable for her to read some of my work.

Not that she couldn't read my fiction and non-fiction writing as she is growing up, but I don't necessarily want to force her to, if that makes sense. Zombie movies, and the people who love them, tend to have an odd stigma assigned from the general public: the common feeling of those who "don't get it" is that there's something inherently subversive about horror fans, that we're all dark and brooding with dirty, deranged, sick little minds. I obviously don't think that's true, but who am I to argue with public opinion, right?

If that's what the masses think, then I guess that makes writing this book a dirty job, and I'm damn sure glad I was the one who got to do it.

Tony Schaab

TAKE 2: ANTHONY GIANGREGORIO

Welcome to Reviews of the Dead, where myself and my co-author, review twenty-five zombie movies that we feel are worth the time to view.

All I will say is this: As far as my reviews go, if you're looking for something new on these films or hoping for some tidbit of information you didn't know if you're already a big fan, then you're in the wrong place. My reviews are just a way for me to share what zombie movies I love, and if you're like me, then you can enjoy them just a little more by seeing them through my eyes.

There are no reviews for zombie movies I disliked here, after all, there's enough negativity in the world as it is, I'd rather not add to it (though I may criticize a little, which is our nature as human beings, is it not?). Instead, every movie listed in this book is of zombie movies I've enjoyed for one reason or another. Whether it has a place in my heart because it's from my youth, or just blew me away with action or gore, it will be in this book.

Many of these movies are what helped me shape my ideas when I first began writing, and in fact, I was actually watching a zombie movie at the

FOREWORD

time I first had my idea for the Deadwater series and I paused the movie, sat down, and wrote the first chapter to *Deadwater (Book 1)*.

To me, every zombie movie I watched was what brought me one step closer to actually wanting to write about them.

And I as a fan, have always enjoyed reading about the movies I love, getting other people's point of views on a film. When I read about *Dawn of the Dead* or *28 Days Later*, it brings me closer to the genre I love so much.

Which brings us to this book and its content.

I will be the first to admit I am no expert on movies or books; I'm just a guy who knows what he likes. Give me great characters I can care about, gore, action, maybe some comedy in the right place, and I'll be a happy viewer.

So please don't get all bent out of shape if you don't agree with me and I promise not to get to upset if I don't agree with you. Just read along and enjoy, and hopefully, by delving into my mind on how I see these films, you can appreciate them a little more or at least reminisce about certain parts that were particularly gory or funny to you.

Zombie movies aren't just about gore and action. They are also about taking down our civilization that has become so corrupt, fragile and unstable with each passing day. Not that I long for the apocalypse, far from it, but at the same time it would be nice if a man could become successful simply because of the brains in his head, the strength in his hands, and the will in his heart.

Sure it can still happen nowadays, that a man can become a success, but not as much as years ago, before the internet and cable television.

The days of a man arriving in the U.S. with a dollar and a dream are long gone, or has morphed into something unrecognizable.

A world of zombies shatters all that to dust, where the rule of survival is the only one that matters, and a full stomach makes you a winner each day.

So come along for the ride and let me tell you about my favorite zombie movies, and I hope, by the end, if by chance you either have seen one or two or didn't like it before, you might give it one more chance by seeing it through my eyes.

Anthony Giangregorio

28 DAYS LATER

YEAR: 2002
COUNTRY: UK/FRANCE/USA
RUNNING TIME: 113 minutes
WRITER: Alex Garland
DIRECTOR: Danny Boyle
PRODUCER: Andrew MacDonald
MUSIC: John Murphy
DIRECTOR OF PHOTOGRAPHY: Anthony Dod Mantle
MAKE-UP DESIGNER: Sallie Jaye
PRODUCTION DESIGNER: Mark Tildesley
COSTUME DESIGNER: Rachael Fleming
CAST: Cillian Murphy (Jim), Naomie Harris (Selena), Megan Burns (Hannah), Brendan Gleeson (Frank), Christopher Eccleston (Major Henry West)

TAKE ONE: T.S.

COMMENTARY

You might call "28 Days Later" the "perfect storm."

The film had three major elements come together at exactly the right time to create its incredibly impressive movie-watching experience. First, it was released in 2003, when the "zombie craze" was just starting to get going full-throttle. Secondly, it was radically different from most zombie movies, so much so that some fans actually refuse to acknowledge it as a "zombie movie" (more on this below). Finally, it was one of the first widely-known movies directed by the amazingly-talented Danny Boyle, who had previously helmed unique films like "Trainspotting" and The Beach," and who would go on to spend the next half-decade making critically acclaimed films like "Sunshine," "Slumdog Millionaire," and "127 Hours" (the latter two earning multiple Oscar, Golden Globe, and BAFTA nominations and wins).

Boyle is a consummate filmmaker, and his talent clearly shines through on "28 Days Later" and is a key reason for the film's success. Taking a story from writer Alex Garland, Boyle brought the film to life using effective imagery and filming techniques, along with maximizing the performances from a relatively unknown cast. The actors and actresses were unknown, but purposefully so, as Boyle and the creative team cast mostly-unfamiliar faces with the intent of adding to the realism and believability factors of the film.

The opening of the story draws similarities to the opening of "The Walking Dead" (both the comic book series and the television series), but "28 Days Later" did it first, beating the comics to the punch by over two years (the movie was in production and filming in early 2001, and the first issue of the comic book wasn't released until mid-2003). After a brief introductory scene, the film opens with the main character, Jim, waking up from a coma in a hospital.

He's shocked and confused to discover that London has been evacuated, and he eventually discovers that the reason is the outbreak of the Rage Virus, a fast-acting disease that turns people violently insane. The story quickly becomes a tale of survival for Jim and the few remaining non-afflicted people he encounters. But can they all work together before their differences—or the Infected—tear them apart?

It's this key bit of information, that the "creatures" are actually living humans infected with a virus rather than reanimated dead folks, which has some fans up in arms about whether the film should truly be considered a zombie film. "Purists" would argue that if the creature featured in the story isn't a dead human being that has come back to life, then it's not a zombie movie. Quite frankly, I couldn't disagree more.

I wrote an entire section about this very question in my book "The G.O.R.E. Score, Vol. 1," and in that book I referenced my answer to a similar question I was asked when I was enlisted to be on a panel of "zombie experts." My response then, which holds true to my opinions today, is as follows (abbreviated here): "Just like there are different types of vampires, werewolves, and a host of other monsters, it is perfectly acceptable to have variations on the characteristics of zombies.

I think lots of people like to hold on to traditions, and as a result, the 'classic' slow zombies get a lot of love from a nostalgic viewpoint. But as they say, 'variety is the spice of life,' and I think that phrase should apply to death and zombies as well; fast or slow, intelligent or dumb, dead or alive, all types of zombie-like creatures are still zombies, and should be enjoyed as such."

But I digress; back to talking about what makes "28 Days Later" a great film. Much like the plot, production on the movie itself was also quite the adventure. The film quickly became iconic for its scenes depicting famous and recognizable places in London appearing eerily empty. Westminster Bridge with Big Ben and the House of Parliament in the background…Piccadilly Circus and the giant Eye of London…the iconic Oxford Street…all shown desolate and seemingly abandoned as Jim wanders the city in his initial state of confusion. In order to get these shots of the normally-busy locations, the film crew was given permission to close off these areas, but only for mere *minutes* at a time.

The shots were normally done very early in the morning, so as to minimize the disruption to the citizens who normally frequented these areas. The film was also shot entirely on digital video cameras, which not only allowed the crew to be extremely more maneuverable and light-packing, but also gave a very "gritty" and realistic visual feel to the movie.

There were also scenes on major streets that had to be shot quickly, including a wide shot of the M1 motorway completely devoid of traffic. For this shot, multiple police cars acted as a "mobile roadblock," slowing traffic down to the point where large stretches of the highway were completely empty for a few minutes and were able to be filmed.

Another scene, on a city street, sees Jim walk by an overturned double-decker bus, and this part of the film was also shot incredibly quickly: the crew took an actively-in-use bus, put it on its side, filmed the scene, and put the bus back upright, all within twenty minutes!

Upon release, the film became both a critical and financial success. Made on a budget of approximately £5 million ($8 million), the movie took in almost £6.1 million ($10 million) in the United Kingdom alone. It became a surprise hit in the United States, showing on only 1,500 screens nationwide but making an impressive $45 million.

Its worldwide gross ended up over $82 million. Additionally, the film has been recognized with honors and awards, including being awarded spot #100 on *Bravo's* "100 Scariest Movie Moments" (one of six films reviewed in this book to be included on the list). The film has also won awards from various institutions for Best Horror Film, Best British Film, Best Director, Best Breakthrough Performance, and Best Cinematographer.

"28 Days Later" has spawned one sequel, "28 Weeks Later" (also reviewed in this book), and from 2007 to 2010 Boyle mentioned in multiple interviews that he was interested in making a third film, "28 Months Later," possibly even directing it himself.

According to the Internet Movie Database, this movie is scheduled to be released in 2013, but as we all know, things can change on in-production projects in a heartbeat, so I recommend you don't hold your breath until you hear something more concrete.

PLAY-BY-PLAY

The movie features non-existent opening credits, opting instead for a black screen with a small "28 days later..." inscription. Before this transition, we see an opening scene at an animal testing laboratory, only it's clear that they aren't doing something as simple as putting cosmetics on bunny rabbits here. The presence and interaction with the primates is not only intense and kicks off a high level of action right away, it's also a very unique approach to the genesis of how people become infected.

After the brief title screen, a "cold open" presents a very naked Jim waking up in a hospital bed–cover your eyes if you're shy! He doesn't waste any time getting up and out of the building, trying to figure out exactly what's going on. The empty London he encounters is incredibly ominous, and the sequence is effective in letting the viewer feel as disoriented and confused as Jim does.

There's a slight suspension of disbelief required here, to allow for the fact that in all of Jim's wandering around, not a single Infected person is attracted by his hollering out "Hello?!" or his accidentally setting off a car alarm. But make no mistake, the Infected do find him quickly, and the scene where Jim stumbles across the diseased creatures in the church is utterly creepy. He manages to escape, with the assistance of a few helpful survivors, and their recap of the situation for Jim also serves to abruptly fill in the viewer as well.

Boyle and Garland combine to make a masterful story-telling team, and the evidence is littered throughout the strong dialogue and excellent camerawork. Both Mark's recounting of his family's demise and the ensuing scene where Jim finds his parents dead via suicide are painfully touching. Jim's moment is especially poignant, with his parents holding a picture of him with a handwritten note on the back: "Don't wake up."

Selena is brutal and unrelenting when she kills the just-Infected Mark, but that's how you have to be in order to survive in this type of world– remorse, emotion, or hesitation will end up killing you. It's scenes and characters like this that should be shown more in zombie movies.

Throughout the middle portion of the film, where Jim and Selena travel with Frank and his daughter Hannah, the audience is given the opportunity to connect with the characters on a deeper level. The quartet tries to find moments of brevity along their journey, and this is crucial to their sanity. Ultimately, Frank meets an unfortunate end, but the scene at the military blockade proves that if literally one drop of blood gets in you, it's over for you, and it's all over quickly.

Dr. Who sighting! Christoper Eccleston, who played the eccentric time-traveling alien in the first season of the BBC's reboot of the series, stars as Major West, the leader of the women-starved military group. The squad, though obviously not as well-manned as they once were, still initially seem great to Jim, Selena, and Hannah, and the squad make the situation appear too good to be true. And, of course, it is, as things take a turn for the deranged once West reveals that he's kept the men from going AWOL because he "promised them girls."

An intense finale reveals that Jim turns out to be quite resourceful in fighting both the Infected and the military men; a product of his new environment, perhaps? There are immediate parallels to some of the more "classic" zombie films, most notably "Night of the Living Dead," in that the deranged creatures don't end up being the only enemy the protagonists have to fight. The survivors' inability to work together leads to their downfall, except this time a lucky few actually do manage to escape the situation.

The film concludes on a very open-ended note, but one that indicates the state of the Infected as they appear to be largely incapacitated as they starve to death. It's a positive note indicating the possible end of the Infected threat, but as any of us who have seen the sequel know, that didn't quite work out!

One final interesting note for owners of the DVD and/or Blu-Ray of "28 Days Later:" the discs contain three alternate endings (four on the Blu-Ray), all ending with Jim dead—did Boyle have it out for this character or what? The most intriguing look at these "what-if" scenarios is easily the "Radical Alternate Ending," a twelve minute storyboard that deletes the military group from the plot entirely and takes the story in a very different direction. If you own a physical copy of the movie and haven't seen these special features yet, I highly recommend you take some time to check them out.

TAKE TWO: A.G.

Jim, a bicycle messenger, comes out of a coma 28 days after a viral outbreak has ravaged London and its surrounding cities.

The plague has caused an evacuation and Jim leaves the hospital to find the city deserted, only trash and abandoned cars filling the streets.

The infection is one of pure rage, changing the population of the UK into bloodthirsty murderers with only one thing on their mind. Can you guess what that is?

Jim meets up with Selena and a father and daughter who stayed in the city for some unknown reason. The four of them leave the city, after hearing a radio message of a battalion of soldiers that say they have the cure for the infection.

The infected themselves are truly horrifying. With blood red eyes and totally psychotic, they can barely reason and think nothing of their own safety. They exist only to kill those that aren't like them and to see a horde of them barreling down on you should be enough to make even the bravest man cringe.

The plague is spread by blood contact. Get it in your mouth, an open cut or eyes, and within seconds the person you once were is gone, replaced by a killing machine. In essence you become a zombie, which is why the movie is in this book.

Though not technically dead, what once made a person is entirely wiped clean, leaving nothing behind but pure rage and instinct. Welcome to the world of fast zombies.

Now this isn't anything new. Twenty years earlier, the Italian movie *Nightmare City* introduced fast zombies for the first time but with *28 Days Later,* they were finally here to stay.

The only hope the island of Britain has is that the infected will eventually die off from starvation, but though the rest of the world is probably fine, the soldiers that our group of survivors come across feel there is no more reason to live unless they can get laid.

Where the first part of the movie is apocalyptic and follows the plot of any good end of the world film, the third act falters with the stereotypical rapist soldiers.

Now, don't get me wrong, though many won't admit it, if the average man knew he could rape and kill who he wanted with no repercussions, I wonder just how many would remain "civilized." Only consequences prevents the average citizen from doing what they want, when they want.

But these soldiers have sex on the mind to the point it gets them killed.

When Jim escapes the soldiers when they want to dispose of him so the men can have the women, Jim sneaks back and releases a captured infected soldier, who is being studied to see how long it takes the infected to die of starvation.

Now, normally, if the infected man escaped and was killing and then infecting your fellow soldiers, the last thing on your mind would be about getting laid, but despite this, at least two solders are more worried about the women getting away then about the infected man running through the mansion they've made their base.

As the soldiers are fighting for their lives, the women are herded up to a bedroom, where Jim is now waiting, as he is using the escaped infected solider as a distraction.

But despite the unrealistic last half, it's still done well enough that these things can be overlooked. And besides, if everyone in a movie got along and wanted to help one another, then the movie would be pretty damn boring. So the same things I'm commenting on as flaws, are also what makes the action, drama and horror happen in the last act of the film.

But despite the flaws, this movie has become one of my favorites in the zombie genre. The atmosphere of a deserted London is done exceptionally well and there are moments that will get your blood boiling. The acting is excellent and the musical score haunting, making this a great thrill ride of zombie fun.

If by some odd chance you have never seen this movie, then stop reading right now and go buy it, pop it in on a dark night, and get ready for one hell of a ride.

28 WEEKS LATER

YEAR: 2007
COUNTRY: UK/Spain
RUNNING TIME: 101 minutes
WRITERS: Rowan Joffe, Juan Carlos Fresnadillo, E. L. Lavigne, Jesus Olmo
DIRECTOR: Juan Carlos Fresnadillo
PRODUCERS: Enrique López-Lavigne, Andrew Macdonald, Allon Reich, Danny Boyle, Alex Garland, Bernard Bellew
EDITING BY: Chris Gill
MUSIC: John Murphy
DISTRIBUTED BY: 20th Century Fox
CINEMATOGRAPHY: Enrique Chediak
CAST: Catherine McCormack (Alice Harris), Robert Carlyle (Don Harris), Amanda Walker (Sally), Shahid Ahmed (Jacob), Garfield Morgan (Geoff), Emily Beecham (Karen), Beans Balawi (Boy in cottage), Jeremy Renner (Doyle), Harold Perrineau (Flynn), Rose Byrne (Scarlet Ross), Imogen Poots (Tammy Harris),
Mackintosh Muggleton (Andy Harris), Meghan Popiel (DLR soldier), Idris Elba (Stone)

TAKE ONE: T.S.

COMMENTARY

Based on the immediate commercial and critical success of "28 Days Later," a sequel was a no-brainer for the Powers-That-Be. With this, though, came a high level of "entertainment danger." So many production companies rush sequel films into production that they lose sight of what made the original film such a success to begin with: whether it was a great plot and storyline, a unique idea, amazing effects, or a combination of factors, much of the attention to detail can easily get lost in the shuffle when a sequel is quickly pumped out in a hurried attempt to cash in on the success of the original.

Fortunately for zombie movie lovers, this was not the case with "28 Weeks Later." While the sequel does feature an entirely new creative team—four different writers are given story credit, one of whom is the film's director, Juan Carlos Fresnadillo, the writer/director team from the original movie, Alex Garland and Danny Boyle, return as producers. This is key, because it helped the filmmakers preserve not only the continuity but the feel of the first film. The end result was a carefully-crafted film with a storyline that not only builds off of the first film, but finds its own unique identity as it adds to the overall lore of the tale. It's an incredibly satisfying film-watching experience, and I wish more sequel-makers would have worked as hard as the "28 Weeks Later" team did to make sure they get it right.

As indicated by the title, the movie picks up seven months after the Rage Virus was first unleashed. The Infected have all died of starvation, and an American-led NATO force has swept the country and deemed it safe for repopulation. Civilians begin to be brought back into the country, but wouldn't you know it, something goes wrong and the Rage Virus rages on. When some of the soldiers discover that a young boy may hold the key to curing the infection, they make it their priority to help him survive not only the attack by the infected, but also the military-mandated citywide "cleansing" in the form of total destruction.

Much like its predecessor, "28 Weeks Later" was an above-average success in both the financial and analytic aspects. The film's budget was $15 million, almost double the budget given to "28 Days Later." It made almost $10 million on its opening weekend in the United States, making an impressive second-place showing at the box office behind cinematic juggernaut "Spider-Man 3." The film went on to gross over $28 million during its American theatrical run, and it's worldwide gross came in at over $64 million. In addition, the movie has garnered over $24 million in home video sales, making it a very profitable motion-picture successor.

An aggressive marketing and promotion campaign may be partly to thank for the film's success. In an age where marketing tactics have become so routine and ritualized that a certain protocol and standard is almost expected, the team for "28 Weeks Later," backed by distributor 20th Century Fox, went above and beyond with a campaign that bordered on the entertainment version of guerrilla warfare.

28 days before the United Kingdom release of the film into theaters, a huge biohazard warning sign was projected against the White cliffs of Dover, the southeastern-most shore of England that faces France and the rest of Europe. The gargantuan sign showed the international biological hazard symbol accompanied by text proclaiming that Britain was "Contaminated, keep out!" (Do an internet image search for "White Cliffs of Dover 28 Weeks Later" if you'd like to see images of the display, it's really quite impressive.) A few months before the movie hit theaters, Fox Atomic

Comics published a graphic novel entitled "28 Days Later: The Aftermath." It featured a story that helped connect the two movies together.

Sounds like a pretty cool advertising campaign, right? But wait—there's more! Removable graffiti was sprayed at various locations in and around London that referenced "contamination" and featured the website address "ragevirus.com." The only problem with this ploy, however, is that the advertising agency forgot to register the actual website address! It was quickly snatched up by some random, entrepreneurial person, and the agency had to pay much more to get the domain name back. Finally, a few months before the movie opened, the entertainment site Bloody Disgusting held an officially-sanctioned film tie-in contest. The winner attained a "District 1 Welcome Pack," the repatriating kit given to returning Brits in the film, complete with an actual ID card and a copy of the *Evening Standard* newspaper with an evacuation headline, both of which were used in the actual film. Stunts and promotions like these easily helped build advance buzz for the film, more so than any "traditional" marketing campaign ever could have.

Of course, we can't talk about either of these films without bringing up the natural question of the possibility of the third movie in the series. In the entry for "28 Days Later," I gave you some of Boyle's thoughts on the matter, so I will leave you here with recent thoughts (recent as of this writing, anyhow) from Garland, whom in a late-2010 interview with *Worst Previews* said the following when asked about the status of a third film: "I'll answer that completely honestly. When we made '28 Days Later,' the rights were frozen between a group of people who are no longer talking to each other. And so, the [third] film is never going to happen unless those people start talking to each other again."

Let's hope they all come to their senses and get real chatty real quick.

PLAY-BY-PLAY

The same grainy-look, erratic-style camerawork from "28 Days Later" appears to be utilized here as well, indicating that at least parts of this movie were filmed with the same digital-style cameras. It's still an effective tool, as the opening scene that seems fairly quiet and relaxed, turns terrible very quickly. Taking place concurrent with the events in the first film, we are treated to an insanely intense opening sequence here, with impressive camerawork and cinematography.

During this initial attack, one of the Infected bites the girl's arm—did they do that in the first film? I don't recall them biting, per se, just attacking "normal" people with an extreme amount of rage. Perhaps an emphasis was put on their biting in an attempt to make them seem even more zombie-like?

Don makes a difficult decision to leave his wife, and is probably seen by many viewers as a bad person. In all honesty, though, who's to say you or I wouldn't do the same in that situation? When push comes to shove, you've got to look out for yourself first…right? It's an interesting debate.

When we first meet the large-scale military operation, we're told that the Isle of Dogs is the only clear zone in London at this point. For those of you not intimately familiar with the nuances of the town's geography, the Isle of Dogs is a business and civic area in the east-central part of London, so named because the chunk of land is surrounded on three sides by a particularly large meander of the Thames River. Once Don is reconnected with his kids in the safety of the Isle, he tells them the tale of their mother's supposed demise, even going so far as to say, "I tried to go back for her." Not true! The important question is: did he lie in order to spare their feelings…or his own?

The kids break the rules by leaving the island to go back to their house, but once they're home they find more than they ever bargained for. Mom's in the attic, and she's alive! How did she survive so long? There is clearly something in her genetics that's the key to immunity, even though she's a carrier of the disease as well. Astute viewers will quickly realize that the two-shaded eye thing is a key, since both Alice and Andy share the feature.

Soon Alice is transported to the safety of the Isle of Dogs, where Don finds her during a moment she's been left alone. When she kisses Don, do you think she knows she's infecting him, possibly as revenge for leaving her alone to die? Probably not, but still…it's something to think about.

So, Don gets infected, the domino effect begins, and shit quickly hits the absolute fan. When the turnaround time from infection to Infected is less than twenty seconds, the odds turn in the virus' favor rather quickly. Once the Infected start mingling with and killing the civilians on the street, there is so much confusion that the military's snipers can't differentiate who is infected from the chaotic masses. So the order comes down to shoot anyone and everyone, and even with all the voracious creatures running wild, this singular moment is one of the most chilling in the entire film.

The action really starts to flow when Scarlet and Doyle work with the kids to help escape the danger zone before they're all killed by the military's mass fire bombings. It's a twisty-turny tale of survival , punctuated by attacks from the Infected seemingly led by a very persistent Infected Dad.

The film ends on a short scene that takes place "28 Days Later," insinuating that the virus has made it to mainland Europe. So, "28 Weeks Later" ends with a perfect setup for a sequel…now, if we can only get one made!

TAKE TWO: A.G.

As the title proclaims, we pick up 28 weeks in from the first movie which takes place 28 days after a viral infection has ravaged London.

The second installment in the franchise is more polished with actors that may not be blockbuster stars, but should be recognized for their accomplishments in Hollywood films.

The movie starts rather slowly, with a group of survivors having a meal in their barricaded home. But that solitude is quickly shattered when a small boy bangs on the door, begging to be let in. He's led the infected right to the cottage and like a cannon going off, we the viewer are blasted with violence as the survivors are attacked and killed one by one.

Only Don manages to escape. He runs for his life while his wife is being killed and though some may call him a coward, if he had stayed, he too, would have been killed or worse, become infected.

Flash forward to weeks later. The U.S. has taken control of London and is slowly allowing civilians back in. As far as they're concerned, the infection died out months ago when the last infected person died of starvation.

But we soon find out that Don's wife wasn't killed and in fact, she's carrying the virus in her blood. A carrier but not one of the infected, she's taken on the role of Typhoid Mary.

When Don goes to see her in quarantine, he kisses her, their saliva mixing. Seconds later he's infected, and after brutally killing his wife, he goes out into the city to infect more and more until a full-fledged outbreak is once again ravaging London.

Not only does this movie blow me away with the violence and blood thrown at the viewer, but the emotional response never seems to not "infect me," if you'll suffer my pun.

As you watch the film, ask yourself, "What would I do in this situation?" And in doing so, it becomes one of the most disturbing zombie films I have ever seen. And throughout the movie there is a familial tie. Don's two children, on the run and trying to survive, come across him multiple times, and right to the end of the move this familial tie is there.

When the outbreak begins again, the U.S. military is ruthless, cutting down infected and survivors alike. The cold-heartedness of the soldiers could be condemned easily, but what is the alternative? To let the virus loose and the entire world become infected? No, there is no choice but to wipe out any possible chance of the contagion escaping London.

The music score takes many of the same scores from the original movie and the haunting chords only add to the element of hopelessness as men and women alike are gunned down mercilessly in the streets. Like rats in an infested building, the military is ruthless. First they firebomb the city, rolling conflagrations shooting through the streets, and then they fumigate, sending gas to every crack and crevice. While all this is happening, our survivors are trying to escape the city, having to deal with both the infected and the U.S. military who are killing anything in sight, infected or not.

A chilling concept to say the least. The people you would run to for help in such a dire situation are the ones who will kill you before they so much as look at you.

One scene that is pure gold in the gore department is when a helicopter takes out a horde of infected by flying low, tipping its rotors and making sushi of them in a glorious spray of blood and body parts.

This movie isn't for the faint of heart. It hits you emotionally and blasts you with blood and violence. Any true zombie fan needs to have this movie in their collection. Though not technically zombies as the infected aren't dead, to me they certainly fit the criteria. They are most definitely not themselves, but are filled with rage and a blood thirst only quenched by tearing their victims apart. They vomit blood like Old Faithful and will use teeth as well as fingernails to kill you. Truly frightening, I defy anyone not to cringe when a horde of infected come over the hill and begin to chase you. And fast is an understatement. Fueled by pure rage, they sprint like an Olympic runner and never stop until they literally collapse from exhaustion. They basically don't feel pain and only a kill shot will put them down for good. Even sliced in half they will keep coming, that is until they finally bleed out.

The end of the movie is the most chilling, setting up a third installment of the series that I for one can't wait to see.

THE BEYOND

YEAR: 1981
COUNTRY: Italy
RUNNING TIME: 89 minutes
SCREENPLAY: Dardano Sacchetti, Giorgio Mariuzzo, Lucio Fulci
DIRECTOR: Lucio Fulci
PRODUCER: Fabrizio De Angelis
MUSIC: Fabio Frizzi
CINEMATOGRAPHER: Sergio Salvati, AIC
MAKE-UP AND SPECIAL EFFECTS: Giannetto De Rossi
DESIGN AND COSTUMES: Massimo Lentini
CAST: Catriona MacColl (Liza Merril), David Warbeck (Dr. John McCabe), Cinzia Monreale (Emily), Antoine Saint-John (Schweick), Veronica Lazer (Martha), Anthony Flees (Larry)

TAKE ONE: T.S

COMMENTARY

"The Beyond" is Lucio Fulci's second installment in the unofficially-named "Gates of Hell" trilogy (with the zombie-centric "City of the Living Dead" being the first and the straight-horror "The House by the Cemetery" being the third). It's considered by many fans to be one of Fulci finest works, and it's an incredibly existential-style take on a zombie film. It's gained a solid cult following since its release, most likely attributed to the fact that, in addition to intriguing plot and atmospheric elements, the film was heavily censored upon its release to the United States and international markets. Much like telling a child they can't have something makes them want that thing all the more, the same principle applies to horror fans and their movies!

Fulci was so engaged by the metaphysical aspects he wrote into "City" that he strongly desired the opportunity to explore them further, thus this film was born. Specifically, he wanted to work more with the ways in which the worlds of the living and the dead might cross over into one another, an idea he was heavily focused on in the second half of "City." He also desired to create a work that could pay homage to his idol, French playwright and Surrealist movement member Antonin Artaud.

Artaud's work in theater prominently featured less emphasis on linear plot and more focus on "cruel" imagery and symbolism with the intent of shocking a viewer into action.

As such the idea for the storyline of "The Beyond" began to form along these non-linear lines. Indeed, the movie bounces around seemingly haphazardly, with the only real connection between scenes being Catriona MacColl's character Liza Merrill, a woman who returns to her hometown in Louisiana upon discovering that she has inherited a rundown hotel. Little does Liza know that the hotel, conveniently named The Seven Doors Hotel, is built upon one of the seven gateways to Hell, and wouldn't you know it, bad things start to happen when she and her restoration team start poking around with the foundation of the building.

This film was made during the peak of the zombies' popularity in the 1980s, so the German distribution company that owned the release rights to Fulci's films at that time insisted that he spice up the story with the undead, as the first draft read as quite the otherworldly haunted-house story. So Fulci acquiesced, adding revenants into various scenes and completely rewriting the conclusion of the story to include a delightfully creepy climax involving a "zombie mega-horde" attacking the main characters inside the local hospital.

Even though the film did have to be altered somewhat from the director's original vision, fans and critics alike applaud the finished product for its "oneiric incoherence," particularly in the movie's final scene. In case you haven't seen the film yet, I'll refrain from describing this scene in detail here, but will of course give specifics in the section below. According to Fulci, the ending is definitely not a happy one, but isn't an unhappy one either; some fans cite the fact that Fulci was a known atheist and that this played heavily into his depiction of the final moment.

The film wasn't released in the United States until two years after its original European release. As was the case with many foreign horror films at the time (as evidenced by a number of other movies reviewed in this book), the title was changed to "Seven Doors of Death" for its limited American theatrical run. The movie was heavily edited to avoid an "X" rating, and the edited version was the only one released on home video in the US, leaving many fans searching for bootleg copies of the uncut film for years.

Things stayed this way until 1998, when American movie-maker Quentin Tarantino (creator of the *Grindhouse* project that spawned the film "Plant Terror," also reviewed in this book) acquired the US distribution rights to the film. He worked with a company to completely re-master the uncut version of the film, releasing it both to DVD and to a limited-screening midnight movie feature at some theaters. The film was also featured recently on *Bravo's* 100 Scariest Movie Moments special, coming in at #60 for the stomach-churning scene where a contractor is slowly eaten alive by a pack of tarantulas. It's Fulci's second film to be featured on the list (and one of six movies reviewed in this book to make the grade), and it's one of the many accolades "The Beyond" has earned the director.

PLAY-BY-PLAY

The film's action gets going right away, with another "confusing" opening scene from Fulci. Of course, the confusion is intentional, as the director doesn't like to explain much right away, giving the viewer instead the slightly uneasy feeling that he/she may not entirely know what's going on. The opening scene is accompanied by a placard that reads, "Louisiana, 1928," and Fulci uses sepia tones to indicate this part of the film is set in the past.

The posse that comes to kill Schweick seems to use some rather extreme measures to get rid of the him, including chain whipping, crucifixion, and burning him with acid. Can't they just shoot him? Maybe not, as we later discover that not only was he the Hellish gatekeeper, the things the posse did to him apparently weren't enough to truly kill him.

Soon, we move forward to the "present," 53 years later, and the switch to color video clearly indicates the shift in time. We meet Liza and her crew, who are starting restoration to the hotel, the very same place where we just saw Schweick brutally murdered. If only Joe the plumber knew about that, then he might not go knocking down strange walls with a sledgehammer. Fulci's running "eyeball gag" comes early in this film—tough luck, Joe!

Any attentive viewer can easily discern that this is a very scary-feeling movie, but not like your "normal" zombie film. For some American audiences, it feels more like a Hitchcock movie, or an early "Nightmare on Elm Street." Very atmospheric and moody, with no clear answers given up-front. The movie is also very fluid, and Fulci is a master of not letting the audience feel where the exposition ends and the action begins.

As things progress, "The Beyond" starts to feel almost like a horror-mystery, where the audience has to try and decipher what's happening. Strange elements like the six-year-old corpse, Mrs. Joe-the-Plumber's unseen and unexplained death in the morgue, and Jo-etta Jr. discovering Mom's face and body acidifying under what appears to be normal water, all add to the utterly confounding but incredibly engaging storyline that Fulci is weaving in front of our eyes.

Soon, we are introduced to a very intriguing character in Emily, the blind girl. Her eyes are glazed over in a very creepy way, but she sure doesn't seem that blind at times, especially when she goes bounding out of the hotel in the middle of the night. Plus, she knows an awful lot about the history of the hotel, which obviously lends credence to the idea that Emily is definitely "more than meets the eye." Soon, we visit Emily in her home, where she "plays" the film's soundtrack on her piano, which is quite a cool effect.

Next we are treated to the infamous "spider scene." As a man with a self-professed case of arachnophobia, I was severely disturbed by this scene! The amount of detail in which the tarantulas attack is unnecessary, at best. One of them eats an eyeball–Fulci hits us with a double eyeball gag in this movie!

Back at the hotel, Zombie Joe appears! He kills Martha the maid with the crucifix spikes, and we are hit with yet another eyeball gag–it's the trifecta! When will the madness end? As mentioned above, the movie does jump around quite a bit, and we travel from location to location quite frequently. Soon, we end up back at Emily's home, where she herself is destroyed by the same evil spirits she was prophesizing about to Liza a short while ago. It seems that Emily's defeat and death are almost a foregone conclusion, even to her, which begs the question: do her powers come and go? How was she so acute and aware at the hotel earlier but so totally incapacitated now that she's under attack?

We're taken again to the hotel, as Liza and Dr. McCabe discover the true nature of the Hellish portal and wisely decide to "abandon ship." As they drive away, we get a really cool shot of the hotel being vacated by the living and occupied instead by the dead. Now that the gate is seemingly thrown open, the dead finally rise en masse. After a hectic and haphazard attempt at escape by our two remaining characters, they try to escape by entering the hospital stairwell, only to exit the stairwell...directly into the basement of the hotel. Mystifying, yes, but not nearly as much as what comes next.

I would probably term this conclusion to the tale as one of the most open-ended I've ever encountered in a film, and it certainly has sparked a lot of debate among fans as to its true meaning. According to Fulci, the extra-dimensional realm Liza and McCabe find themselves trapped in is a sort of refuge that exists outside of normal time and space. Whether it's meant to be purgatory, a different plane of existence, or something else entirely, as we see the two wander aimlessly amidst mummified bodies, eventually succumbing to blindness and fading into oblivion, we're given a conclusion to this zombie story that is, quite frankly, unlike any ending ever seen before.

TAKE TWO: A.G.

Liza Merril has a problem. It appears the hotel she's inherited was built over one of the seven gateways to Hell, and it has now awakened and has become a malevolent abyss that sucks in the bodies and souls of all who enter its dilapidated walls.

As Liza tries to unravel what's going on, the dead and spirits are killing off her staff and soon the entire town is threatened to be sucked into Hell.

But she's not alone. The mysterious Emily, blind but beautiful, will try to help her and well as Dr. John McCabe.

Along the way, acid will eat faces, chains will tear bodies to bloody ruins, bodies will be impaled, gory crucifixions, flesh-eating tarantulas will tear off faces, heads will be impaled on spikes—with eyes popping out of their sockets—seeing-eyed demon dogs will tear out the throats of their owners, and the dead will rise to slaughter the living, all in eye popping color, the splatter non-stop.

For any true gore hound, this movie is a must see. Though the zombies are not flesh-eaters, they are murderers, and usually in very gruesome ways. Like Romero zombies, a bullet to the head will put them down, and they are slow to the point that Romero zombies act like sprinters.

What *The Beyond* lacks in plot structure, it makes up for in sheer over-the-top gore and atmosphere. Filmed on location in Louisiana, for American audiences it adds a little something more. While most Italian horror movies are filmed in Italy or overseas, such as Africa or New Guinea, to see a city within the United States adds a little something to it, or at least it always has to me. I suspect it's merely simpler to relate when the movie is based in the country you live in.

Though if you examine the outside of the hospital, it's painfully apparent that the building is not a hospital. And why does the doctor get to park on the walkway outside the front of the building, ten feet from the main doors? Does he hold some powerful position? There's nothing that says he's not simply another doctor on staff.

Though the plot is loose, there is one, and as long as you don't study it too much, it's a fun ride. Like many of Fulci's movies, he will begin a plotline only to toss it away ten minutes later. But despite this, there is still a thread to tie the movie together.

At the end of the movie, when the characters find themselves in a barren landscape with strewn corpses in all directions, the answer is still not blatant. It's up to the viewer to decide what the end result is, whether they are in limbo or Hell or somewhere else, or whether they are still alive or now dead.

But back to the gore.

Where most movies give you a glimpse or an action sequence, where if you blink, you've missed the gore, Fulci puts it on display in glorious color. As the tarantulas feast on a man's face as he lays paralyzed on the floor from a fall, the camera not only holds still, but gives the viewer close-ups as his eyes are torn out and his tongue is devoured. Sixty seconds of gore, never once does the camera pull away, this is what makes Fulci's others and this movie great. He's never apologetic about what he shows us and he challenges the viewer not to turn away.

Blood splatters in gallons as victim after victim is slaughtered mercilessly. Even children aren't safe. When Liza is attacked at the morgue, the girl attacking her has her head blown off, the impact so over-the-top it's like a grenade has gone off inside her skull.

Much like in *City of the Living Dead*, these zombies seem to be more ghost than undead. They can bend time and space, appearing out of thin air and are more inclined to kill you than eat you.

Like many Italian movies, this film has it flaws, such as when Dr. McCabe shoots the zombies in the chest to see they won't die. Then he shoots them in the head and they drop to the floor, dead. So then why does he continuously still shoot them in the chest? And many times he fires again and again without reloading, though it's a six round revolver.

And here's a fun one. Because of flooding and water seepage, Louisiana buildings don't have basements, but the hotel does for some reason. Not that these holes in the film matter. Oh no, they only add to the charm. The Italians are well known for making movies on shoestring budgets and they don't always worry about authenticity, but rather rely on the gore to keep their audiences entertained.

The Beyond is a link to the rich, imaginative world that is Italian horror, a bloody harvest of the sins of the flesh that should not be missed by a true horror connoisseur.

If you have seen this movie already, then it's worth another viewing and if you haven't, then man, are you in for a treat.

CEMETERY MAN (DELLAMORTE DELLAMORE)

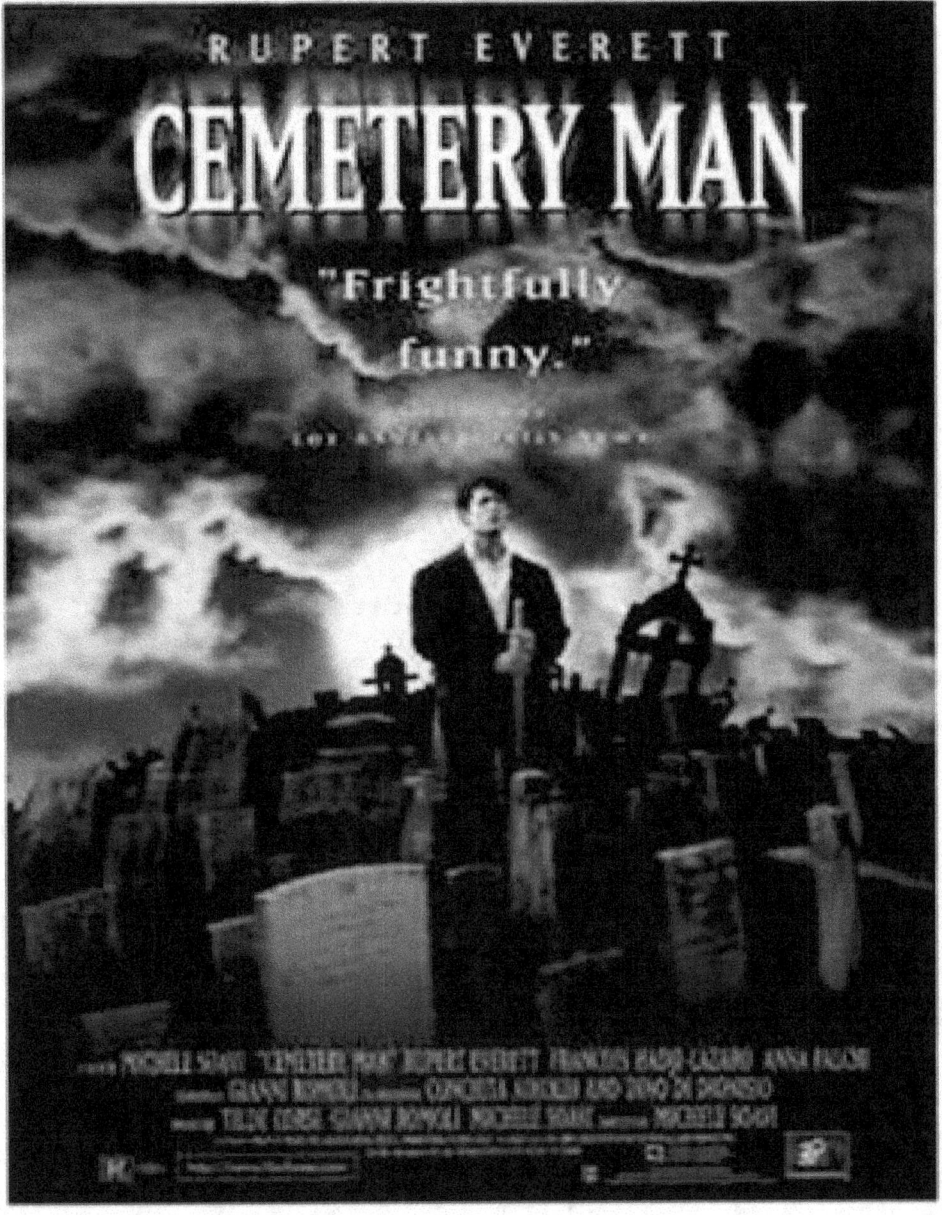

YEAR: 1994
COUNTRY: Italy/Germany/France
RUNNING TIME: 99 minutes
NOVEL: Tiziano Sclavi
SCREENWRITER Gianni Romoli:
DIRECTOR: Michele Soavi
PRODUCER: Tilde Corsi, Gianni Romoli, Michele Soavi
MUSIC: Manuel De Sica
CINEMATOGRAPHOR Mauro Marchetti
SPECIAL EFFECTS: Sergio Stivaletti
MAKE-UP DESIGNER: Sergio Stivaletti, Gino Zamprioli, Enrico Jacoponi
PRODUCTION DESIGNER: Massimo Antonello Geleng
COSTUME DESIGNER: Maurizio Millenoti, Alfonsia Lettieri
OSSUARY DESIGNERS: Francesca R Di Nunzio, Sergio Stivaletti
CAST: Rupert Everett (Francesco Dellamorte), Francois Hadji-Lazaro (Gnaghi), Anna Falchi (The Widow, Mrs. Martin, Mayor's Secretary, Laura), Mickey Knox (Marshall Straniero)

TAKE ONE: T.S

COMMENTARY

"Some films defy such terse summation." A quote from the DVD liner notes gives a fairly accurate representation of trying to summarize the one-of-a-kind movie-watching experience that is "Cemetery Man."

Indeed, in reading other reviews that have been written about this movie, many reviewers spend more text trying to explain the movie and its plot than they do talking about their actual thoughts on the film. It's a very surreal viewing experience, trying to ride the fine lines between black comedy, sweet romance, and zombie horror; the thing is, it not only rides the lines, it lives comfortably in all three areas without alienating the viewer or ever feeling like things have gone off track. It is, in my humble opinion, likely the most critically underrated zombie film in existence.

It is an Italian film, but it comes to us from the mid-1990s, a full decade after most of the other Italian zombie films reviewed in this book. As such, director Michele Soavi was able to utilize elements of those movies that had come before him, while keeping his creation well-removed from being directly associated with that "clump" of films which all came out so soon after one another that many viewers started to think they were just clones of each other. Based on the 1991 novel by Italian author Tiziano Scalzi, "Cemetery Man"—or, as it was called upon its original Italian release, "*Dellamorte Dellamore*"—tells the following tale, which I shall do my best to summarize as succinctly as possible.

A caretaker of a small town's cemetery, Francesco Dellamorte, stays much busier than your average graveyard watchman. That's because in his cemetery, the dead return to life seven days after they die, and it's up to Dellamorte and his sweet-but-stupid assistant Gnaghi to send them back to death permanently. Things are "business as usual" for the duo until the arrival of an unnamed widow, who captivates Dellamorte in a way he has never felt before. From here on out, his life is a twisting conflagration of lust, death, undeath, and hallucinations, not necessarily in that order. Along the way, Gnaghi tries to find love as well, becoming attached to the severed head of the dead Mayor's daughter, and through all the madness that ensues for the two men, even the specter of Death himself appears, leading up to a baffling conclusion that makes Dellamorte (and his viewing audience) question everything about his life.

Oh, the things I could tell you about this film, they could probably fill a book of their own. It's an incredibly captivating movie, one you'll most likely want to watch over and over again, to see what you catch on the current viewing that you didn't in previous viewings, and just to see the ending again and again to see if you can decipher it any further.

The sheer uniqueness of the film can be attributed directly both to Soavi and to the source material provided by Scalzi's writings. Soavi was no stranger to the film industry before he directed "Cemetery Man," as he studied under Italian horror great Dario Argento and eclectic film-maker Terry Gilliam. This obviously helps to explain the combination of horror and existentialism present in this film. In the early '90s, Soavi read Scalzi's best-known creation, the comic book "Dylan Dog," about a troubled paranormal investigator whose adventures were often dark and comedic all at once. Soavi enjoyed the stories so much he called the public information service to get Scalzi's telephone number. He then called the comic creator just to tell him how much he liked his work! Soon after, a friendship formed, they stayed in touch, and a few years later, Scalzi sent Soavi a 400-page script manuscript of "*Dellamorte Dellamore*." While Soavi enjoyed it, it wasn't quite ready for the big-screen, so he set the script aside for some time until he connected with writer/editor Gianni Romoli, who worked with the director to cut down and fine-tune the script until it was perfected as the story they wanted to tell. A conglomeration of European financiers backed the film, and the process of creating the film was officially set in motion.

Creation of the film was truly an international production, and nowhere was this highlighted more than in the casting of the film's three main characters. British actor Rupert Everett, years before he came to know American cinematic success opposite Julia Roberts in "My Best Friend's Wedding," was cast as the everyman-hero Dellamorte; this was an especially ironic bit of casting, as Everett was the very actor that was the inspiration for Scalzi in creating the physical appearance of Dylan Dog. An Italian model born in Finland, Anna Falchi was relatively unknown for her acting skills when she was chosen for the part of the unnamed widow, often referred to as "She," which actually ended up being three parts in one, which you'll read more about in the Play-by-Play section. A French musician named François Hadji-Lazaro was hand-picked for the understated-yet-crucial role of Gnaghi, the rotund groundskeeper who is infinitely endearing to all who come across him, character and viewer alike.

"*Dellamorte Dellamore*" saw moderate success in its European release, and after a stint at the Toronto Film Festival, the American production company October Films optioned it for US theaters, changing the title to "Cemetery Man" and giving it a campy ad campaign to promote a limited-market release. While the film performed poorly in its American theatrical release, it found new life stateside on home video, with renowned director Martin Scorcese going as far as calling it "one of the best Italian films of the 1990s."

PLAY-BY-PLAY

We are treated to a rather unique and intriguing opening with a "zombie salesman," knocking at Dellamorte's door. He nonchalantly shoots the revenant in the head while talking on the phone to Franco, the cemetery's accountant and his only real friend. This is also the beginning of Dellamorte's little double-entendre quips: "Life goes on."

The cemetery set is lit w/a red candle on each gravesite, which gives the whole area a very serene-yet-spooky look. I use the term "set" very loosely, as the production was actually situated outside and was built upon an actual deconsecrated gravesite for maximum realism. The ossuary (bone crypt) we see later on is also quite real, and quite creepy.

As Dellamorte and Gnaghi go to re-bury the zombies who have unearthed themselves, we see a lot of unceremonious dumping of the corpse back into the grave. There is clearly no love lost here, it's just a job and "business as usual" for our duo. We do, however, get some fun special effects and unique zombie kills early on in the movie, including shovels and memorial crucifixes through skulls, before Dellamorte seems to settle down and routinely resort to the old bullet-through-the-brain later on in the film.

Fortunately, the headshot does actually stop the "Returners," because these clearly aren't your normal undead. Even though it's never explicitly referenced in the film, Soavi tells us in the behind-the-scenes action that the undead's ability to reanimate comes from the mandragola roots that crisscross the cemetery. As for the Returners themselves, they are quite a talkative bunch. The second zombie we see surprisingly says "eat!"...*twice*...before he is put back down! Many other zombies talk as the film progresses, including an entire pack of Boy Scouts who sing a campfire song as they are sent back to Hell, but whether this speech is a byproduct of the undead's actual abilities or Dellamorte's quickly-unraveling psyche, we're never really told.

The viewer can see early on that it's going to be a very artistic movie, with exceptional camerawork and very distinctive approaches to filming, giving the audience shots from the grave, from the viewpoint of the zombie, and so forth. It a film that actually borders on being a beautiful piece of artwork on more than one occasion.

Falchi, in her multiple characters, is damn near perfect...for the role, I mean. Her sultry glances eschew sexiness without coming across as "slutty," and her facial expressions and body language are matched only by her other, shall we say, ample assets. She is, in a word, stunning. I can understand what Soavi saw in her when he decided to cast her in this multi-role. Her first character, that of the widow, is oddly kinky, wanting to have sex on her dead husband's grave, but this kind of perversion seems fitting for the kind of story being woven here. Too bad her husband had to reanimate while she was doing the deed with Dellamorte, and come ruin the party. Did I hear the husband say "that's life" as he bit the widow?

Dellamorte isn't the only one who seems to have been shot by Cupid's arrow. During a trip into town, we see Gnaghi fall in love with the Mayor's teenage daughter. She pays him a compliment, and he answers with a typical guy response—he throws up on her! Gnaghi is very "Three Stooges" Curly-esque, in many ways.

Soon after, the Mayor's daughter meets her untimely demise. I have to admit that I saw it coming, but had no idea it would be so gruesome! Her death and ensuing zombie attacks let the special effects team further highlight their work on the undead. In addition to her decapitated zombie head that Gnaghi takes home to dote his simple love upon, we also get the pack of Boy Scouts who are literally chomping at the bit to get to Dellamorte, as well as a zombie biker-boyfriend of the mayor's daughter, who gets fun makeup replete with transmission tubes and bit of still-blinking tail light in his undead head. We're also treated to a rather evil-looking zombie nun whom Dellamorte bludgeons back to death with a statue. Seems wrong somehow...

The dialogue in "Cemetery Man" also deserves recognition, as we get not only some great one-liners (one of the best coming from a teenager who tries to dismiss Dellamorte as her zombie lover begins to eat her: "Mind your business! I shall be eaten by whomever I please!") but some thought-provoking speech as well.

There is a trippy scene where Dellamorte meets the Grim Reaper, and their conversation is not to be missed. Even in the name of the title character lies some fun with words, as he himself explains in the film, *Dellamorte* means "of death," while his mother's maiden name, *Dellamore*, means "of love. This obviously makes for an interesting and soul-searching dichotomy for Francesco.

Soon, the rigors of the job combined with the loss of the widow in his life take their toll on our hero, and Dellamorte seems to just stop caring what happens to his life. A perfect example is given when the Mayor comes around to the cemetery to dig up his daughter's body. Dellamorte doesn't care that the body's head is missing. It's almost as if he's content to ride whatever wave life puts him on, instead of steering his own fate.

Along this same line, the town's police chief seems to take everything in stride, including the Mayor's death. He didn't witness the Mayor's daughter's head biting him, but he doesn't go out of his way to ask any questions as to why her head is out of the coffin.

As mentioned previously, the zombies get more vocal as the movie progresses, either in "real life" or in Dellamorte's head. Some, like the Mayor, even try to rationalize with him before he destroys them. The closer we get to the ending of the film, the stranger things become in general.

A large question that goes unanswered is the significance behind Falchi's playing of three separate roles, all seeming to be the same person but...not. Then comes the super-trippy ending when Dellamorte and Gnaghi try to leave town, which is quite entertaining but also quite confusing. It's all very hard to explain, but I suspect that's exactly what Soavi wanted.

And look at me–I've written more words trying to explain the movie than I have in giving my actual commentary about the movie, just like I said many other reviewers have done. Well, to quote Dellamorte himself: "In the end, who cares? I'm just doing my job."

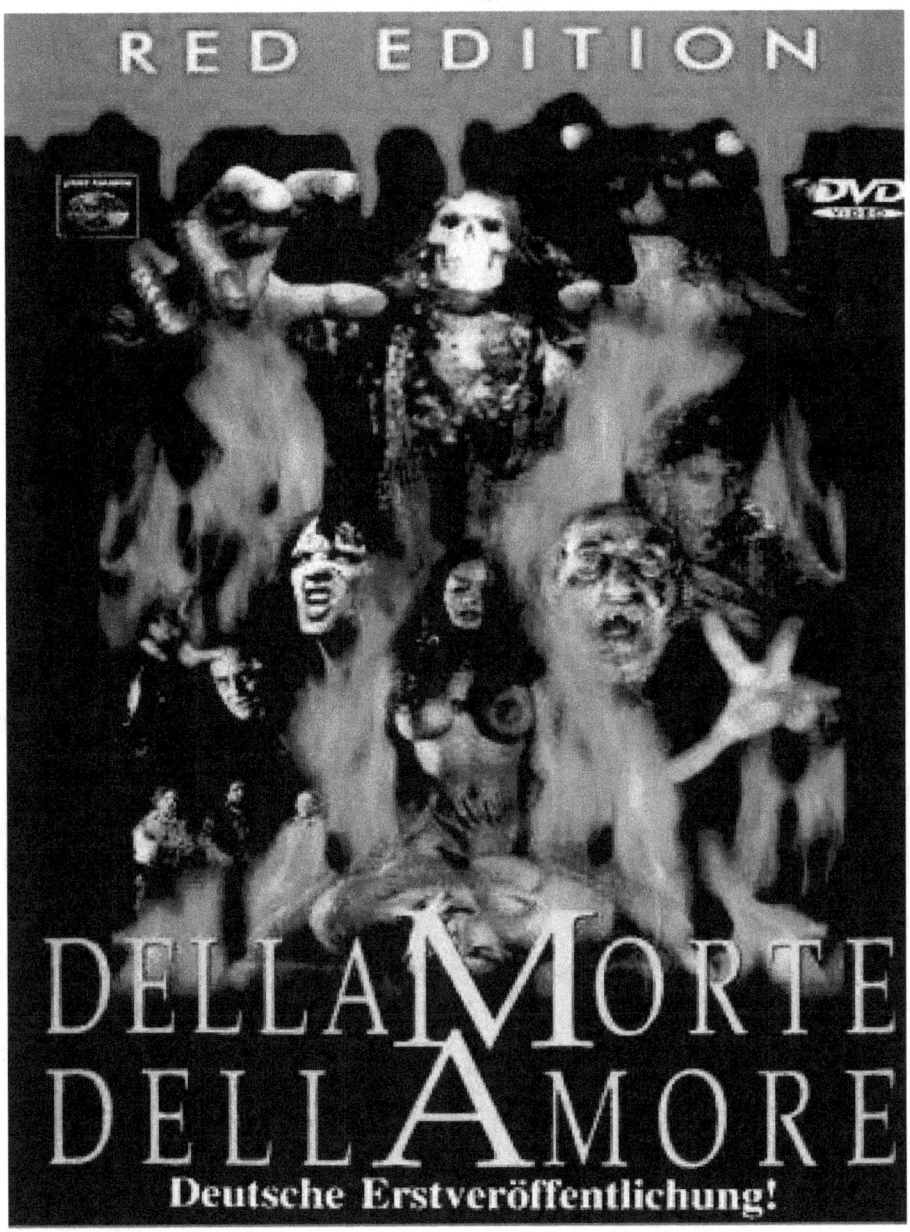

CEMETERY MAN (DELLAMORTE DELLAMORE)

TAKE TWO: A.G

Francesco Dellamorte has a problem as the caretaker of the Buffalora Cemetery in Northern Italy. It seems the recently laid to rest sometimes return from the dead after being buried for seven days.

Not wanting to lose his job if the cemetery is shut down because of this odd occurrence, Francesco takes it upon himself to re-kill the zombies and thus save his job. To help him is his loyal sidekick Gnaghi, a Curly (from the Three Stooges)-like man who doesn't talk but grunts. He seems a little slow in the head but as a gravedigger is more than competent.

It's a hard life as a caretaker, and in fact he can't even get overtime for all the nights he spends chasing down the deceased, but what's a man to do?

Simple…shoot them in the head, for that is the only way to put a "Returner," as he calls them, down for good.

Along the way, Francesco meets the beautiful widow who has just buried her geriatric husband. For some reason, she is drawn to Francesco and a torrid love affair begins, which always has them making love in the cemetery. One time, they do it right on her late husband's grave. In fact, pay close attention to the old man's picture on his tombstone, and see how it changes with what's happening.

When he comes back and attacks his wife, she's bitten and passes out from shock. Later, Francesco waits for her to return as he sits silently with her corpse in the ossuary.

Gnaghi falls in love, too, with the Mayor's daughter. But when she dies in a motorcycle accident, Gnaghi sees a chance to be with her. A simple thing like being dead isn't a problem for him. He digs her up, and her eyes open. Her head was severed in the accident and Gnaghi takes it home, propping it inside a damaged television set. There, the two carry on with a romance, happy in its innocence.

Though the zombie's don't seem to be particularly ravenous, they do feast on human flesh and will attack and kill if given the chance.

In the middle of the movie a bus of Cub Scouts goes off a cliff and the cemetery becomes inundated with new "guests." One of my favorite lines is here. As coffin after coffin is carried into the cemetery for internment, Francesco turns to Gnaghi and says, "We're gonna need a lot more bullets."

Later, true to form, the Cub Scouts, as well as the chaperones on the bus, return in droves and Francesco, trapped in the locked cemetery, has to deal with them.

For those who have never seen the movie, at the very beginning, when the credits roll, pay close attention to the snow globe. It will have a direct impact on the end of the movie.

Over the course of the film, Francesco meets three women, all the same actress, playing different roles. I've always wondered if it is Francesco who meets these women and imagines they look alike, not that they are truly all the same person. See, the entire film in many ways is like a dream; whether it's Gnaghi or Francesco dreaming is unknown.

When Francesco gets a visit from an angel of Death, he's told not to bother with killing the dead, but to get a step up on his job and just kill the living now. After all, we're all dying anyway, he reasons. He then goes on a killing spree and despite this, he stays a character you care about.

Unlike many Italian movies, Cemetery Man has excellent zombie effects and cinematography. Rupert Everett as Francesco Dellamorte is a talented actor, and so is the supporting cast. The dialogue is sharp, not cheesy like many Italian zombie flicks and the special effects are more than acceptable given the date of the movie. Note the small fire flies that hover around Francesco and the woman as he makes love. You can see the strings. And later, when he's with her in the ossuary, her now dead, and a fly crawls on her shrouded face, you can see the thread as the fly is pulled along. But none of this takes away from the movie, in fact it adds to the charm.

The musical score is excellent as well, a haunting theme that only adds to the gothic atmosphere.

While not the traditional zombie movie with the dead wanting to eat the living, Cemetery man is a love, sex, and violence movie, as well as a few tongue-in-cheek moments.

Recently it's been released on DVD by Anchor Bay and though there are no real extras about the movie, there is a thirty minute documentary about director Michel Soavi.

Filled with a gloomy atmosphere, a haunting score, and a troubled main character, Cemetery Man should please even the most discerning zombie fan and is one of this reviewer's favorite zombie films.

And remember, much like in the movie, perhaps life is merely just a dream, and no matter what we do or say, in the end, it's all futile, for death comes to us all.

CITY OF THE LIVING DEAD

YEAR: 1980
COUNTRY: Italy
RUNNING TIME: 93 minutes
STORY: Lucio Fulci, Dardano Sacchetti
DIRECTOR: Lucio Fulci
PRODUCER: Giovanni Masini
MUSIC: Fabio Frizzi
DIRECTOR OF PHOTOGRAPHY: Sergio Salvati
MAKE-UP EFFECTS: Franco Rufini
COSTUME DESIGNER: Massimo Antonello Geleng
CAST: Christopher George (Peter Bell), Catriona MacColl (Mary Woodhouse), Carlo De Mejo (Gerry), Antonella Interlenghi (Emily Robbins), Giovanni Lombardo (Bob), Daniela Doria (Rosie Kelvin)

TAKE ONE: T.S

COMMENTARY

Lucio Fulci had a vision.

The man, quite simply, wanted to make horror films. He had made quite a few productions in many different genres throughout his early career, but his true passion belonged to the scare. Building upon the release of his first internationally-successful film, "Zombie," Fulci was ready to branch out and try his hand at presenting other kinds of horror stories, but the undead were still wildly popular across the globe at the time.

As such, his financers and distributors requested more movies from him that incorporated the walking dead, so the resulting films that Fulci produced were interesting mash-ups of the existential-type stories he wanted to tell, with a healthy dose of zombie for good measure.

The best examples of this can be seen in the first two movies of Fulci's unofficially-named "Gates of Hell" trilogy. So named because each movie revolves around the existence of one of the Seven Gates of Hell, the final film in the trilogy, "The House by the Cemetery," does not incorporate zombies but the first two, "City of the Living Dead" and "The Beyond," certainly do.

The trio of movies is so graphic and gory that they originally received ratings of "X" or equivalent upon their theatrical release around the globe, and in some countries the films were banned outright.

"City of the Living Dead" is probably the creepiest zombie film I've ever seen, and I absolutely mean that in a good way. When I say "creepy," I mean more along the lines of an eerie, supernatural feeling, and not the other kind of creepy that involves shady characters with minivans and bad comb-overs. It's definitely a mesh of the classic supernatural horror/suspense type of film mixed with some of the more typical traits of early zombie movies.

The plot is a little convoluted, as some horror films tend to be: after a Catholic priest hangs himself in a cemetery in the town of Dunwich, the city built on the remnants of Salem (of the Witch Trial fame), the gate to Hell is opened. Evil spirits are unleashed, many of them manifesting themselves as zombies with a variety of extra abilities, such as teleportation, super strength, telekinesis, and more. A recently-returned-from-death psychic and a newspaper reporter head to Dunwich after learning of the gate's opening, and together with the ever-dwindling number of the town's survivors, they attempt to close the gate before All Saints Day, when all the spirits of the dead can come through and take over the Earth.

If the description sounds intense, it's because that's exactly how it plays out on screen; many scenes are incredibly eerie, especially those that take place in the cursed town of Dunwich, and Fulci really did manage to capture a very sinister and spine-chilling feel throughout the film, especially in the climactic, drawn-out final sequence.

While the storyline may be a challenge to follow at times, you definitely have to give Fulci credit for being able to shock the viewer with a variety of tactics. Believe me when I say that absolutely no one we meet on-screen is safe in this film; Fulci has no problem taking a main character who we get to know throughout the film and kill that character in a heartbeat.

Moments of shock also come from some of the particularly disturbing scenes, including the infamous "head drilling" scene that single-handedly got the film banned from England and Germany.

Of equal stomach-churning note is the scene where actress Daniela Doria sees the evil spirit of the hanged Father Thomas impel her to purge her entire intestinal system through her mouth; Fulci strove for so much realism that he had Doria vomit actual, whole sheep entrails out of her mouth for the scene.

Now *that's* dedication to the craft.

PLAY-BY-PLAY

The viewer is treated to a spooky opening scene in a graveyard that may stir up some thoughts of similarities to the opening scenes of "Night of the Living Dead." It certainly doesn't take long for Fulci to establish that this is clearly one of his movies, as the "slow reveal" strikes again early and often here.

Following the presentation of this film as less the "standard" zombie film and more similar to the paranormal/mystic style of horror film, things move quickly in this direction. There is quite a supernatural tilt at the séance, especially with the ball of flame that appears and disappears seemingly at will. You can tell that this is not your typical zombie flick so far.

There is an equally bizarre scene up next, at an abandoned farmhouse—more "Night of the Living Dead" similarities! The important question is: is this mere coincidence, homage, or a good old-fashioned rip-off?

We are given a very interesting back-story that is slowly filled in about the town of Dunwich and how its ancestors were the Salem witch burners. Some of the plot here revolves around how no one really knows where Dunwich is, which is strange for a few different reasons. For one thing, it seems like a decently-sized town, so I'm surprised it "isn't on any of the maps" as the characters claim, and for another thing, the real-life town of Salem, which actually changed its name to Danvers, is located in northeastern Massachusetts, and its whereabouts are very well-known, especially in the New England region.

One of the most intriguing aspects of this film, at least for me, is Mary's return from death. No real explanation is ever given for this, which makes me wonder if it was meant to play a bigger role in the film. Fulci notoriously ran short on funds towards the completion of the movie, as you'll read more about below, so it certainly is a possibility that this was a plot thread that will forever remain unexplored.

Following the tone he established in "Zombie," Fulci continues to infuse his films with a high gruesome content, and it's probably most notable here in the scene with the couple in the car who are confronted by the specter of Father Thomas. As mentioned in the final paragraph of the Commentary section, this is the scene where the girl's innards fall out through her mouth, and it is—pardon the double-meaning pun—quite stomach-churning. A close "second-place" example would be the scene where the spirits break the windows of Gerry's office and quite literally make it rain maggots on the four main characters for what seems like an eternity.

Seems like these evil spirits keep "upping the ante," making things worse and worse for the living. It's raining maggots!

I really feel like I can't state enough that, from start to finish, this movie really feels like a cross between a zombie film and a ghost story/supernatural thriller, which is exactly what Fulci was going for. Almost every scene is very slow-developing and the entire look of the story presented on screen is highly atmospheric; these two elements help build an incredible amount of suspense for the viewer.

Continuing another "Fulci-esque" trait that he developed during his previous films, some very unique camerawork is utilized here. A prime example of this is during the scene in the home where the old lady's body is found in the kitchen: lots of swooping movements, odd angles, and unusual cross-screen pans add to the feeling that something isn't quite right for the characters in the scene.

Strangely enough, everyone in town seems to trust Gerry the psychiatrist more than they do the police! They call him first when there is trouble: Janice with her dead old lady in kitchen, Jon-Jon when his dead sister Emily reappears and kills their parents…it's too bad everyone in the town ends up dead, otherwise he would have a booming business with a schedule full of highly-disturbed people for years to come!

If it seems to you that many of the characters aren't really trying to fight off the zombies, it's probably because its true – the living are too paralyzed with fear to even think fast enough to fight back! Personally, I think this is probably one of the most realistic depictions of how many people would react to a zombie attack I've ever seen. Plus, these zombies are slow, but seemingly intelligent, as they are very deliberate in their movements and attacks. Very disturbing indeed.

It takes a brave man to hop into the partially-opened pitch-black tomb of the demon-priest ringleader of the zombie horde. Gerry the psychiatrist, I salute you! And what does he find down there but a walkway to a veritable catacomb of the living dead, replete with an ultra-creepy "ceiling cemetery."

Here, at the thrilling conclusion, the movie continues to kill off lead characters with reckless abandon, and I love it! There is lots of gruesome brain-squeezing from the zombies…I'm sure there's a "headache" joke in here somewhere…

As I mentioned above, the ending of the film is one of the ultimate "what the…?" type endings of all time. Even among fans who love the film, this final scene is much maligned, and for good reason: it is wholly and utterly confusing, and any possible explanation from the director or creative team is conspicuously missing from any special features, commentaries, etc., that I can find. Jon-Jon running towards the survivors, the scream, and the cracked screen; it all combines to make, if nothing else, one of the most talked-about endings to any zombie film ever.

TAKE TWO: A.G.

Before I begin to talk about this movie, I have to add a little history about what this movie means to me.

Back in the 1980's, there was this run-down theatre in my city. It was old, very old, with a balcony and that musty smell when you walked into it. The screen was old, with imperfections in it, but that only added to the charm.

Because this theatre was on its way out, it used to show over the top horror and grindhouse movies. One such movie was called *The Gates of Hell*—the edited version of this movie for U.S. audiences.

Every Saturday, my friends and I would go see this horror movie. It was rated R, but the clerk at the ticket counter could have cared less that we were under seventeen.

So every Saturday, I would sit in the grungy theatre, with its scratches and banged-up screen, and watch Lucio Fulci's zombies rip into brains and make victims regurgitate their insides.

Back then, before CGI and all the makeup effects we have now, to see the zombie at the end burning or Bob getting his head drilled right there on the screen, was absolutely fantastic.

So when I talk about this movie, no matter what, I'm already far from impartial.

But despite all this, most zombie fans agree that *City of the Living Dead* is a classic.

Now the first thing anyone who is a fan of the movie will tell you is don't study the plot too hard. Fulci has a penchant for going left one second and for no reason whatsoever stopping and then going right or backing up and going the wrong way. He's all over the place with his plot and only the barest of strings keeps it all from unraveling.

But despite all this, there is a fun plot here.

It's rather simple too. When Father William Thomas kills himself in the small town of Dunwich, Mass., for some unknown reason, he inadvertently opens the gates of Hell. If the deceased Father isn't stopped, on All Saints Day, the dead will walk the Earth and mankind will be doomed.

A reporter and a psychic team up and off to Dunwich, Mass. they go.

But they're a little late and the dead are afoot. They are already killing the residents of the town.

Now these zombies aren't Romero's zombies. They are more supernatural. They can teleport from place to place and though a few are fresh from being dead, they come back looking like burn victims and have supernatural strength. With a one-handed grip, they can tear the top of a person's skull off, squeezing the brains in their hand.

They also seem to have the ability to make a victim either bleed blood from the eyes or regurgitate their insides.

All in all, it's zombie fun for all, even if they aren't true zombies the way most of us are used to them.

But that's okay, because in the middle of all the undead hijinks, there is plenty of blood and gore and tense situations to go around.

When the psychic is thought to be dead and then buried—no autopsy or embalming for her I guess— she's buried alive and the reporter uses a pick-axe to set her free. I remember sitting in the theatre and watching this scene, and back then I considered it the most terrifying thing I had ever seen on a movie screen. Even now, thirty years later, it still brings chills. Each time the pick-axe goes into the coffin lid, it either misses the woman's face by an inch or comes in on her side. It's unknown what the reporter was thinking as he used a pick-axe to blindly break into the coffin, but in the end she's okay. I defy anyone not to cringe during that scene.

The other scene that should give anyone goosebumps is when the town pariah, Bob, is caught with a girl. The father of the girl decides to dish out a little vigilante justice. This is accomplished by the industrial power drill that gets turned on by accident.

Ever seen a man get his head drilled from one side to the other? Sure you have, but back in 1980, this was rather over-the-top and gore-filled for the time. Surely one of the all time best horror movie moments.

But if that isn't one of the best, then the girl in the car having to puke up her insides, intestines liver and all, must come in as a close second. Serves her right for necking in the middle of nowhere.

The atmosphere is gothic, as is Fulci's trademark in these horror movies and the score is foreboding. Some of it has been reworked from Zombie, another of Fulci's movies, and also reviewed in this book.

So whether you have fond memories of this movie like I do or are seeing it for the first time, this film is one of the classics that has made zombie cinema what it is today. Don't miss out, go see it and if you already have, hell, man, go see it again!

DAWN OF THE DEAD

YEAR: 1978
COUNTRY: US/Italy
RUNNING TIME: US Theatrical Cut, 128 min/ Extended Cut 140 min; European Cut, 120 min
WRITER: George A Romero
DIRECTOR: George A Romero
PRODUCERS: Richard P Rubenstein, Dario Argento
MUSIC: The Goblins and library tracks
DIRECTOR OF PHOTOGRAPHY: Michael Gornick
MAKE-UP EFFECTS: Tom Savini
VISUAL EFFECTS: Arthur J Canestro
COSTUME DESIGNER: Josie Caruso
CAST: David Emgee (Stephen), Ken Foree (Peter), Scott H Reiniger (Roger), Gaylen Ross (Francine)

TAKE ONE: T.S.

COMMENTARY

If "Night of the Living Dead" is the classic Mustang—a muscle car that might look a little outdated today but still maintains a high level of awe-some-ness—then "Dawn of the Dead" is the Mustang re-issue of its time, updated with current technology while still maintaining the "bad-ass" feel of the original.

"Dawn" is hailed by many fans of the "Dead" movies as the high point of the series, and rightfully so. Even though many folks, myself definitely included, will always have a special place in their heart for "Night of the Living Dead" and the way it changed the horror genre, there is no denying that its first sequel takes not only the story but the horror, acting, and effects to a new level. Released theatrically more than a decade after Romero's first zombie film, "Dawn" reportedly wasn't even on the creator's mind until a series of random events set things in motion.

According to information from various behind-the-scenes documentaries, in 1974 Romero was visiting his friend and fellow Carnegie Mellon alumni Mark Mason at the Monroeville (PA) Mall, which was managed by Mason's company, Oxford Development. As Mason showed Romero some of the hidden parts of the mall, Mason jokingly suggested that people would easily be able to survive in the mall if an emergency ever occurred. The mental wheels started turning for Romero, and the idea for "Night's" sequel was born.

Frustratingly for Romero and his team, "Night" hadn't quite reached a terribly popular and successful status by then, so no domestic investors opted to back the film financially. By sheer chance (and good karma), news of the potential sequel reached all the way across the Atlantic Ocean to Italian horror director Dario Argento. A big fan of "Night," Argento was eager and willing to help the classic movie receive the sequel he felt it easily deserved. He met with Romero and his producer, Richard Rubenstein, and helped them secure enough financing to get the project green-lit, with the condition that Argento would hold the international distribution rights to the film. The deal done and the two horror icons working together, Argento invited Romero to come to Rome while he was writing the screenplay, for two main reasons: so he could have a nice change of scenery while writing, and so that the two could collaborate even further, discussing the story and how it would play out on the big screen, and so forth.

The developmental aspect came full-circle for Romero when he was able to use the Monroeville Mall, the same location which first hatched his ideas for the movie, as the location for the actual movie shoot. Returning with the strength of Argento and his financers behind him, Romero was also able to secure additional funding for the film through his connections with Mason and Oxford Development. Even though shooting at the mall proved to have its inconveniences—filming took place primarily through the busy holiday months of December, January, and February, hence the holiday decorations we see on screen, and the crew only shot overnight during the mall's closed hours of 11 p.m. to 7 a.m.—it easily paid off, contributing heavily to the realistic feel in the finished product of the film.

Of course, the entire movie wasn't shot in the mall. Certain parts of the mall shown in the film, including the group of survivor's hideout in the upper area as well as the department store elevator and the gun shop, didn't actually exist in the real-life mall, so sets were built specifically for these locations. Although the movie is best known for the iconic scenes in the mall, much of the film actually revolves around a storyline line that takes place outside of the shopping center, so a wide variety of other sets and location filming helped give the production a much broader scope and feel.

Running at 126 minutes, "Dawn of the Dead" finally saw its theatrical release in the United States on April 20, 1979, but this edition of the movie is actually one of many versions in existence. Romero wanted to premiere the movie at the 1978 Cannes Film Festival, so in order to make the deadline he put together a hastily-edited 139-minute version of the film. This version is what is now sold and promoted as the "Extended Cut" or the "Director's Cut." Additionally, since Argento held the international distribution rights, he was able to re-edit the movie and make some changes he deemed appropriate. As a result, the version of the movie shown overseas is missing a few "dialogue-heavy" scenes of exposition, and clocks in at 119 minutes. In an odd quirk, "Dawn" was released internationally in Italy in September 1978, almost nine months before the movie was shown in America. The Italian release of the film was titled Zombi: L'alba dei Morti Viventi, translated as "Zombie: The Dawn of the Living Dead Men." This title led to the confusion with Lucio Fulci's soon-after released undead films, so much so that Fulci's movies have actually been called "pseudo-sequels" to "Night of the Living Dead." (See my review of "Zombie" in this book for further information on this entertaining story.) All three versions of the film, including different commentary tracks for each version and a host of other behind-the-scenes documentaries and extra features, were released in 2004 in the "Dawn of the Dead Ultimate Edition DVD" set.

Through all of this, "Dawn of the Dead" emerged unscathed as an amazing story of a zombie apocalypse and humans' attempt at survival. Romero was seemingly at the top of his game in creating this film, and it easily earns all the accolades and recognition from the multiple "best-of" lists the film graces from various publications and websites. It's legacy is so long-spanning that in January 2010, over 30 years after the film's original release, the website Bloody Disgusting announced that MTV was planning a television series that was to be a spin-off of the story presented in "Dawn." Even though the project seems to have now stalled, it's a testament to the longevity of the high entertainment value that the film provides for audiences both then and now.

PLAY-BY-PLAY

The film opens with a hectic scene at a television news station. The newscasters and producers are desperately trying to keep the station on the air, even though many of the line-level employees are ready to "abandon ship" and get home to their loved ones. The station is running names of rescue stations along the bottom of the screen – a nice tie to original "Night of the Living Dead," which employed the same tactics on the television station shown in that movie. Indeed, many people have questioned whether "Dawn" is a direct sequel to "Night" or if the films just share common plot elements. With the exception of "Survival of the Dead," the most recent "Dead" movie to date, Romero does not consider any of his "Dead" films to be true sequels, since none of the major characters or specific aspects of the story continue from one film to the next. It's usually easiest to say that the sequential films follow the scenario set up in "Night," primarily in the existence of the zombie epidemic. This situation advances with each film, but each movie utilizes an entirely different set of characters, and the time moves ahead to the time when the movies were filmed. This makes the world's progression the only true interlocking aspect of the series (again, with the exception of "Survival," which is in fact a direct sequel to "Diary of the Dead"). See my reviews of all of these movies in this book for further details.

Okay, I'm back to movie.

The mass confusion at the news station captures nicely the feel of "general insanity" that is no doubt permeating the entire country, perhaps the world. Even through all of this, here in the beginning of the movie it still feels like there's still a well-functioning government and law enforcement. The early scenes with the SWAT team raiding the ghetto apartment building give the film less the feel of a zombie movie and more of a "cops & robbers" flick with zombies thrown in.

Inside the apartment building, the feeling of utter confusion translates well to the viewer. Zombies jump out of every corner and every room, people have committed suicide and continue to do so right in front of the SWAT team, and mass mayhem abounds. As I mentioned above, everyone remembers this movie most for the scenes that take place in the mall, but these opening scenes really sets the tone of the film. Here, and in other scenes throughout the film, astute viewers will notice pieces of the original "Night" soundtrack being used.

During the initial helicopter ride, Peter and Roger talk about "the island," a plot element that Romero references and even uses in his later films in this series. It's nice to see that, even early on, Romero had this idea brewing.

The scene with the Army and rednecks hunting zombies (they're actually listed in the credits as "rednecks") has the feel of a very festive atmosphere, almost like a party. This scene is essentially an extension/re-hash of the "posse" scene at the end of "Night," and it's a good way to carry on tying the two films together.

The zombie action continues to come fast and furiously as our quartet of main characters maintain their journey. We are treated to some very cool zombie kills throughout the film, starting with the poor undead fellow who gets the top of his head chopped off by the spinning helicopter blades. Also of note here in the hangar scene is that at this point in the series, Romero still has some of his zombies moving faster than others. A few of the undead folks have a rather clipped gait, and the two children zombies that attack Peter in the hangar office are downright spry!

For as good as the quartet was with planning to get the chopper and make their escape from the city, they really have no clear direction after that. They have no clue where they're going or what they want to do! Fortunately they stumble across the shopping mall, replete with a convenient helicopter landing pad on the roof. Once the characters are inside and have shop set up in the storage area, it starts to become clear that the two civilians have ideas that clash with the two SWAT members' thoughts and opinions. In classic military/authoritarian style, Roger and Peter are not content with just making do.

The viewer is treated to some signature Romero-style subtle comedy in the mall, most noticeably with the zombies on the mall's escalators and the poor undead souls listening to the shopping center's still-running muzak. Later we see the muzak utilized in a different way, as we bear witness to the absurd dichotomy of the light tones playing in the background as the men are hauling away the heaps of re-killed zombie bodies.

Something to take particular notice of in "Dawn" is the intriguing and inventive camerawork Romero utilizes. Throughout most of the mall scenes, Romero used numerous cameras running at the same time, in various locations and angles, to give himself a wide array of possibilities during editing; he could choose to do "quick cuts" between angles, show a particularly unique view of a moment, or simply shorten or extend a scene using this technique. This approach, and the resulting amount of extra footage that was captured, directly contributed to the ability for multiple cuts of the movie to exist as they do. As for inventive camera work adding to the "horror" feel of the film, nowhere is this more evident than the scene in the boiler room, when a zombie is essentially stalking Stephen. The way the scene is shot makes things feel very claustrophobic on screen, and is incredibly well done.

Even with some of the undead moving a little faster, as I mentioned previously, this movie really established the slow, shambling "Romero-type" zombie. Yes, we saw a lot of these zombies in "Night," but the sheer number of the living dead in this film really launched the idea that a horde of slow-moving monsters could exist and still be scary as Hell. On the flip side of this, the "Hare Krishna zombie" that finds its way up to the quartet's hideout and terrorizes Francine proves that one lone zombie in an enclosed space is just as frightening, if not more so, than a whole horde!

Francine's pregnancy brings up an interesting question in the face of zompocalypse – would the average person truly want to bring a child into this strange new world? Obviously if the human race has any chance of surviving, they not only have to fight back against the undead, but they will also have to propagate the species at some point. However, the challenges of raising a child are, to put it lightly, numerous; as a first-time parent with a very young child myself, I can tell you that my hands are full day in and day out, and I'm constantly busy and distracted in tending to my young one – and that's not even with any hordes of ravenous undead monsters hunting me and wanting to eat the flesh off my bones. I couldn't fathom raising a child in that kind of environment, so I certainly can empathize with Francine's debate on whether to keep her unborn child or not.

This leads us to an interesting bit of trivia that not many fans know about the end of this film. In addition to the ample consumerism commentary at the conclusion of the story, and of course the nice, ambiguous ending that has become a staple of the Romero zombie film, the writer-director actually had plans for a very different tone for the final scenes of the movie. According to the original screenplay, Peter was to actually follow through with his plan to shoot himself in the head instead of changing his mind at the last minute. Not only that, but Fran was actually going to commit suicide as well by thrusting her head into the moving helicopter blades. The end credits were then going to roll over a stationary shot of the helicopter's blades turning until the engine gives out at the end of the credits, indicating that Fran and Peter would not have had enough fuel to get very far anyway.

This ending was so close to being a reality that rehearsals for the final scenes were actually run with the actors. In addition, the special effects team created an appliance of a duplicate head for Fran, a malleable skull that was to meet a grisly fate in the chopper blades. Since Romero decided at the last minute against this ending, the head was re-purposed as the head of the African-American zombie that was blown off by a SWAT team member's shotgun. A lot of the scenes setting up the "alternate ending" are actually present in the finished film. Fran stands on the roof directly under the moving helicopter blades, waiting for Peter, as the zombies close in on her, and we see Peter go as far as actually putting the gun to his head, preparing to shoot himself. But as we all know, Peter changes his mind at the last second, deciding to join Fran in escaping into an uncertain future.

TAKE TWO: A.G.

From the second you see that blood red carpet on the screen, you know you're in for a treat. There's just something about the color red that seems to grab the attention of most of us.

Fran looks vulnerable as she tries to get some sleep and as we see her shocked awake, as if from a bad dream, we see how beautiful she is.

Of course, she and us as viewers quickly find out that her nightmare isn't only in her head, but a reality. And all this thanks to George Romero, the creator of the modern zombie.

For the dead are walking and the world will never be the same again, on or off the movie screen.

We only get to see Fran in her workplace for a few minutes but when she's there, we see a strong, decisive woman. The same for our first impression of Stephen. When he talks to her, he's confident and sure of himself, quite the difference once we get to know him. Then, we find a man who is so far out of his element it's riduclous, especially when he's thrown in with two trained SWAT officers.

Peter is strong and confident, and it's not just for show. He's a man not afraid to make a decision, which we see when he shoots Wooly in the back (another SWAT officer who goes crazy during a raid). Though Wooly was out of control and what happened was necessary, if the world hadn't collapsed, then Peter would have either been brought up on murder charges or would have become a pariah from the other officers.

Roger is also a strong role model for men everywhere. While short on stature, he makes up for it with his charisma, wit and bravado. The two officers are a perfect counterpoint to one another.

In the tenement building we get our first look at the zombies. Unlike *Night of the Living Dead*, we now get to see the dead in glorious color. Of course in many ways this detracts as they all look blue and some green. In many ways, the black and white predecessor was able to hide the faults in makeup.

But where that may be a disadvantage, seeing the spray of bright red blood makes up for it. Sure, the blood is too red, but that's what makes it fun. It's so vibrant you can't help but look and want to make sure you see every last drop splatter across the screen.

Here, Peter and Roger battle the walking dead and first become partners. If you look at Roger's face when he's in the basement, when he turns and sees Peter and recalls that this is the man who killed Wooly, you have to wonder if Roger believed he was about to be next?

The Priest that startles the two men is priceless and utters two of the wisest statements in movie history.

"You are more powerful than us but soon, they will be stronger than you."

And, "When the dead walk, we must stop the killing or lose the war."

Those statements can be taken and used in so many wars and conflicts across the globe it's frightening.

One of the next scenes that always grabbed me was when Peter is shooting the zombies in the basement, a tear rolling down his cheek. He is feeling what all the officers must have been feeling as he shot men, women and children.

Though all the SWAT officers must have been running on adrenalin alone, when they finally had a chance to slow down and take in what they were doing, the slaughtering of people—or what looks like people—well, it had to be a lot to deal with.

Which explains why Roger's buddy shoots himself in the head in the tenement apartment after they take down two zombies.

Move forward a little and we're at the police dock. As I'm talking about the extended version, we get a sneak peek at the man who will play Rhodes on Day of the Dead, though now he is playing a different character.

I wonder what might have happened to Stephen and Fran if Peter and Roger hadn't arrived right then. Would the rogue cops have killed Stephen and taken Fran for themselves? Or left them in peace.

And as the rogue cops float away in a boat, searching for an island, you have to wonder whatever happened to them. There is another whole adventure right there.

Jumping a little further, we get to the abandoned airfield. When Peter goes into the small building, there's a scrawled note on the wall.

"Joe, gone to Druckers Farm."

Makes you wonder who left that and what happened to them and Joe.

When the two kids charged out of the closet and attack Peter, have you ever had a look at how fast they run? They aren't slow and plodding, they're whip fast, leaping at Peter and wrapping their arms and legs around him.

Not relevant, but amusing as I have never seen anyone comment on it. Were these the first "fast" zombies?

Maybe they were so fresh they were still able to move fast.

Here we see how bad a shot Stephen is and how great a marksman Roger is.

One question I always had is when Stephen leaves the old hangar and has the mallet in his hand. When he tells Fran to run, instead of cracking the zombie over the head, he kind of belly flops the ghoul. They fall to the ground and he then whacks it. Just strange is all.

Moving forward once more, we get to see our first view of the shopping mall as the helicopter flies over it. Even now, thirty years later, who doesn't get excited at the sight of a shopping mall? And to have the run of one, with no one to stop you from taking what you want? Still probably on most people's wish list.

Here's another item no one has pointed out that I'm aware of. When the group looks down into the mall from the roof to see zombies wandering around, the floors of the mall are pristine. Not so much as one spot of blood. Zombies are gross, and have wounds, shouldn't there be even a little blood or maybe dirt?

And the zombies themselves are nice and clean. Only two or three have soiled clothing, the rest look like they just put them on. If you get killed and then turn into a zombie, shouldn't your clothes get bloody? Just having fun in pointing this out, not trying to be negative.

Once the group is inside the office space above the mall and Peter and Roger go "shopping," the fun really starts. After all, they're doing what all of us can only dream of, and it's all for the taking.

Of course, college boy Stephen follows and almost gets killed. Here I think we see that Stephen really has no street smarts. He goes for the maps in the back office, as he's an intelligent man, but common sense...well, not so much.

He shows this when he's a hairsbreadth from getting killed while he keeps shooting erratically in the pump room. If he had stayed calm, he could have shot the security guard zombie with one bullet. But then, isn't that the theme of the entire movie? When you don't stay calm and keep your head, you are your own worse enemy.

When Stephen joins Peter and Roger, we can see how much fun he's having, the pure comradery of being with two macho men. One has to think how Stephen's personal life was as far as how he dealt with other men. I figure it's highly unlikely he had friends such as Peter and Roger.

Here is where Stephen's intelligence comes in and he shows the other two the map of the duct system and becomes a valued asset, and not just their pilot.

After saving Fran from the Hare Krishna zombie, we see a new dynamic forming as far as Stephen and Peter are concerned. Peter respects Stephen a little more, seeing the pilot can do more than just fly a helicopter.

This is where we find out Fran is pregnant and Peter asks if Stephen wants to abort it. Can you imagine how Fran must have felt upon hearing that?

As if she didn't count and she was a second class citizen, the "men" were deciding her fate.

Later, as Peter, Roger and Stephen move the trucks to block the mall entrances, we see Roger begin to lose it. Here is where his wild side runs loose and he become careless.

After being attacked in the cab of a truck, he changes. Now, killing zombies has become personal, and that change is his downfall.

Taking far too many chances when they weren't necessary, he gets bit.

Though off screen we know the group manages to get all the trucks in front of the mall doors to block the zombies, it comes at a terrible price.

Roger is doomed to become one of the living dead.

But not yet, and we get to have some more action as the team races to lock the shopping mall doors from the inside. Lots of fun and gore here. One of my favorites is when the show car on display pulls away and the woman zombie is hanging on the back, but when she's shot in the face it's now a stunt man.

Once the group gets the doors locked, they're good to go; all they have to do is kill the zombies still trapped inside the mall. As Peter says, he and Stephen are "going on a hunt."

And the shopping mall is theirs; they own it by rite of battle.

Now it's time for leisure. As the world falls apart, they pass the time playing games and relaxing.

A few days later, as the TV drones on, letting the four friends know how bad things are getting outside the shopping mall, Roger dies and returns and Peter is there, ready to do what has to be done.

In many ways, losing Roger hits the three remaining friends in a very different way. The reality that they can die, too, something none of them had really faced before Roger was bit. They were just going on auto pilot, taking risks, and with Roger dead, their reality hits home in a whole new way.

Now this is where the film slows down but for me it's always been my favorite.

With Roger gone, the three live on, the mall theirs to do as they please.

We see how time passes in a few ways. One being Fran's growing belly. But also in the way their living space is decorated. From a bed on the floor and a sanitation barrel as a nightstand, we soon see they have actual furniture and are living quite well for themselves.

Of course, once the TV stops broadcasting their moods change, realizing that while they're safe, the world is in dire straits.

Fran learns to fly the helicopter which is a great thing for her self esteem as well as the safety of the group. Unfortunately this calls attention to their haven. A roving motorcycle gang has come across the shopping mall and has spotted the helicopter. Surviving on the road through the apocalypse, they want what's in the mall and aren't afraid to take it.

This adds a new challenge for the trio of survivors. The zombies have been tamed so to speak, but other humans are another story.

This is a theme throughout Romero's movies, all about how if we all worked together we would be fine, but like always, we're always out for ourselves, each with his or her own agenda.

In the last chapter of the movie the bikers attack, Peter and Stephen closing all the store gates to make it harder for the bikers to take items. But Stephen, in a ridiculously foolish act, decides it's the group's mall and shoots at the bikers. Here is the classic losing your head Romero always talks about.

Why Stephen did this is so foolish it's mind boggling and in the end, it gets him killed when he's trapped in an elevator after being wounded by a biker. He dies and comes back and this is an interesting part as he has some remembrance of when he was alive. He goes right to the false wall he and Peter built to hide the stairwell to their living space from intruders.

Now this shouldn't be a big deal. The living space of the trio has a door.

But for some reason, Peter doesn't bother to lock it. This has always driven me crazy. If they're going to go to all the trouble of building a fake wall, then why the hell wouldn't they bother putting a two dollar lock on the door to their apartment? I mean, a two-by-four would have worked.

Then to keep the movie going in a realistic fashion, the zombies could have pushed the door in with their weight.

But beside this small plot hole, the end of the film is wonderful. Peter sends Fran to the helicopter and decides to give up and commit suicide, but at the last second he wants to live and he fights off the zombies and climbs onto the roof just as Fran is about to leave.

Peter climbs into the helicopter, and she flies off into the coming dawn.

The helicopter is low on gas and they have lost Stephen, but the rising sun gives us hope that they will make it to someplace safe.

DAY OF THE DEAD

YEAR: 1985
COUNTRY: USA
RUNNING TIME: 102 minutes
WRITER: George A Romero
DIRECTOR: George A Romero
PRODUCER: Richard P Rubenstein
MUSIC: John Harrison
DIRECTOR OF PHOTOGRAPHY: Micahel Gornick
MAKE-UP EFFECTS: Tom Savini
ART DIRECTOR: Bruce Miller
PRODUCTION DESIGNER: Cletus Anderson
COSTUME DESIGNER: Barbara Anderson
CAST: Lori Cardille (Sarah), Terry Alexander (John), Joe Pilato (Rhodes), Jarlath Conroy (McDermott), Antone DiLeo (Miguel), Richard Libery (Logan), Howard Sherman (Bub), Ralph Marreo (Rickles), John Amplas (Fisher), G Howard Klar (Steel), Gregory Nicotero (Johnson)

TAKE ONE: T.S.

COMMENTARY

A friend once shared with me this opinion: "Day of the Dead" is the "Return of the Jedi" of zombie movies—the end to a classic trilogy." While I whole-heartedly agreed with him on the "classic trilogy" part, I had to quickly correct him on his usage of metaphor; Romero's trilogy started to grace the silver screens nine years before Lucas', so the more accurate statement should actually be that "Return of the Jedi" is the "Day of the Dead" of sci-fi movies—the end to a classic trilogy.

Semantics, I know; but it's the thought process like my friend's that underscores how sorely under-appreciated "Day of the Dead" is amongst film aficionados. Heck, in one of the special features interviews on the Divimax Special Edition DVD of the movie, Romero himself states proudly that "Day" is his favorite film of the original trilogy. He goes on to describe the film in his own words as a "tragedy about how a lack of communication causes chaos and collapse even in this small little pie-slice of society." What he may be indicating is that, while all three of his original trilogy films highlight how things can go from bad to worse if we lack even the most basic trust and compassion for our fellow man, "Day" may best illustrate the utter collapse of a tenuous situation due to humans' inability to simply get along with one another. And after having watched this classic story many times, I'm hard-pressed not to agree with him.

"Day" was originally intended to be much more sweeping and vast in its nature, "the "Gone with the Wind' of zombie films," as referenced by The Homepage of the Dead. Sadly, concerns over the amount of gore Romero wanted to show and his desire to release the film unrated caused United Film, the distributor of the movie, to cut the budget in half, from $7 million down to $3.5 million. Even with this dramatic reduction, "Day" still sported the highest budget of the original trilogy, but Romero was forced to significantly alter his story. Through multiple script rewrites and adjusting his original vision for the film, he finalized the final draft, and filming for the movie began in the fall of 1984.

Since Romero was living in Florida at the time, the in-film location, as well as much of the actual shooting, took place in the state, a departure from the other two movies being filmed exclusively in Pennsylvania (although parts of "Day" were shot there as well). To help save on budget costs, the zombie extras were infamously paid $1 for their services, as well as receiving a hat that said "I was a Zombie in Day of the Dead." Romero's producer and special effects coordinator from "Dawn," Richard Rubenstein and Tom Savini, respectively, returned to their roles for the new film.

Speaking of Savini and the special effects group, his return to working with Romero is not the only "zombie connection" this movie has. Greg Nicotero was featured on screen as one of the military men, Private Johnson, and he has gone on to continue to work in the effects field in Hollywood, notably as the cofounder of KNB Efx Group and most recently as part of the special effects team for the AMC television series "The Walking Dead." Joseph Pilato, who was one of Savini's production assistants on "Dawn" (in addition to playing a police captain in the film), starred in this film as the main villain, Captain Rhodes. Savini himself would go on to direct, with Romero's blessing, the 1990 remake of "Night of the Living Dead." Clearly, the movie-making zombie community is a close-knit one!

Once the film was released into theaters, it met with mixed reviews from both critics and viewers. Many were disappointed that the nature of the plot, which had allowed our view of the zombie-infested world to be considerably expanded from "Night" to "Dawn," had been re-constricted here to only showing us one small group of survivors and nothing else. In addition, the film has a considerably darker tone to it than either of the other two, and most of the characters come across as unsympathetic and unpleasant, bordering on downright unlikeable. The film was considered a "flop" when it was released in American theaters, grossing only $5.8 million domestically. Thanks to its strong international showing, the movie ended up grossing over $34 million in theaters worldwide.

Scenes and bits from "Day" have been referenced in a multitude of pop culture idioms, including music, television, video games, and even other movies, probably most notably in the film "Resident Evil" (which is also reviewed in this book), which pays homage to "Day's" ghost-town newspaper headline "The Dead Walk!" by duplicating the same headline in a newspaper shown in its final scene. From a personal standpoint, I can't even count the number of times I've heard or seen someone in another zombie movie, book, comic, etc., scream "Choke on 'em!" in reference to Rhodes' last words in the film.

In 2008, "Day" received the unauthorized-remake treatment, much like "Dawn" before it in 2004. Unlike "Dawn's" remake, however, the remake of this film has very little entertainment quality, and is really not even worth seeking out by anyone except the most hard-core horror fans. There also exists a "Day of the Dead 2" film, subtitled "Contagium," which was produced by Taurus Entertainment, the company who holds the rights to the "Day of the Dead" name.

To call "Contagium" terrible would be, quite frankly, an insult to the word "terrible." News was released in February 2010 that Taurus plans yet another pseudo-sequel, "Day of the Dead: Epidemic;" nothing new has been mentioned about the project since this initial release, so let's all continue to say our prayers that this film never sees the light of "Day."

Talks of other movies aside, all good trilogies must have a concluding chapter, and even though this film ultimately didn't end up as our final cinematic glimpse into Romero's "Dead" world, it remains as one of his best pieces of work, and will always be highly regarded by the intelligent zombie lover.

PLAY-BY-PLAY

The film begins with a "dream opening," which is a moderately-used tactic among filmmakers, but a decidedly different tactic for Romero. It works, though, and provides for the beginning of a nice "bookend" feel with the closing scene of the film as well.

Right away, you can tell this movie will sport much of the same kind of feel as its two predecessors, but will also be a different entity altogether. Romero and his crew do an excellent job of keeping the "Dead" movies separate but still connected via the common element, the walking dead. One noticeable difference in "Day" as opposed to the other two: the zombies are a lot more vocal in this film, with almost all the members of the hordes moaning loudly, almost bordering on screaming. In "Night" and "Dawn" we witnessed a few moaners here and there, but certainly nothing on the level we are given in this third film.

Every human survivor in the rag-tag group in the underground bunker is dealing heavily with the effects of stress, which is surprisingly not something that's addressed too much in many zombie tales, but a definite underlying factor in all of them. The writing here deftly shows the characters suffering in their own way, as each individual's personalities dictate how they act and react to each situation they encounter. It's an excellent dose of realism injected into the film.

There is a death of one of the military men early in the story that is not shown on-screen. The unit's commander, "Major Cooper," is killed, leaving Captain Rhodes in command and setting up the conflict between Rhodes and the survivors that will permeate the rest of the story. A nagging question for me, though: could this Major Cooper be a relative of "Night's" Harry Cooper, maybe? One can dream!

The "zombie corral" is an interesting idea, and one that's been "borrowed" more than a few times by creators of other undead stories. The revenants also seem much more animated in this film, but also more decomposed, which makes for an interesting dichotomy.

This film obviously highlights Romero's none-too-secret, tell-us-how-you-really-feel commentary about the negativity of the military. What started with "redneck" posses in the first two movies has slowly transitioned into the full-blown, anti-military sentiment we see here. Even though the opinion is very prevalent in the film, it fits with the tone of the story without beating us over the head with it, so I really can't complain too much about it.

We're given a significant amount more relating to the actual science surrounding the undead than in the previous films, mostly through the work of the "main" scientist, Dr. Logan. However, for as intelligent as Logan obviously is, the strain of the situation is clearly wearing on him as well. A perfect example of this comes as we see him operating on the reanimated corpse of Major Cooper. This is the first bit of the film where I felt like things were getting disturbingly past "the point of no return" for the characters.

Romero loves to throw bits of comedy into his horror movies, and even though "Day" is fairly dark in its tone, we still get a few opportunities to chuckle. One of the military men mentions that "all the shopping malls are closed," a nice direct reference to this film's predecessor, and we even get to hear some musical cues in "Day" that are lifted directly from the muzak featured in "Dawn's" shopping center.

At first glance while watching the movie, most people think there are two main factions of people in the bunker, the military and the civilians, but upon closer inspection we actually find that there are three: the contracted workers, John the helicopter pilot and Bill the radio technician, make a third party.

They keep themselves separate from both groups until the time for action comes, after a very tense meeting that really highlights the desperation and hopelessness of the group's situation. After Sarah visits the two men in their trailer in the mine, isolated from the military and civilian quarters, there is a definite shift in the feel of their allegiances. A rather deep philosophical conversation ends up bringing Sarah closer to them, and this relationship plays a key role in the tense climax of the film.

Who are we kidding, really—I can spend lots of time talking about the human characters and their interactions with one another, but the true stars of this film are the zombies themselves. Romero shows them in a drastically new light; they learn, react, and even exhibit some emotions, all very unzombie-like things to do, especially up to the point when the movie was first released. Blazing the trail in this new direction is "Bub," Dr. Logan's prize specimen who possesses quite a bit of ability to recall information from his "past life" as a human.

He recognizes items such as toothbrushes, razors (which he tries to use and awkwardly cuts off a thin slice of his undead flesh), books, telephones, and even a gun. The latter he points at Rhodes; it's not loaded, but the mere act makes an already-pissed-off guy like Rhodes all the more outraged. The scene where Bub finds the murdered Dr. Logan is actually quite touching.

Even more gruesome than the zombies here are the way they kill humans. I mean, these undead folks really rip the survivors to shreds! In the final scene with Rhodes and Bub, I feel confident saying that I don't believe an audience has ever rooted so much for a zombie to kill a human before.

Of special note is the final scene in the film, as it completes a very interesting transition for Romero. The endings of the trilogy's individual films go from bleak ("Night") to indifferent/uncertain ("Dawn") to actually rather positive ("Day"). It's an interesting transition that shows not only growth on the part of our beloved director, but possibly the hint that he may have had an idea of a bigger story from the get-go, from all the way back in 1968 until seventeen years later when his third film would conclude the trilogy.

Even if that may not be true…it sure is a nice thought.

TAKE TWO: A.G.

Just like in the previous movie—*Dawn of the Dead*—*Day of the Dead* has more zombies than you can shake a stick at.

From the first scene where Sarah is staring at the calendar and zombie hands reach for her, you know you're in for a zombie-good time.

As the helicopter flies over Florida, the haunting Caribbean music begins to play. In many ways it's lighthearted and upbeat, much to the contrary of the world below.

The musical score is one of my favorite things in *Day of the Dead*. The synthesized beat has had me viewing the movie multiple times, if only to hear the score. When I finally got the music CD of the movie, I was a happy little zombie.

As Miguel calls out "Hello!" the zombies in the small town in Florida begin to rise and we get our first look at a true zombie. Missing his lower jaw, the tongue hanging low, we see the state of the ghouls after at least five years or more. The exact time is never told, but we have to assume almost ten years has passed since the second movie.

As the town's streets fill with zombies, and money—now worthless—blows about the street, we see a world where the dead have won.

As the moans fill the air and John says it's so loud it can be heard over the engine of the helicopter, a chill should run down any zombie fan's spine.

As they leave and head back to their base, we now have a clear picture of the world we're thrown into.

The base is an underground facility, old and outdated. Soon, we see the vast walls and the massive cave where the zombies are being stored. Now in most movies, we would have had our peek at the zombies and then would have more than a half hour of talk amongst the characters, but not here. No sooner does the team arrive then they are going to the cave where the large pen is set up to catch the zombies. Dr. Logan, aka "Frankenstein" is waiting for more lab specimens and it's the job of the soldiers to fetch them when needed.

Here we see how messed up Miguel is and how he's barely holding it together. Lot's of great zombie action as they struggle to grab the ghouls and get them to Dr. Logan.

When Miguel screws up as they're capturing the ghouls and almost kills Rickles (another soldier), we get a little insight of the dynamics of the men. Steele is a racist jerk, but is no doubt a capable man.

He's someone that though you might not like, you'd want him at your back in a fight. Rickles is his sidekick, and also seems competent, though has an "I don't give a shit attitude."

And then there's Captain Rhodes.

Now years ago, when I first began watching *Day of the Dead*, I considered Rhodes to be an asshole. He was a jerk, with no respect for the scientists or the men under him. He's abusive, crude and obnoxious. He's the bad guy in the movie, the guy you want to see killed.

And then I grew up and now look at life a little differently than when I was younger.

Now I see Rhodes isn't an asshole at the beginning of the movie. Not really. What he is, is a man who will tell you like it is. He's a man that when his commander dies suddenly—Major Cooper—he's left in charge and he's not ready for it. Everyone is under pressure and stress is rampant and now Rhodes has had it all thrown in his lap. He's overwhelmed and scared. He reacts by lashing out, demanding things, and Sarah, who is also a strong-willed woman, yells back.

At the meeting when he threatens to shoot her, in a way it's something he has to do. If he lets her disrespect him—the commander—then what will stop his men from listening to his orders?

And if you look at the science team, they have little to no respect for the soldiers keeping them safe and doing their dirty work, such as getting zombie specimens for Dr. Logan.

There's a lot of yelling in *Day of the Dead*, a lot of anger and swearing, and that's why most people don't like it. But you know what? That's why it's so great. *Day of the Dead* is one of the realistic movies ever made.

Stick different types of people in a cave for years, with a world that's gone to Hell and little to no hope, and you know what you'll get? People freaking out, lashing out, and snapping at one another. In time, they will even kill each other. (A reality show in the making, perhaps?)

And then there's Bub. A zombie that can think, even if it's only barely. In many ways, he has more of a soul than the humans who occupy the bunker. The scene where Dr. Logan fixes his headset and Bub grabs his arm, but doesn't take a bite, says that zombies can learn, that they aren't simple eating machines. Of course, this would be followed further in the next movie more than twenty years later in *Land of the Dead*.

The theme of *Day* to me is a simple one. People need to work together. When we don't, we're all doomed to failure.

And that's what happens. It all comes to a chilling ending when an insane Miguel (after being bit by a zombie and has his arm cut off…ouch!) lets the zombies inside the bunker. As he's torn apart, the dead take over the bunker, killing everyone but the few heroes we liked from the very beginning.

As for Captain Rhodes, well, he has one of the best death scenes in the history of cinema. "Choke on 'em!" is absolutely classic, and is one of the goriest scenes in zombie cinema. And the fact that Bub could have shot him and put him out of his misery and didn't, adds yet another layer to the zombie that he can actually think and reason. Hell, he even saluted as Rhodes is about to be torn apart by the horde of zombies!

Romero originally had a grander theme planned for the movie but lack of funding caused him to cut back. Though his original vision would have been much larger, in many ways what became the finished work is far superior.

The movie *Day of the Dead* is about people. It's close to home, deep inside what makes us tick, and in years to come may be considered the best and truest of the zombie films Romero has made.

Because the entire movie takes place in an underground bunker, there is nothing really to place it at a particular date in time in history, so out of all of Romero's zombie films, this movie holds up well as the years slip by.

Filled with zombies—even if it's just one zombie such as the scenes with Bub—from beginning to end, and a few choice moments that have been duplicated by other filmmakers over and over, *Day of the Dead* is one of the best zombie films out there, even after twenty-five years.

They just don't make 'em like this anymore.

DEAD ALIVE (BRAIN DEAD)

DEAD ALIVE (BRAIN DEAD)

YEAR: 1992
COUNTRY: New Zealand
RUNNING TIME: 100 minutes
SCREENPLAY: Peter Jackson, Stephen Sinclair, Frances Walsh
DIRECTOR: Peter Jackson
PRODUCER: Jim Booth
ASSOCIATE PRODUCER: Jamie Selkirk
MUSIC: Peter Dasent
DIRECTOR OF PHOTOGRAPHY: Murray Milne
SPECIAL EFFECTS: Richard Taylor, Stuart Conran
PRODUCTION DESIGNER: Kevin Leonard-Jones
ART DIRECTOR: Ed Mulholland
COSTUME DESIGNER: Chris Elliot
CAST: Timothy Balme (Lionel), Diana Penalver (Paquita), Elizabeth Moody (Mum), Ian Watkin (Uncle Les), Stuart Devenie (Father McGruder)

TAKE ONE: T.S.

COMMENTARY

It's been said by many folks that Peter Jackson's "Dead Alive" is the goriest film of all time.

I'm here today to add my name to that list.

Not only do the blood and guts flow like a river throughout the film, culminating in the unbelievably-entertaining shock-fest of the ultimate final zombie fight sequence, the movie is damn entertaining from nearly every other aspect as well. The writing is tight, with laugh-out-loud funny moments, and even a hint of emotion (and romance!) for good measure. The cast does a great job of acting to the level of the movie. In other words, they seem to know that they're part of a film that probably won't be winning any Oscars, so no one tries to be overly dramatic, but they also avoid "hamming it up."

It just looks like everyone wanted to have some good old-fashioned fun with this film, and the result is easily one of the best zombie movies ever to grace the screen.

"Dead Alive" was originally titled "Braindead" in its native country of New Zealand, but the title had to be changed upon its theatrical release in the United States due to copyright issues with another film that shared the original title. Even though the movie was a financial flop in U.S. theaters, it has gone on to become a cult classic on video, and to avoid too much confusion here in this review, I'll continue to reference it as "Dead Alive," with all deference to its original name. Directed by the über-talented Peter Jackson long before he "made it big" by helming the mega-bucks "Lord of the Rings" cinematic trilogy, the story took a fairly standard horror trope and twisted the presentation into so-shocking-it's-funny territory.

Set in the late 1950s, the film sees human poachers visit Skull Island (yes, inferred to be the same Skull Island from the "King Kong" franchise, another film that Jackson would later give the big-budget Hollywood remake treatment to) and ensnare a mythical Sumatran Rat Monkey, putting it on display in a zoo in Wellington. Prototypical dweeb Lionel takes his new girlfriend Paquita on a date to the zoo, and when his overbearing mother follows him and gets bit by the monkey, she gets extremely ill.

Eventually she passes away and reanimates, and then the real fun begins. Lionel tries to keep up appearances to the neighbors and townspeople that all is well, even though he doesn't have the heart to kill Mum and tries to keep her from killing other people by locking her (and a few other zombies she's already turned) in the basement. Of course, it's hard for Lionel to keep something like this a secret indefinitely, and before long zombies are everywhere and havoc is officially being wreaked.

"Dead Alive" was actually Jackson's third feature directorial effort, behind 1987's schlock-fest "Bad Taste" and 1990's black comedy "Meet the Feebles." Both of these movies, while entertaining in their own right, truly helped Jackson hone his craft and the lessons he learned from them are directly responsible for helping him to make "Dead Alive" the highly-entertaining story it is.

Through everything the movie has to offer, it is most discussed among genre fans for its climactic scene, in which the zombie kills are plentiful and the amount of gore is copious.

Of particular note to fans, and often described as the "best zombie killing tool of all time," is Lionel's attack on the horde with a lawnmower. Not only is it an amazingly enjoyable and effective way to—pardon the pun—mow down the undead, but in a sea of zombie films where protagonists repeatedly choose to put zombies down by shooting them in the skull, cutting off their heads with a knife or sword, or burning a revenant, Jackson's choice to have his hero use the ultimate lawn-care tool to help him eliminate the undead with extreme prejudice is a refreshing change of pace. And damn fun to watch.

DEAD ALIVE (BRAIN DEAD)

PLAY-BY-PLAY

As mentioned previously, "Dead Alive" begins with a very "classic horror" opening scene of the oppressive, know-it-all civilized man taking what he wants despite warnings from the natives. I love that Jackson specifically stated directly in the film that this sequence takes place on Skull Island, a direct homage to one of his favorite films, "King Kong." Also of note here is that the scene was shot at the Putangirua Pinnacles, a very unique geological formation of rocky outcroppings in New Zealand, and a site that Jackson would revisit as a director for the key "Paths of the Dead" sequence in "The Lord of the Rings: The Return of the King."

Jackson establishes that he is going to give the viewer a very gory film right out of the gate with the decapitation of the Wellington Zoo's representative on Skull Island. It is here, within the first few minutes of the movie, that he sets expectations for his audience, and they are expectations that he easily lives up to throughout the remainder of the film. When we get our first visual exposure to the Sumatran Rat monkey, we are reminded of the limitations of some of the types of special effects in the early '90s, when this film was made—wow, is that monkey some bad Claymation! But now, in retrospect, it has a kitschy appeal to it, and even though it's no Harryhausen-esque effect, the graphical representation was passable for its time.

After a fair bout of exposition to introduce us to the main characters and their personality traits, the bloody action gets flowing again at the Wellington Zoo. When the Sumatran Rat Monkey attacks Vera, Lionel's mother, it's one of those moments that you know is coming but is still shocking when it actually occurs.

Of course, Vera being Vera, she can't let the little bugger bite her and get away unharmed, so naturally, she steps on its face. Her yelling and the ensuing ruckus has drawn a crowd, and as she kills the monkey with her shoe, a man in the crowd (the actual J. Forest Ackerman, nonetheless) takes a picture excitedly, giving one of many perfect examples of the good blend of comedy plus horror Jackson was able to achieve throughout this story.

As Lionel cares for his mother, Vera's condition gets exponentially worse, as does the visual state of her wounds—the initial monkey bite arm wound gets extremely gruesome, and the disturbingly-disgusting damage quickly spreads across the rest of her body. Vera's final human-to-zombie transformation during the dinner scene with guests is absolutely hilarious, including the gag-inducing pus she squirts in one visitor's pudding, and the fact that she eats her own ear!

The film has some great dialogue, and some classic one-liners abound. Among some rather hilarious exchanges are, "Your mother ate my dog!" "Well, not ALL of it..." and "They're not dead, exactly, they're just sort of...rotting." Then comes one of my all-time favorite zombie movie quotes, one I bandy about quite often: Father MacGruder's emphatic exclamation of "I kick ass for the Lord!" And he does!

"Dead Alive" also gets bonus points for tackling a few of the more off-kilter questions that most zombie films never get around to addressing. As Lionel can attest to, it's hard to keep a nice house and clean up after a zombie.

At this point in the film, Jackson switches into full-on comedy mode, often putting things in the storyline simply for the attempt at going for the extreme gross-out. The stomach-churning yet laughable situations are plentiful. They include Lionel's attempts to sedate his mother and the other zombies by sticking tranquilizer injections directly into the undead's pus-popping eyes and nostrils, and the embalming "mishap" that causes Vera to literally explode with formaldehyde—extra appalling points for the undertaker that still eats the sandwich that was resting on her chest during the explosion. Lionel still tries to maintain some semblance of civility, even going so far as to serve breakfast to his mother and his other undead guests. Of course, this goes about as well as you'd expect, with the reanimated monsters shoving forks through the back of their heads, having eggs fall out of slits in their throats, and eating one another's post-digested eggs. I guess no matter what kind of story, zombies just don't have any manners!

But wait, there's more gross-out to be had! Thanks to Jackson and his twisted mind (along with the twisted minds of his co-writers Stephen Sinclair and Fran Walsh), we get to see what unprotected zombie sex leads to—horrible little zombie babies! Again, Lionel tries in vain to take the "high road," going so far as taking the zombie baby for a walk, but once again he meets with fairly disastrous results. In all honesty, once Lionel drops his attempt at gentility, he gets to do what most parents feel like doing some days, and really beats the crap out of that junior zombie.

Just when you think this film couldn't possibly break any more taboos and show you anything more "wrong" than what you've already seen, along comes the final portion of the movie, when the zombie virus has spread to hundreds of revenants and it's up to Lionel and his rag-tag team of survivors to take them all out. The attention to the gory, disgusting, comedic detail is actually quite impressive: from the dismembered hand that picks Lionel's nose to the dismembered zombie internal system complete with an exposed anus that farts, GROSS is the only word that comes even remotely close to describing the mayhem you're exposed to here. And for those of you who haven't seen the film yet, make no mistake—even though it sounds incredibly odd, the zombie internal organ system, which has been ripped out of the body of another reanimated corpse, is easily the most persistent of all the undead pursuers.

When it's all said and done, the unbelievable amount of gore in the final scenes is actually incredibly impressive, and a testament not only to Jackson's story-telling abilities, but the faith that the movie studio had to have in him in order to put this crazy experience on the big screen in front of the public. Thank goodness they did have that faith in their director, because the result is a truly one-of-a-kind movie that should be on every zombie fan's "must-see" list.

TAKE TWO: A.G

Over the top, excessive, surreal, bizarre, and more blood and gore than any other zombie movie ever made at the time. *Dead Alive* is all of these things and more.

Peter Jackson's zombie masterpiece is not for the faint of heart.

The movie begins with a prologue that mimics both King Kong and Jurassic Park.

Here, Jackson explains how the zombie outbreak will begin. A rare, Simian rat-monkey is captured on Skull Island, near Sumatra, one whose bite is fatal and contains a form of viral disease.

The explorer who has captured the rat-monkey finds himself being chased by the local natives. When the explorer is bitten by the rat-monkey during the chase, the natives then proceed to graphically dismember him a limb at a time, hacking him to pieces so he can't spread the infection.

All this is just the prologue to the actual film and despite the horror, comedy and gore, there is a deeper meaning to the movie, one where Lionel has a tenacious relationship with his authoritarian mother, who has completely dominated him. Not so much a Momma's boy as merely a good son, Lionel is constantly being ordered around and controlled, despite his willingness to want to spread his wings.

When Lionel meets Paquita, a supermarket clerk, it only adds to the relationship troubles between Lionel and his Mum.

When Lionel takes Paquita to the zoo, Mum follows, rather stalkishly, and is accidentally bitten by the rat-monkey when she gets too close to its cage. Later, in bed, we see the wound is pulsating and putrefying, a sign of what's to come.

We get our first taste of how over-the-top this movie is when Mum and Lionel are having lunch with another couple and Mum's wound spurts globules of blood and pus, some of it landing in one of her guest's custard bowl. Oblivious to the pus and blood, the man scoops up a heaping bowl of custard and swallows it whole, the entire time complimenting how creamy the custard is.

When Mum's ear falls off, she scoops it and eats it in her own custard, making sure to spit out the pearl earring as she chews and swallows. Mum is pretty much gone by now and on the verge of death.

The fun really begins when Paquita arrives with her dog, Fernando, who is promptly eaten by Mum, who then bites and kills and thusly infects the nurse who was treating her.

Lionel, not knowing what to do with two zombies on his hands, panics and throws Mum and the nurse into the cellar.

Wanting to keep it all quiet, he now does his best to keep the zombies his little secret.

But Mum doesn't stay in the cellar and the next day when Lionel is out seeing Paquita at the grocery store, Mum escapes and is then run over by a trolley car, and sent flying through the air to crash into the grocery store. With the jig up, so to speak, Lionel has to bury her, but not before making sure she's doped up on horse tranquilizer to keep her looking dead.

Even being embalmed does little to slow Mum down.

When Mum dies a bit later, and wakes up as a zombie, Lionel is at the cemetery ready to dig her up.

The gore and madness continue when three hooligans confront Lionel at the cemetery and begin to beat him up. But as one of the hooligans pees on Mum's grave, she reaches up through the dirt and disembowels him, then kills the other two hooligans and infects them.

Enter the ninja-priest who kicks ass for the Lord. As he goes on a rant, punching and kicking the zombie hooligans, he is soon bitten and killed. With nothing else to do, Lionel tranqs them all and gets them back to his house, and thus keeps his secret a little longer.

As Lionel tries to keep all the zombies sedated, it seems the dead priest and the nurse like one another, in a hilarious scene, they hump each other on the table. Meanwhile, Lionel is trying to keep his greedy Uncle at bay, who wants Mum's money for himself.

Later, in the cellar of Lionel's house, the bizarre comedy horror continues as the nurse gives birth to a baby in record time. Lionel, not knowing what to do, takes the small tot for a walk, trying to mimic other mothers at the park. But the zombie baby is mischievous and laugh-out loud hijinks ensue.

More fun ensues until Paquita finds out about the zombies and convinces Lionel to kill his zombie mother, telling him she's long gone and that the zombie isn't her any more. But when Lionel thinks he's using poison to kill her and the other ghouls, it's really an animal stimulant and it sends all the zombies into overdrive.

When they literally explode out of the ground in the cellar after being buried, they head upstairs where Lionel's Uncle is throwing a party after finding out about the zombies, and thinking they're only corpses, he blackmails Lionel for the house and money or else would go to the police.

As the amped up zombies leave the cellar, a house full of partygoers become zombie chow, and as each dies, they then come back to join the ranks of the undead, and soon Paquita and Lionel are fighting for their lives in a house full of ghouls.

Dead Alive has some of the most extravagant, gore-filled special effects ever committed to film. There is everything from mutated bodies, which are hacked, dissected, gutted and ripped apart, to walking torsos, decapitated corpses, animated intestines and organs, and disembowelings by the truckload.

Everything from lawnmowers, to blenders, to rakes and shovels are used to kill zombies, even a lawn gnome!

And in the climax of the movie, amid the carnage and chaos, we find out the truth behind Lionel's father's disappearance and what his Mum did to him and how it affected his entire life.

DEAD AND BREAKFAST

YEAR: 2004
COUNTRY: USA
RUNNING TIME: 88 minutes
STORY: Matthew Leutwyler, Jun Tan, Billy Burke
SCREENPLAY: Matthew Leutwyler
DIRECTOR: Matthew Leutwyler
PRODUCERS: Jun Tan, E.J. Heiser
CO-PRODUCERS: Julie Sandor, Francey Grace, Michael K. DeVaney (Assoc. Producer)
EXECUTIVE PRODUCERS: Joe Madden, Wang Ching, Miranda Bailey
MUSIC: Zach Selwyn, Brian Vander Ark
ORIGINAL MUSIC: Brian Vander Ark
CINEMATOGRAPHY: Cinematography by David Scardina (director of photography)
EDITING BY: Peter Devaney Flanagan
DISTRIBUTED BY: Anchor Bay Entertainment
CASTING: Kari G. Peyton
MAKE-UP DEPARTMENT: Suzette Mariel, Michael Mosher, Richard Redlefsen, Nicole Sofios
ART DIRECTION: Guy Harrington
SET DECORATION: Lisa Clark
PRODUCTION DESIGN: Don Day
COSTUME DESIGN: Molly Grundman
CAST: Ever Carradine (Sara), Brent David Fraser (The Drifter), Bianca Lawson (Kate), Jeffrey Dean Morgan (The Sheriff), Erik Palladino (David), Oz Perkins (Johnny), Gina Philips (Melody), Jeremy Sisto (Christian), David Carradine (Mr. Wise), Diedrich Bader (Chef Henri), Miranda Bailey (Lisa Belmont), Vincent Ventresca (Doc Riley), Mark Kelly (Enus), Portia de Rossi (Kelly)

TAKE ONE: T.S

COMMENTARY

On the DVD cover of "Dead & Breakfast," Harry Knowles of Ain't It Cool News says that this movie is "the U.S. answer to 'Shaun of the Dead.'" After reading that, I was a little concerned: "Shaun of the Dead," also reviewed in this book, is an amazing film, and a rom-zom-com (romantic zombie comedy) is amazingly hard to pull off correctly, as evidenced by the piles of praise for "Shaun" and the piles of many other movies that have tried and met with varying degrees of success (see "Boy Eats Girl," "Zombie Honeymoon," and "Zombie Strippers," to name just a few).

Imagine my relief when I found myself laughing out loud several times while watching the movie. "D&B," while light on the romance portion, is in fact a very entertaining film with a surprising amount of fairly-good-looking gore included. It does have a few shortcomings, including trying too hard to make some scenes too funny and issues with editing jarring the viewer in and out of moments, but on the whole it is a vastly pleasant surprise for a movie that not many folks seem to know of or talk about too much.

For a self-proclaimed "independent film," the cast is surprisingly recognizable and above-average, including David Carradine and his daughter Ever, Gina Phillips (of "Jeepers Creepers" fame), Jeffrey Dean Morgan (probably best known among fans these days as The Comedian from "Watchmen"), Portia de Rossi, Jeremy Sisto, and Deidrich Bader (most recognizable as the weird neighbor from "Office Space" and one of the main characters of "The Drew Carey Show"). The story revolves around a group of five friends traveling to a wedding, but wouldn't you know it, they get lost along the way and have to stay the night in a very odd bed and breakfast on the outskirts of a small Texas town chock full of quirky characters. Murder, mayhem, and dancing zombies ensue.

As I mentioned above, I found myself laughing out loud quite a bit throughout the film. There are moments when it seems that writer/director Matthew Leutwyler, tries to squeeze in too many jokes for a film with a scant 88-minute run time. On occasion, some of the would-be comedic moments do fall flat, but there are more than enough jokes, gags, and tongue-in-cheek references to keep you laughing. The comedy aside, the story and pacing are also good, and the movie definitely keeps the viewer engaged and interested.

This film scores high in the "originality" category for two main reasons. First, the explanation of how the zombies came to exist is a fairly unique one, involving a "Far Eastern" ceremony and a soul-collection box. The zombies in this film can run, think, and speak, but they are all controlled by the primary spirit that inhabits the body of the person who possesses the box. Through a series of missed connections and bumbling accidents, the geeky character Johnny ends up accidentally opening the box, and it's a fun turnabout to have him completely change into the maniacal spirit and leader of the undead horde.

The second original plus for this film is its music, much of which is original content and was written and performed by Zach Selwyn.

Selwyn gets to play one of the locals who turns into a zombie, and his songs are catchy and humorously describe what's going on in the scenes without feeling over the top or forced. The rest of the plot elements and storyline are fairly standard horror fare, but kudos to "D&B" for taking enough chances to make it stand out from the pack.

As is the case with most zombie comedies, the low point comes from its predilection to throw most things related to realism out the window, and "D&B" is no exception here. The little town the friends get stuck in, Lovelock, is small enough to not show up on any maps, but they've got no problem having huge parties with people who seem to come out of nowhere and return to nowhere just as quickly. The townspeople we do meet are fun and unique, but the details don't quite add up. Why is an eccentric Zen Master like Carradine and his professional French chef running a dingy bed and breakfast in the middle of nowhere? Why does the lady who runs the town's hall of records have semi-automatic guns and high-tech crossbows coming out of every nook and cranny? These characters definitely make for entertaining storytelling, but they feel a little out of place and unrealistic in the grand scheme of things. In movies like this, however, these kinds of "gaps in reality" can be forgiven in the grand scheme of trying to tell a fun story.

There is a surprising amount of good-looking blood and guts in "Dead & Breakfast," and as mentioned previously, the original music really adds a great and unique element to the film—you'll be surprised how easily the songs get stuck in your head. If you're like me, after you've watched the film you'll find yourself humming the tunes and mumbling lyrics without even realizing it. As you're viewing the movie, you'll be having such fun enjoying the story that the minor errors that tend to come with smaller, more independent-style films are pretty easy to overlook.

PLAY-BY-PLAY

Many films we've included in this book sport some very interesting and unique opening credits, and "Dead & Breakfast" is no exception. Black and white drawings with blood-red accents help fill the viewer in on the backstory while we get our first audio exposure to the singular style of music that will be presented throughout the movie.

The group of friends traveling in the camper seem like your standard horror-movie characters, and that's really exactly what they end up being. The quirkiness of the film doesn't really derive from them, but rather the other characters they meet during their unexpected stay in Lovelock. The gas station attendant they first meet is none other than music-maker Selwyn himself, and indeed he is outside by the pumps, playing guitar with a drummer and a bassist! These musicians add an odd but entertaining touch to the movie, in addition to being pretty damn funny.

The music and musicians pair up with more comic-book-style panels from the opening credits to make for very unique transitions from scene to scene. Before long, we end up at the titular home-turned-hotel, and after getting settled in, some of the group wants to explore the house. This is where Sara (played by Ever Carradine) finds Mr. Wise (played by David Carradine) in his bodega, which brings up an interesting question: is this the first-ever father/daughter Carradine scene in the entire history of film? We're witnessing something special here!

Cut to the scene where David goes into the darkened kitchen and sits at the table to eat the pie...the viewer is just waiting for something bad to happen, almost anticipating it, but the reveal of Henri the chef, dead in the corner with the knife still in his throat is pretty rough! The scare is broken up pretty quickly, though, as we revert back to comedy via the old "slipping in blood" gag, replete with accompanying kitschy old-style music.

This story gets quite the convoluted back-plot, and there are moments when the viewer really does have to pay close attention if they want to make sure they get it all. But fear not, even if you do miss pieces about the Far East mystical practices and how their ceremonies relate to exactly what kind of evil is being unleashed here, you'll still be fine to enjoy the rest of the story. Just know that there's an evil spirit in Johnny that wants to not only kill people, but have a little fun while doing it, and you'll be fine.

The big town hoedown has an innocent, fun little feel to it...until possessed Johnny shows up and the carnage begins! It quickly turns into quite the messed-up scene. One thing I do want to give Leutwyler credit for is that in this movie, he's not afraid to kill off his main characters, seemingly at the drop of a hat. Other films want to give their characters big speeches or heroic moments when they die, making for a prolonged moment of departure that the audience becomes well aware is coming at them, but not here. It's a jarring tactic, to be sure, but it gives the viewer a moment of true surprise, like "Ohmigod! He's like, totally dead, just like that! I can't believe it!" Pardon the gratuitous use of Valley-Girl-speak, but I wanted to get the point across of just how shocking the moment can truly feel, and it's a great source of unexpected entertainment value. After the massacre at the hoedown, the survivors retreat to the bed & breakfast, with Johnny and his zombie horde soon to follow. I must say, though, that it's not a very menacing horde of the undead. Not only is it comprised of goofy rednecks, but soon the group actually starts to sing and dance! Did I catch some "Thriller" moves in there? The story gets even more convoluted as the zombies prepare to attack and some of the characters have to head off to the cemetery to dig up Mr. Wise's corpse, but it's forgivable stuff because the movie is just so darn full of random fun. Johnny possesses David, who abruptly and brutally kills his girlfriend, and Leutwyler again surprises us with the sudden eradication of a main character.

The zombies finally do attack the house full-scale, and Sara ends up being the only survivor left to fend them off. Seems like easy pickings, right? Not so much–Sara's a headstrong gal, and not only is she going to fight back with everything she's got, she's not taking any prisoners! Her counter-attack has a very "Home Alone-ish" vibe in the amount of prep work she does, but since she actually survives the onslaught, I guess it works out okay for her. The gore really gets ratcheted up in these final scenes, with copious amounts of blood, guts, and body parts flying around. It's a satisfying finish to an oddly-satisfying film.

TAKE TWO: A.G

Not many zombie movies can pull off an equal share of horror and comedy.

Luckily, this movie does and then some.

The first half of the movie is a little slow in the blood and guts department, but that shouldn't be a problem as the acting and dialogue is more than adequate for an independent movie. In fact, many other independents should learn a thing or two from this film.

The actors have been taken from mostly television, but that makes the movie only more fun as you should recognize more than one actor or actress from a past show. I like when I see this as I then know the acting will be good, compared to the many one-shot actors who do a low budget horror movie and then never act again, probably because they were a friend of the director or producer.

The plot is rather refreshing for a zombie movie as well.

When a small box is opened, it unleashes a spirit/demon that immediately takes control of the person who opened it. This demon then goes on a killing spree, and each victim joins his army of the undead.

Soon, the entire town are zombies and our small group of survivors hole up at a bed and breakfast and battle the attacking dead.

Once they're in the bed and breakfast, it has the feel of *Night of the Living Dead*, but ups the ante on blood and gore. Everything from pipes made into homemade shotguns, to chainsaws cutting off heads, is used to make us laugh and cringe. The movie soon changes gear and become more like the cult zombie movie *Dead Alive*.

The sheer amount of blood, bones and gray matter splattered in this film will rival any zombie movie out there, the only difference is this one doesn't try to be serious. Laughs abound, as well as slapstick moments such as feet slipping on a floor of blood and a severed head that becomes a puppet for the lead zombie.

My personal favorite is when the zombies start dancing while the song "We're comin' ta getcha!" plays. There are many jingles in the film which adds to the lightheartedness of it.

By the time the movie ends, more than half the cast is dead and there's enough body parts scattered everywhere to fill a truck.

This movie has been called the American version of *Shaun of the Dead*. I can't say I agree with that. Just because a movie is a mix of comedy and horror doesn't mean it's comparable, but if you love your gore mixed in with a side of laughs (and who doesn't) then you need to check this movie out.

Released direct to DVD, it's something of a sleeper movie and that's a shame, because quart for quart of blood, this movie holds up as well as any zombie movie out there, and that includes the big budget ones out of Hollywood.

So come and visit the small town of Lovelock, there's plenty of room at the local bed and breakfast.

Just don't plan on leaving any time soon.

DIARY OF THE DEAD

YEAR: 2008
COUNTRY: US
RUNNING TIME: 95 minutes
WRITER: George A. Romero
DIRECTOR: George A. Romero
EXECUTIVE PRODUCERS: Steve Barnett, Dan Fireman, John Harrison
PRODUCERS: Sam Englebardt, Peter Grunwald, Ara Katz, Art Spigel
CO-PRODUCER: Paula Devonshire
ASSOCIATE PRODUCERS: Donna Croce, Michael Doherty
MUSIC: Norman Orenstein
CASTING: John Buchan
CINEMATOGRAPHY: Adam Swica (director of photography)
ART DIRECTION: Jon P. Goulding
EDITING: Michael Doherty
MAKE-UP EFFECTS: Sid Armour, Chris Bridges, Mark Ahee
PRODUCTION DESIGN: Rupert Lazarus
STIDIO: Artfire Films Romero-Grunwald Productions
SET DECORATION: Justin Craig
COSTUME DESIGN: Alex Kavanagh
DISTRIBUTED By: The Weinstein Company
CAST: Shawn Roberts (Tony Ravello), Joshua Close (Jason Creed), Michelle Morgan (Debra Moynihan), Joe Dinicol (Eliot Stone), Scott Wentworth (Andrew Maxwell), Philip Riccio (Ridley Wilmott), George Buza (Biker), Amy Lalonde (Tracy Thurman), Tatiana Maslany (Mary Dexter), R.D. Reid (Amish Farmer), Tino Monte (Newscaster), Megan Park (Francine Shane), Martin Roach, Alan van Sprang (Colonel) (Stranger), Matt Birman (Zombie Trooper), Laura DeCarteret (Bree), Janet Lo (Asian Woman), Chris Violette (Gordo), Todd William Schroeder (Brody), Gregory Nicotero (Zombie Surgeon), George A. Romero (Chief of Police), Alexandria DeFabiis (Zombie), Nick Alachiotis (Fred) Boyd Banks (Armorist)

TAKE ONE: T.S

COMMENTARY

Sometimes, you just want to go back to square one and start fresh.
That was George Romero's thought process when he created "Diary of the Dead," a re-boot of his "Dead" series mythology, with new characters

and a new story of the undead apocalypse updated for modern times and audiences.

The tale follows a group of college students who are shooting a horror movie in the woods when word starts to trickle in about strange happenings with dead bodies reanimating. Before long, it's a full-blown zombie uprising, and the kids capture it all on film as they attempt to travel home together in their camper. This decision to record all the events on their video cameras doesn't sit well with everyone in the group, as well as groups of looters and National Guardsmen they come across. Eventually the group of students makes their way to the seemingly-well-fortified home of one of their friends, where they try to "hole up" until things get better.

The fifth film in Romero's "Dead" series, "Diary" is familiar to fans of his work yet alien at the same. The movie does pay direct homage to earlier films in the series, most notably when the same television news track from "Night of the Living Dead" can be heard playing on the TV in the looters' warehouse area. The movie also features the slow-shambling style of walking dead that the director is famous for making popular (remember, Romero's zombies didn't always shamble; see my reviews for "Night" and "Dawn" in this book for more information on this).

Indeed, very familiar notes to remind us that this is a movie that comes directly from the "Grandfather of Zombies" himself. Yet at the same time, this entry into the series is decidedly different and utilizes a vastly different approach than its Romero-ed brethren. The film and the story are removed from the previous four "Dead" movies by returning to the beginning of the outbreak. Yes, zombies are still the focus of the story, as is the common bond that ties together the other films in the series, but "Diary" doesn't propagate the main storyline that connects the other movies—following the zombie outbreak as it progresses through time—instead, it takes the viewer back to "square one" with the genesis of the plague set in the current time period.

The production itself had a very low budget, produced directly through Romero and his friend Peter Grunwald instead of leaving those responsibilities to a production company. A production company or film studio would have given the director an increase in the financial realm but also a significant decrease in the area of creative control. For "Diary," Romero used computer-generated effects rather extensively, a departure from his normal tack but an approach he felt was a necessity for a film like this. It allowed him to film the scenes much quicker than normal, since he could add much of the special effects in later during post-production.

This movie also strayed far from the director's usual tactic of using multiple camera angles and piecing the movie together scene-by-scene in the editing room. In a *Hollywood Gothique* interview, Romero spoke at length about how "Diary" was instead filmed using the strange-to-him approach of shooting in long, continuous takes: "The camera was 360 [degrees], so everybody was an acrobat, ducking under the lens when the camera came past you. The cast was great. They had a lot of theater experience. I think they could have gone from scene one all the way to the end of the movie, all in a single shot."

One thing that Romero was able to do by utilizing the magic of extensive post-production was to involve many big names in horror in minor off-camera roles. Famous folks and Romero fans such as Quentin Tarantino, Wes Craven, Guillermo del Toro, Simon Pegg, and Stephen King all lend their voices as in-movie radio newscasters, and it makes for quite the treat for true horror fans to try and identify whose vocals appear where throughout the film.

The biggest difference that "Diary" brings us is an intriguing and sometimes-polarizing one for fans: instead of the film telling the viewer a story, the story tells the viewer about the film. This is Romero's first tale set in "The Digital Age," with the ever-present and all-encompassing pervasiveness of the internet, cell phones, bloggers, and constant news and opinion influx from all sides. So he decided to use this "24/7 media" mentality to tell us a story through a computer and a camera's eyes, and the movie is shot in the "verité" style where all characters involved know that they are being filmed as they go about their business. It makes for a definite shift in the feel and tone of the story being presented, and the outcome is a Romero film like one we've never seen before.

Even though some reviews of the film, which was released directly to DVD, were mixed, Romero won a 2008 Critics Award for the film, and many reviewers, regardless of their opinion of the nuances of "Diary," reiterated the fact that Romero is still the master of the zombie genre.

Absolutely no argument here.

PLAY-BY-PLAY

One thing that "Diary" definitely shares with Romero's other films: it begins with another news-centric opening scene/introduction. This seems to not only be a favorite way for Romero to dispense information to viewers, it's also a very effective approach.

Many reviews I've read and fans I've talked to about this film have lamented the usage of the monotone, almost uncaring narrative given by Deb; could it be that Romero gave her instruction to speak this way on purpose, to indicate how detached and aloof this generation has become? The "film within a film" is definitely an interesting approach, and the eye-rolling title "The Death of Death" is a moniker I would absolutely expect a college kid to come up with!

Jason's direction to his in-film actor of "dead things don't move fast" is a "wink" to fans and a fun commentary on the usual complaints and criticisms of zombie movies in general. The early scenes here in the forest have a very "Blair Witch Project" type of feel to them.

Soon it becomes clear to the characters that something serious is going on, so they pack up and head back to their college, the University of Pittsburgh. Extra kudos to Romero for continuing to set most of his tales in and around this area (even though all shooting for "Diary" took place in Toronto). Jason, camera in tow, heads to the women's dorm to find Deb. Has the girl's dorm been ransacked, or is it always a disaster area? Obviously it has indeed been quickly "looted," but I've seen many college dorms look just as bad (or worse) on an average day.

The scene where Jason is "interrogating" everyone on-camera in the Winnebago feels odd, uncomfortable, and forced...until you realize this is exactly what the paparazzi and the entertainment news industry does every day, and this is obviously the point that Romero was trying to get across to his audience here. He's interrupted by the group's first direct exposure to the undead in the form of a fiery car crash and the undead wandering down the middle of the road. Mary's reaction to killing these zombies (possibly living people, unknown to her at the time) is one of remorse and contrition, a response we haven't seen much of in zombie movies lately. Everyone is normally so seemingly cavalier to pick up a gun or other weapon and start mowing the creatures down, her reaction is a nice change of pace–before she gets so upset that she shoots herself, of course.

The viewer is once again treated to fun and unique zombie kills, a welcome staple with Romero's films. Some early highlights are destroying the zombie nurse with defibrillator paddles to the head (or at least trying to kill her, anyhow) and the revenant who has to be dispatched using his own IV pole. In between the zombie mayhem, a few key moments of alone time gives Jason the opportunity for some interesting internal rhetoric about the nature of disasters and his supposed "responsibility" to capture it on film. Here, and later in the climax of the film, the characters talk about the two different kinds of shooting, both with the camera and with the guns, and the irony is definitely not lost here.

The group hits the road again, and we travel with them to a few interesting locations. The first stop is Samuel's, the deaf Amish man's farmhouse—Romero managed to work in another farmhouse to his films, awesome! After this, we head to the looters' warehouse, where a member of this group who dies alone and reanimates adds a little zombie action to an otherwise pretty low-key situation.

Make sure to note when the group is watching the newscast on the TV that not only is this where the original "Night" broadcast can be heard, but Romero cameos in his own movie as Police Chief Arthur Katz. I wouldn't mind seeing more story from this group of "looters," and indeed Romero himself has stated that if he were to make another "Dead" film, he would like it to follow the exploits of either this group or Tracy, the member of the college friends who does seem to head off on her own adventure towards the end of this story.

Eventually the friends arrive at Deb's house, where all is not as calm as it seems. Now, I know it's done for suspense and all, but I have to roll my eyes just a little here…two zombies in the house, one of whom can jump on your back, don't attack when they hear the house alarm AND Deb screaming their names? Really?

Soon after we hit the road again, we run into Crockett's military unit, the group that Romero's next film, "Survival of the Dead," follows. Note that the members of the unit that we see here, aside from Crockett who is the only one with actual dialogue, are not the same people we see in "Survival." This isn't a complaint, really. I can easily forgive Romero for not thinking a movie ahead!

In classic horror-movie style, the arrival of the group to the "too good to be true" safe mansion, of course, is actually too good to be true, and our survivors start dying off rather quickly. The story wraps up with another great nod to "Night," with the footage of the good old boys (rednecks) shooting up zombies, seemingly more for sport and pleasure than for "Survival."

It just goes to show that in any good "Diary," there are parts that cast people in a negative light that they may not want you to know about…but the truth must be told.

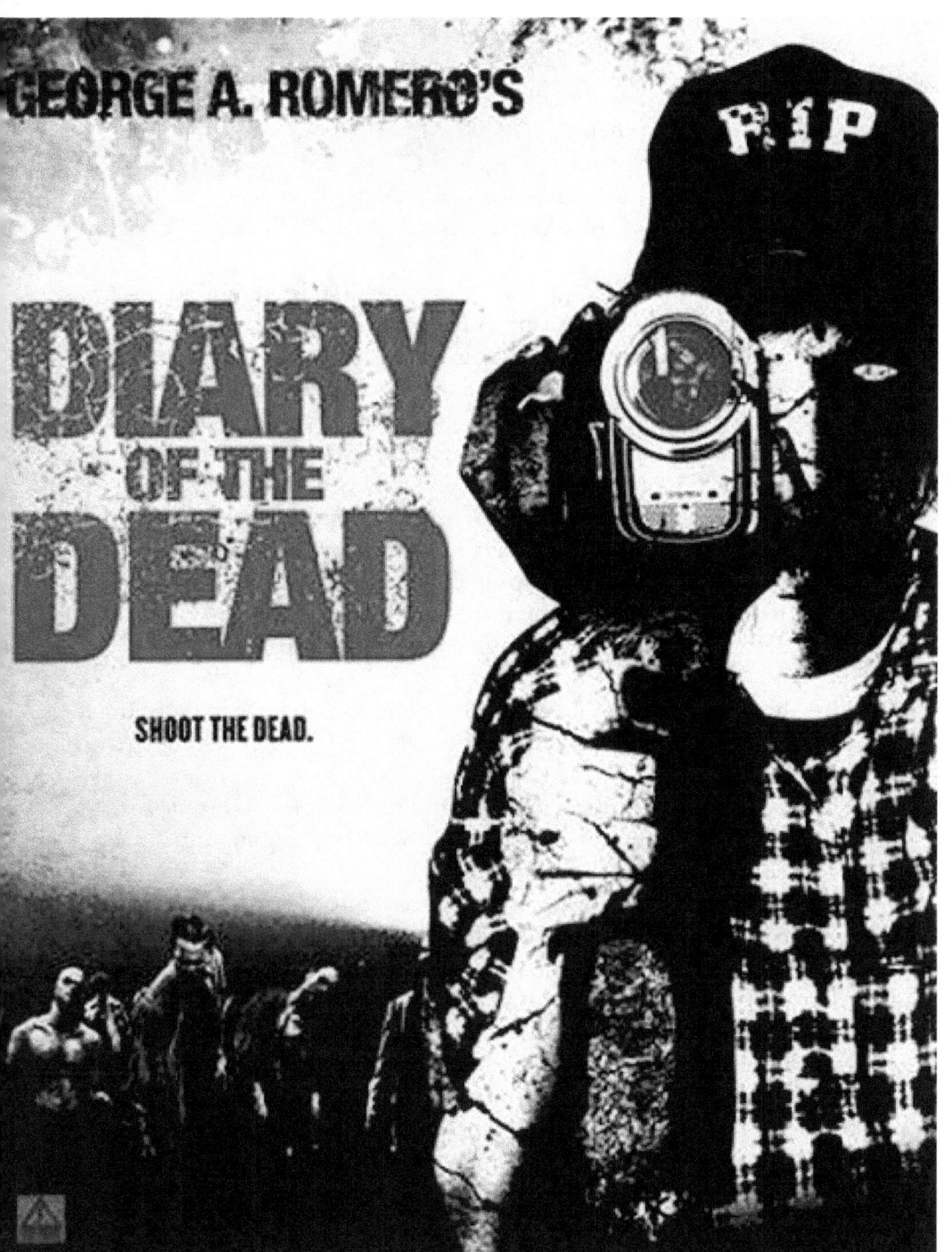

TAKE TWO: A.G

Note: Make sure to read my full review. First I share my concerns and dislikes about this film, then I share what I liked about it to even it out.

Like most fans of zombie movies and George Romero, when I found out there was going to be a new Romero movie, I was ecstatic. I mean, Romero hadn't done a zombie movie since *Land of the Dead* and finally, he was going to make another.

When it came out on DVD, I was there the first day to buy a copy and when I watched it, I found I wasn't very satisfied with the results.

For one thing, the style of filming, is terribly annoying. I'm not a fan of *Cloverfield* and movies that use a documentary feel to them and *Diary* fell into this trap. But worse still, when some of the characters were in danger, their so-called friends wouldn't put the damn camera down to help them. I found this terribly unbelievable and each time this happened, I was pulled from the movie and back to the real world by the sheer ridiculousness of it.

Another thing that drove me crazy was the heavy-handed way Romero was getting his point across. Perhaps it was because the movie was geared to a younger fan base, but each time I was told by one of the characters that "we are the news and that every one of us can report it," I died a little inside.

One thing I have always loved about Romero's movies is the subtle way the point he wants to get across is delivered.

Not this movie.

Here, the point he wants to make is not only force fed to the viewer, it's shoved in your mouth and you're made to swallow it at gunpoint.

I was so disappointed it was tangible.

Where normally, I will eagerly look forward to the next viewing, this time I placed the DVD on the shelf and wondered if I would ever want to watch it again.

Here's an example. When one of the characters in the movie, a student from Queens named Tony, is handed the camera to film for a while, he says he doesn't want to do it. In fact, he's been giving shit to the main character, Jason, about filming for the entire movie. But when Tony gets the camera, he whines for a second and then, guess what? He keeps filming, like his father had ordered him to and he has no choice. Here's an idea, Tony, put the damn camera down if you don't want to do it?

Later, when a female character is running from a zombie, Jason refuses to help her, but only follows her to get it on film. Really? He's that obsessed to the point he would watch his friend get killed and eaten because he doesn't want to "miss" anything? Sorry, folks, but it's just way too over-the-top in a bad way for me to enjoy it.

And where there is usually some humor in Romero's movies, I challenge you to find some. It's few and far between and not blatantly obvious.

So what do we get in the end? We get a bunch of college students in a Winnebago, trying to get home while whining and bickering the entire time.

I believe one of the reasons I'm not a fan of this movie is because I'm over twenty years of age. There is a college professor in the film, but he feels like an after thought, as if either Romero or someone on the movie said, "Hey, no one is over twenty in this movie, you need to add an adult!"

And for some reason they made him a drunk and someone that doesn't like guns, even though he knows one will likely keep him alive in a zombie-infested world.

Next let's talk about the zombies.

There aren't very many in this movie, I'm sorry to say. Other than a scene at a farm where there are more than five at a time, do we ever get the idea there are actually millions of walking dead in the world. To any fan of zombie films, hey, you need to actually put zombies in the movie.

And last but not least. When the college kids arrive at their friend's home, another student called Ridley, we find he is still wearing the mummy costume he'd been wearing from almost two days ago.

What, he never even once considered changing? And if you look at the costume, no way is it comfortable, hell, after he went to the bathroom he wouldn't have bothered to put it back on as it was wrappings and time consuming.

No, I'm not trying to nit-pick. But I have found to make a zombie movie feel real, as if yes, this is really happening, you need to follow the rules of normality with the exception that the dead walk. Otherwise it all falls apart.

So, to wrap it up, though I am a big Romero fan, this movie left me wanting to the point I stared at the screen when the credits began to roll, I was so shocked that that was it.

Okay, now the positive.

Since watching the movie the first time, I have read about it, listened to Romero interviews about the movie and learned other things that put it all in perspective.

The biggest thing to take with you before viewing this movie is that it's very low budget. Yes, Romero wanted to go back to his roots with this one, a shame but there it is, so he only had so much cash to make the film. Too bad; he does even greater things when he has a big budget.

Now, knowing this, the movie takes on an entirely new perspective. The use of stock footage of riots and by using the television and radio to express what's happening in the world is an excellent way to give the viewer a feeling of a society collapsing.

And if you know this going in, the viewer can be more forgiving, knowing they aren't going to be getting a *Land of the Dead* type production, but more of a *Night of the Living Dead* feel, with a smaller budget.

So, keeping this in mind, Romero did a great job making a zombie movie of the first days of the dead walking. With the help of CGI, he was able to give us a few good moments mixed with some heavy atmosphere as well.

Not counting the actual script, which unfortunately can be a little corny, the cast of actors are excellent. I found them all believable and thought they gave great performances. There are also a couple of cameos from actors that were in *Land of the Dead*. I counted four or five and I wasn't really looking for them, either.

This time when I watch the movie so I could give this review with the film fresh in my mind, I found it was more enjoyable, but that's only because of the information I've learned since its release.

But still, I found I enjoyed it more and learned to appreciate the atmosphere as much as the appearance of zombies.

So in the end, I would say this movie is a mixed bag, depending on what you want to get out of it. Though not my favorite of Romero's zombie films, (it's last actually) I'm still very thankful it was made and is there to be watched.

What we should all ask ourselves even if we watch a movie we aren't happy with is, "Would I have preferred if the film had never been made?"

My answer is a resounding, "Hell no." I'm very glad it was made and we have yet another Romero movie to add to our zombie collection.

Just next time, maybe he could put some more zombies in it.

FIDO

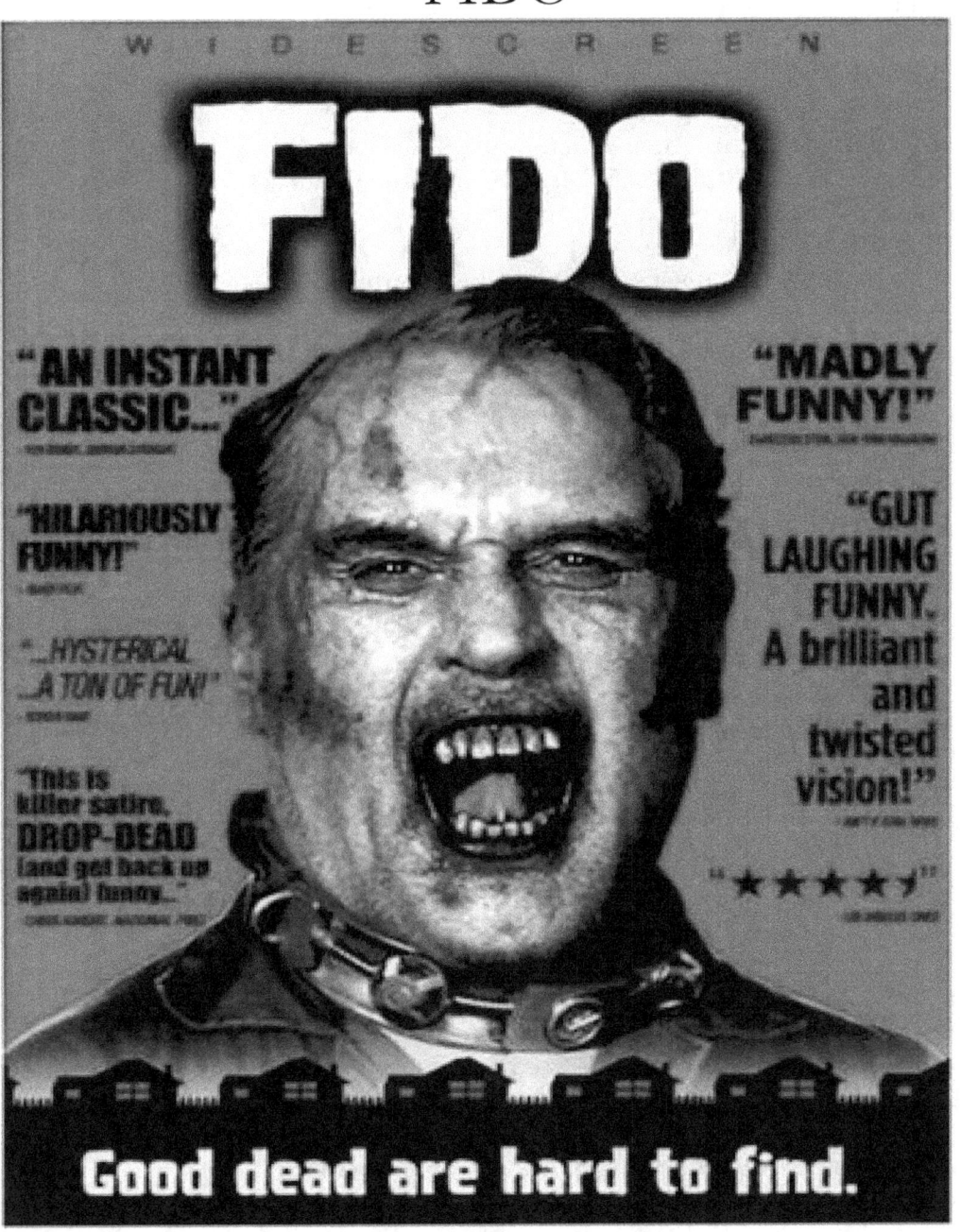

YEAR: 2006
COUNTRY: Canada
RUNNING TIME: 93 minutes
WRITERS: Robert Chomiak, Andrew Currie
DIRECTOR: Andrew Currie
PRODUCER: Mary Anne Waterhouse, Blake Corbet
EXECUTIVE PRODUCERS: Jason Constantine, Patrick Cassavetti, Peter Block, Daniel Iron, Shelley Gillen
CO-PRODUCERS: Trent Carlson, Heidi Levitt, Kevin Eastwood
ASSOCIATE PRODUCERS: Bill Stephens, Michael Shepard, Ki Wight, Erin Smith (line producer)
FILM EDITING: Roger Mattiussi
MUSIC: Don MacDonald
SET DECORATION: James Willcock
CASTING: Lynne Carrow, Heidi Levitt
CINEMATOGRAPHY: Jan Kiesser (director of photography)
PRODUCTION DESIGN: Rob Gray
COSTUME DESIGN: Mary E. McLeod
ART DIRECTION: Michael N. Wong (as Michael Norman Wong)
CAST: Carrie-Anne Moss (Helen Robinson), Billy Connolly (Fido), Dylan Baker (Bill Robinson), Kesun Loder (Timmy Robinson) (as K'Sun Ray), Sonja Bennett (Tammy), Jennifer Clement (Dee Dee Bottoms), Rob LaBelle (Frank Murphy), Aaron Brown (Roy Fraser), Brandon Olds (Stan Fraser), Tim Blake Nelson (Mr. Theopolis), Alexia Fast (Cindy Bottoms), Henry Czerny (Mr. Bottoms)

TAKE ONE: T.S

COMMENTARY

As more and more movies are created and released with stories involving the living dead, it becomes increasingly difficult to find a truly unique tale. Now, that's certainly not to say that a film whose plot or storyline shares some elements with another movie is automatically bad–far from it. Indeed, many of the films we included in this book share some type of common element with one or more other zombie films.

However, when you find a zombie movie that truly "breaks the mold" and tells you a story that is so fresh and unique, you've got to give credit to the creators for thinking so far outside the box, and when the same film effectively combines moments of comedy, horror, emotion, and social commentary, you've got to include it on your "best-of" lists. And when that same film is named "Fido," you can't help but smile and talk about it right now.

From start to finish, "Fido" is simply good old-fashioned fun, presented in a very kitschy retro-1950s feel, where everybody has a sunny disposition and the "ignorance is bliss" mentality takes center stage. Taking place in an alternate-reality version of the '50s, a quick "newsreel" film gives viewers the film's back-story: years ago a comet passed by Earth, dousing the planet in radiation and causing the dead to rise.

The ensuing Zombie Wars pitted living against undead, and the living humans actually won the battle. However, the lingering radiation still causes every person who dies to reanimate, unless they are decapitated or cremated. A government-like company called Zomcon helps to keep the revenants at bay with two key products: reinforced fences around entire towns to keep zombies out in "the wild zone," and a gadget-heavy collar that keeps zombies sedated (i.e. they don't try to kill humans) and makes them ideal slav—er, helpers.

A fairly in-depth origin tale, but with a movie like this, that is so vastly different from our usual undead romp, it's a necessary evil, to be sure. This information helps set the tone for the bulk of the story: Timmy Robinson's parents finally decide to get their very own zombie–actually, Timmy's mom Helen makes the decision, as his father Bill is a zombie-phobe stemming from the traumatic experience of having to kill his own father. After a brief period of uncertainty, goofy and nerdy Timmy warms up to the zombie as it becomes his only friend, even going so far as to name the monster "Fido."

As Fate would have it, Fido's collar starts to malfunction, and when he starts to kill and eat the neighbors, Timmy has to work hard to keep covering up the murders, and it all leads to a thrilling (though still innocently-presented) conclusion to the tale.

Shot in Canada and produced by a Canadian film company, "Fido" premiered at the 2006 Toronto International Film Festival, and also played at the 2007 Sundance Film Festival. Even with all the positive buzz it generated, when it opened in the U.S. on June 15, 2007, it was only shown in two theaters (one in Los Angeles and one in New York City) and a month later "expanded" to four more screens in other cities. The film made under $300,000 in domestic theatrical revenue, and another $120,000 in an even weaker global theatric showing. With an estimated budget of $8 million, to say that "Fido" was a massive financial failure is no understatement. According to BoxOfficeMojo.com, it's one of the lowest returns on investment for any film ever recorded.

Sounds depressing, right? Well, the entire rest of the world's loss is your gain when you sit down to watch this film. It's off-the-charts unique, highly comedic, stylistically impressive, and features some fun acting by some moderately-recognizable faces. "The Matrix's" Carrie-Anne Moss is probably the most well-known of the group, although Billy Connelly, without saying a word throughout the entire film, turns in an undead-tour-de-force performance as the decomposing-yet-entertainingly-emotive title character.

PLAY-BY-PLAY

As mentioned above, the movie opens with an awesome retro-newsreel opening, replete with kitschy '50s-style music and jokes that might have been funny at the time. As shown by so many zombie movies, from "Night of the Living Dead" to many recent undead films, it's a well-proven and time-honored tactic to open with the news-centric presentation, and it works to great effect here.

The newsreel itself is the "property of" Zomcon, which preaches "a better life through containment." It's a thinly-veiled propaganda video, but it is effective at introducing not only the basic plot points but the zombie domestication collar to the movie-watching audience.

We see that the newsreel is being shown to an elementary school class, which looks like your typical group of school kids for the time period. Two young boys who sit up front are dressed like Boy Scouts, but closer inspection reveals they are actually part of a group called the Zomcom Cadets! They must be this storyline's equivalent to the Scouts.

If there was any question that we've got a zombie comedy on our hands, it's quashed right away through the back-and-forth dialogue between the students and Mr. Bottoms, the head of Zomcon Security. Pay close attention when he says "Without Zomcom, we'd all be dead! And then where would we be?" You'll hear a little voice from the back of the room reply "…dead…" and your funny bone will be off and running!

Soon the class moves on to "outdoor education," which is the school system's politically-correct term for target practice. The children sing a fun little limerick as they shoot their rifles at paper zombies that just may get stuck in your head: "In the head and not the chest, brain shots are the very best!"

We get to see much of the rest of the town of Willard (named in homage to the town with the rescue station in the original "Night of the Living Dead"), and we quickly discover that those domesticated zombies are everywhere! They are mailmen, newspaper boys, delivery drivers, crossing guards, movers, welcome-to-town-sign wavers, gardeners...and concubines?

Once Helen makes the move to get their family a zombie, the parallels between the undead servants and a family pet go quickly beyond the name of the titular character. Quotes in this scene like, "Everybody has one except for us!" and "We can't afford a zombie!" help to drive the point home to even the most clueless of viewers (not that any of you reading this are clueless, mind you...I'm talking about other viewers).

When Fido's collar malfunctions for the first time, we get our first true zombie action–*vaya con dios*, Mrs. Henderson! Since most of the folks who get eaten are the meaner characters or people the viewer hasn't really been allowed to get attached to, the human deaths don't seem so bad, and this is a theme that permeates through the entire movie. It also helps that, as the movie progresses, Fido is seen more and more as a sympathetic character, so he doesn't seem so bad to the audience when he kills.

There is an interesting internal dichotomy between "domesticated" Fido and "feral" Fido when his collar malfunctions. Somewhere along the way in this story, Helen starts to get "into" Fido, and it's hard to pinpoint exactly where this shift first takes place.

The more interesting question: is it lack of attention from her husband that drives her to this paradigm shift in thinking, or something...eerier? It's not just Helen, though, the entire Robinson family is very dysfunctional, but much like many families of the time, they simply choose to hide it from others and live in a semi-state of denial themselves.

As you might expect, soon enough there is a zombie outbreak within the town, albeit one that is initially surprisingly subdued and almost seems expected by local law enforcement. It starts small and then grows, and as things get worse in town, there is still plenty of opportunity for comedy. The scene where Fido leads Helen to Timmy is ridiculous, yes, and draws immediate comparisons to the classic television show "Lassie," but how can the film's creators *not* take advantage of this connection, really?

Before the final horde scene at Zomcon headquarters, we get an odd scene at the Robinson home. Bill (who is humorously reading a magazine called "Death" instead of "Life") can't help but revert to his base thought process when Helen tells him about her pregnancy, even going so far as to say "I don't think I can afford another funeral." This scene helps solidify the viewer's dislike of Bill, who isn't necessarily a bad guy, but a man who seems to have a different set of priorities than his wife and son.

It's this dislike for the character that doesn't make it seem so bad when Bill dies at the end, by getting shot at the hands of Mr. Bottoms. Indeed, Timmy doesn't even shed a tear for his father. Something else interesting to note in this scene is that after his father's death, Timmy could have easily shot Mr. Bottoms with the gun in his hand, but he had Fido kill the man instead by going "feral" on him.

In the end, though, everything goes back to being "peachy" in typical '50s style: a news story with plenty of spin covers up the shadiness behind the outbreak, Bill gets the funeral he's always wanted, Mr. Bottoms comes back as a domesticated zombie for his family (on a leash with a nice pink scarf, no less), and Fido takes his role as surrogate father to Timmy and the new baby. In the more-than-slightly-off-kilter world presented to us in "Fido," the ending really is a perfect fit.

TAKE TWO: A.G

Welcome to suburbia, circa 1950.

Only this isn't the suburbia from our history. In this one, there has been a zombie uprising and the resulting Zombie War.

At the end of the war, the humans have taken the upper hand and have managed to build fences around towns all across the United States.

Enter ZomCom, a conglomerate that has made use of the zombies by an electronic metal collar that controls their bloodthirsty urges.

Now, the zombies are our slaves and do everything from cook our meals to walk our dogs.

At the beginning, it's hinted that if ZomCom will soon know everything about you, in effect controlling you like a fascist state would want to. Privacy over safety is the choice and with ZomCom the savior of the world, who would argue? In time, if they have their way, they will become a dictatorship.

The story revolves around one family, the Robinsons. Little Timmy is eleven and is smart and aware of his world. He questions everything. Not as a rebellious boy, but as an intelligent boy who isn't afraid to wonder if his world is really all that exists. His mother, Helen, played wonderfully by Carrie Ann Moss, wants to fit in and when her family is one of the few in the neighborhood to not have a zombie-butler, she goes ahead and buys one, despite her husband's protests.

See, where the world embraces the slave labor of zombies, Bill Robinson has always been terrified of them, ever since his father turned when he was a boy and he had to kill him.

Enter Fido, the name Timmy gives their new zombie. At first, Fido is nothing more than a servant but as time passes, Timmy and Fido form a bond of friendship.

One reason I believe this happens is because Fido is a little more human than the average zombie. There are special humans in our world, whether they are geniuses, prolific writers or scientists and inventors. Why not zombies, too?

The zombies wear a collar and if the red light turns green, it's time for a zombie to start munching, as his urges aren't contained. But even when Fido's collar malfunctions, he refuses to harm Timmy.

In many ways, you expect Lassie to come running down the street at any second, the feel of the old time TV show is so prevalent.

When Fido accidentally eats an old lady, Timmy scrambles to contain the misdeed but soon the old bag is up and around and feeding on anyone she can get her hands on.

A small zombie outbreak ensues and ZomCom quickly quells it.

Timmy is found out to be the owner of the culprit zombie and Fido is taken away to be used as factory labor.

But before Fido was taken, Helen was growing attached to him, for the simple reason that her own husband, Bill, was so distant. In many ways, Fido had more emotion in him than Bill did, who would leave his family to play golf and never seemed to care what his wife and son were thinking.

Timmy gets help from a neighbor and a desperate plan is put into action to save Fido from the factory.

When Helen and Bill find out, they race to ZomCom to save their boy who has been captured and then forced into the wildlands, which is anywhere outside the perimeter fences of the town, where ravenous zombies still roam free in a blighted landscape.

Timmy's father saves the day at the last second by taking down the leader of ZomCom security. As the two men struggle, Bill is shot, but Fido then attacks and takes out the man. Timmy is saved and in the ensuing influx of "wild" zombies, the family escapes.

This movie is fantastic to me. The production values are excellent, the old cars, the music, the homes and clothing, all remind the viewer of Leave it to Beaver or Lassie, only with zombies.

The way the townspeople accept zombies is part of the humor, as if having a wild animal cut your lawn should be fine. Many zombies do tasks so menial that it becomes redundant.

Who needs a zombie to hold up a sign, when a steel post would do the same thing? How about a zombie who delivers your milk, while the actual milkman reads a magazine in the truck?

The humor in this movie is always perfect, causing you to chuckle in just the right moments while also having a lot of emotional value.

Helen is fantastic as the ignored housewife who loves her husband and just wants to be noticed, while Timmy is the perfect son of eleven, with wide eyes and a cute face that begs you to give him a hug.

Billy Connolly plays Fido and he's excellent. He never says one world of actual dialogue but with his eyes and facial gestures he manages to speak volumes.

When he has a smoke, doing what he did before he died, it's hysterical. Imagine a zombie smoking…and enjoying it!

If you haven't seen this movie then you're missing out on a true gem of zombie cinema.

HELL OF THE LIVING DEAD

YEAR: 1980
COUNTRY: Italy/Spain
RUNNING TIME: 102 minutes
STORY AND SCREENPLAY: Caudio Fragasso, Jose Maria Cunilles, Rossella Drudi, Bruno Mattei
DIRECTOR: Bruno Mattei (as Vincent Dawn)
PRODUCER: Isabel Mula
EXECUTIVE PRODUCER: Sergio Cortona
MUSIC: Goblin
DIRECTOR OF CINEMATOGRAPHER: John Cabrera
MAKE-UP DESIGNER:
MAKE-UP: GIUSEPPE FERRANTI
CAST: Margit Evelyn Newton (Lia Rousseau), Franco Garofalo (Zantoro), Selen Karay (Max), Jose Gras (Lt. Mike London), Gaby Renom (Osborne), Josep Lluis Fonolli (Vincent)

TAKE ONE: T.S

COMMENTARY

Every genre has their "guilty pleasure;" the movie, book, or TV series that is so bad it's good. The one that you own but keep in a closet and refuse to admit to your friends that you have. The "train wreck," where you don't *want* to watch but can't turn away.

These guilty pleasures are fun for us because they represent our low-brow side, the part of us that doesn't feel the need to be sophisticated or explain ourselves to anyone, when we want nothing more than to just hunker down with a pizza or a bowl of ice cream, turn our brains off, and simply enjoy some good old-fashioned nonsense.

Welcome, my friends, to this book's guilty pleasure: "Hell of the Living Dead." It's a rambling, partially-incoherent story that draws many parallels to George Romero's "Dawn of the Dead" (see the Play-by-Play section for further details). To make a long and convoluted story as short as possible, an accident at a chemical company in New Guinea releases a toxic gas that reanimates people and some animals as flesh-eating zombies, and it's up to an "elite" European SWAT team to travel to the exotic island location and uncover the cause of the accident.

Like so many of its Italian-horror-film counterparts, "Hell" has a long and dubious production history. It also shares it's brethren's penchant for having multiple titles bestowed upon it in various international markets; in addition to its Romero-and-Russo-impinging title, the film is variously known as "Virus" (Italy), "Zombie Creeping Flesh" (United Kingdom), "*Zombi 2:* Ultimate Nightmare" (also Italy), "Night of the Zombies" (USA), "*Inferno dei Morti-Viventi*" (Surprise! Italy again), and in various areas as "Cannibal Virus," "Zombie Inferno," and "Zombies of the Savanna."

Beginning its life as the simply-titled "Virus," the film treatment written in 1980 by Jose Maria Cunilles was expanded into a large script by the husband-wife team of Claudio Fragasso and Rossella Drudi. In all honesty, saying the script was "large" may actually be an understatement, as Fragrasso and Drudi actually created a massive, bloated, rambling story that didn't have much of any kind of coherent plot to it. But the horror-movie market of the early '80s was, pardon the pun, hungry for new zombie movies after the success of films like "Dawn of the Dead" and "*Zombi 2*," so the film was rushed into production.

Two different movie studios, Dara Films in Spain and Beatrice Films in Rome, jointly optioned and financed the film. These two studios were notorious for working specifically in low-budget horror, and their approach here was no different.

They hired Bruno Mattei to direct the film (with the help of Fragasso), largely based on his reputation as a director who could effectively work within constrictive budget limitations. Many, many people like to blame Mattei for the shortcomings of this film when in reality, he's probably to be owed a debt of gratitude for saving the film from being downright unwatchable; more on this below.

Parts of the original script, specifically those set in Africa and major scenes involving ships full of dead bodies and a corpse mincing plant, were deemed by the studios simply too large-scale to be included in the film's budget, so these parts were cut out of the narrative. Unfortunately, nobody apparently bothered to tell this to Mattei or Fragasso, who continued to shoot the rest of the scenes as normal. Only when the cast and crew returned from the majority of the on-location filming in Barcelona did Mattei review the footage and discover that not only was it insufficient and partially unusable, but the story just didn't make any sense!

Mattei and the production companies were left scrambling. In a stroke of what I'm sure he thought was genius (or at least smart enough to avoid a total re-shoot), the director recommended the cost-saving move of inserting footage from the 1972 French pseudo-documentary *La Vallée* into the film, with minimal additional footage being shot to augment this part of the storyline. Dara and Beatrice readily agreed, as they were eager and willing to do whatever it took to get this film completed as quickly and cheaply as possible. Hastily-constructed sets were built to mimic the tribal village seen in the documentary, and a plethora of haphazard gore-filled special effects were created to be randomly inserted into the film to help "bloody" it up. A new ending was slapped on the film, and some of the band Goblin's music that was featured in "Dawn of the Dead" was inserted into the film (without getting the band's authorization, leading to a legal dispute that almost stopped the movie from being released).

The last-minute edits were meant to enhance the film, and while they probably did save "Hell" from being a total disaster, they certainly were not the film's savior by any stretch of the imagination. This movie is a true-blue head-scratcher, and viewers should probably win an award if they can piece together the thinly-constructed plot line from start to finish.

Regardless, watching this movie late at night with a couple of friends and a couple of alcoholic beverages can all combine to create an oddly sublime event that you simply have to experience for yourself, if for nothing else than to be able to say to your friends that you've lived through "Hell."

PLAY-BY-PLAY

Right away, the opening credits set a tone of "urgency" with the upbeat, insistent song coupled with a man on a loudspeaker counting down to zero over the shot of the industrial Hope Center. The tense atmosphere continues through the opening scene, as lots of people are urgently checking and re-checking readouts on their computers, but…for what?

Soon we discover what all the fuss is about: it's a leakage of toxic gas! The technicians locate the actual cause of the disturbance–that's one pissed-off reanimated rat! The rate gets bite-y, as undead rats tend to do, and it doesn't take long before this zombie outbreak is in full swing. Give "Hell" credit for championing the "toxic gas as cause of monster problem" shtick well before many other movies of the 1980s did.

The SWAT team, or as they are referred to in the film, the "special squad" of four men that are sent to take out the terrorists, definitely seem like guys who graduated from a "special" school, all right.

In all fairness, some of the disconnect from the characters could be attributed to the dubbing of their lines into English, which always seems to create problems when the editors are trying to find words that allow the new dialogue to sync up with the way the character's lips are moving. Also of note here is the blatant similarity to "Dawn of the Dead" in the fact that the SWAT team members are wearing identical dark blue uniforms as those worn by the SWAT team in Romero's film, right down to the goofy work-hats.

The first three locations in the film—the industrial complex, the American consulate in a European country, and the native jungle of New Guinea—are vastly different from one another, and give an interesting look at how a storyline can exist (albeit loosely) in extremely different environments.

In a Mission isolated in the jungle, we're given our second big zombie attack. The zombie priest is trippy, but not nearly as much as the zombie boy who wakes up, looking no different, and just kinda scrunches up his nose to indicate that he has "turned." It certainly doesn't stop him from munching on Dad, though! Elsewhere in the compound, zombies pop up out of the lake, and the photographer has the audacity to say "They could be drunk, or drugged…or maybe it's a leper colony." In denial much?

In a theme that will recur throughout the movie, one of the SWAT guys, Santoro, informs the rest of the team that in order to kill a zombie you have to "shoot them in the head," and then the team immediately proceeds to continue to empty their clips directly into the zombies' torsos. This is most likely done for the benefit of special effects, but any good zombie fan will agree that it detracts heavily from the perceived reality of the situation.

Now we arrive at the part of the movie that has been heavily spliced with the nature documentary. In true classic B-Movie style, Mattei fulfills his quota of "topless girl" here, as Lia strips down and puts some war paint on, and she is conveniently ignored amongst the natives for about twenty minutes, since these natives are the ones from the different film.

The biggest positive the film has, by far, is the effects and graphic representation of death and reanimation, which are pretty impressive by the standards of the time.

I could do without the blue faces and the ketchup squirted on shirts to indicate blobs of blood, but once we are given some close-up looks at head kills, dismemberment, and a few zombie feeding sessions, the true effects work shines through.

Even though the dialogue makes the interactions themselves a little iffy, the dichotomy of the military and civilian trains of thought is all too real, and is a theme that is explored in many a zombie movie. One thing they all seem to enjoy doing together, though: they all sure do chew the scenery like it's nobody's business

Through all the jungle scenes and into the portion of the movie where the group finds the abandoned plantation, the SWAT team continues to give zombies body shots! Santoro again tells them to shoot for the head, which he does to one (spectacularly), but then he inexplicably runs into the horde while not shooting, choosing to taunt them verbally instead.

The writers and/or directors probably wanted to use this scene to indicate the fragile mental state the men are in when faced with a crisis like this, but the whole thing just comes across as a little odd.

Here at the plantation we are given one final typical "zombie megahorde" scene, with people making bad mistakes—leaving their guns laying around, standing in front of windows, and so forth—before they get eaten. And the SWAT team *continues* with the body shots!

Finally, we are taken back to the Hope Center industrial complex, and give Mattei credit for bringing us back here so we can get a sense of the story trying to come "full circle." Once inside, we get more bad decisions by our characters that ultimately doom them all. Lia's transformation in particular was quite a surprise.

She was such a headstrong woman earlier, but now all she does is stand around, scream, and look up as blood drips in her mouth from the ceiling. We do get a pseudo-explanation of the initial outbreak—"Operation Sweet Death?" Who chose to call it *that?*—before the zombies rip the last two survivors to pieces (more gruesome kills and good effects here).

Sadly, the film ends on an even more dour note, with one of the schlockiest endings ever—totally unrelated to the rest of the film's plot and absolutely tacked on in an attempt to make the movie seem more connected to the other undead films being produced at the time. In all fairness, though—Mattei was well-known as a director who could cut whatever corners needed to get things done with a film, so I guess you could call this one "mission accomplished" for him.

TAKE TWO: A.G.

The first to thing to say about this movie—as well as many others like it—is don't take it seriously.

How can you? The plot is terrible and some of the dialogue will make you cringe, it's so bad.

But despite all this, if you're a fan of zombies then this movie has to be in your library.

Why?

Well first off, anyone watching the movie may find the musical score rather familiar. See, it's Goblins' score for *Dawn of the Dead*, blatantly ripped off and placed in the movie, most times the score not fitting at all. In the beginning, when the SWAT team goes on a raid, the animated Goblin score beats away as the SWAT team slowly walks and creeps. It's just wrong.

But it is fun to hear the familiar score in an entirely different movie.

Like similar Italian movies from the 1980's, there are multiple scenes of what is basically stock footage from documentaries. Animals, natives and scenery are edited into the movie to basically add time to it.

A blatant *Dawn of the Dead* rip-off, this movie is amazingly unashamed of this, as were most of the Italian zombie movies made at this time.

But if you're looking for gore, then look no further, for though the Italians never made an A horror zombie movie, they most definitely know how to make a B one. And that's B for blood.

The camp value of this movie is priceless and if by some chance you haven't seen it, then I recommend it highly. Just don't expect to get nightmares that evening after the viewing.

Now, some fun tidbits that I find so amusing in this movie that they have to be listed here.

1) For some reason in this movie, when anyone is in danger, they don't seem to know how to run away. They just stand there and wait to be attacked.

2) When someone near you is being attacked, don't help, just stand there with eyes wide and watch.

3) The four troopers are such a blatant rip-off of *Dawn of the Dead* it hurts to watch.

4) When a woman falls from the ceiling and hangs there, her mouth opens and she spits blood, though she's clearly very dead.

5) When the troopers meet their first zombies, they barely hesitate before shooting to kill. And when they find a child eating his father, they repeatedly shoot the child in the chest until another trooper shoots the boy in the head, telling the others that's the only way to kill them. "Them"? How does he know they're zombies and not very sick?

6) Why do only four troopers go into another country on a mission if there is some kind of global catastrophe about to occur or had occurred. I've heard of a low military budget but seriously?

7) In the village when the troopers are attacked by zombies, they don't use their guns but swing with the butts of their weapons. The zombies flinch and duck away. If they are truly dead, then why would they flinch?

8) Despite the SWAT team knowing they need to shoot the zombies in the head to stop them, the team repeatedly chooses body shots over and over again.

9) And my favorite... Every time Santoro (one of the Swat members) runs into a horde of zombies they never do anything to him. They just stand around and hiss. Why don't they bite and attack him?

In the end, this film is here for one reason, to give the viewer gore, violence and believe it or not, a chuckle.

The director wanted to play on *Dawn of the Dead's* popularity, but wanted to keep the tone lighter. And whether on purpose or not, that's what you get as the dialogue is said with straight faces, despite being absolutely terrible.

So am I saying this is a bad movie? Hell yes, But is it a fun movie, hell yes again.

Filled with buckets of blood, gratuitous nudity, and hilarious dialogue, this movie is one for the history books.

YEAR: 2005
COUNTRY: USA/Canada/France
RUNNING TIME: 97 minutes
WRITER: George A Romero
DIRECTOR: George A Romero
PRODUCER: Mark Canton, Bernie Goldmann, Peter Grunwald
CO-PRODUCER: Neil Canton
EXECUTIVE PRODUCERS: Lynwood Spinks, Ryan Kavanaugh, Dennis E Jones, Steve Barnett
MUSIC: Reinhold Heil, Johnny Klimek
DIRECTOR OF PHOTOGRAPHY: Miroslaw Baszak
MAKE-UP EFFECTS: Greg Nicotero, Howard Berger (KNB EFX Group Inc)
VISUAL EFFECTS: Spin, Jeff Campbell, Switch VFX, Rocket Science VFX, Deluxe
ART DIRECTOR: Doug Slater
COSTUME DESIGNER: Alex Kavanaugh, Stephanie Lees
CAST: Simon Baker (Riley), John Leguizamo (Cholo), Dennis Hopper (Kaufman), Asia Argento (Slack), Robert Joy (Charlie), Eugene Clark (Big Daddy), Joanne Boland (Pretty Boy), Tont Nappo (Foxy)

TAKE ONE: T.S

COMMENTARY

At the time of this writing, it's been over half a decade since "Land of the Dead" was theatrically released, and I think many of us nowadays have forgotten how simply plain excited we were when this film opened. I mean, really–George Romero's first new entry into the "Dead" series in twenty years? What true zombie fan wouldn't be excited beyond belief?

Drawing on unused plot elements from its predecessor in the series, "Day of the Dead," "Land" was not only blessed with the highest budget of any movie in the series to date, it also claims the highest grossing revenue of the series to date. Rated "R" upon release, it's the first film in the series to receive an MPAA rating, the previous trio being unrated either by choice or by virtue of the rating system not existing at the time.

The film follows the story of the zombie outbreak as established in Romero's original trio of "Dead" films, with "Land" taking place at an indeterminately-later point in the chronology. Due to its unique geography,

Pittsburgh has been successfully isolated from the living dead, and survivors continue their existence at varying levels of economic and social status, from poverty-stricken individuals crowding the streets to the elite and wealthy occupying a gleaming shopping-and-living-center skyscraper called Fiddler's Green. Through frequent raids to nearby towns (usually successful thanks to the existence of the ultimate armored transport-and-defense machine, "Dead Reckoning,") the community has been able to "survive and advance," as it were.

But the zombies aren't simply out in the world milling around doing nothing. They have started to learn and adapt, and under the unofficial leadership of an ahead-of-the-curve revenant nicknamed "Big Daddy," the undead soon come together as a "mega-horde" with the intent on infiltrating and destroying the humans' refuge.

Theater-going fans weren't the only ones excited to see Romero return to the big screen. A generation of award-winning directors and film makers had grown up watching and loving his "Dead" trilogy, and they were just as enthused for "Land" as you or I. Acclaimed horror director Guillermo del Toro said in an interview with Spike TV that, "Finally someone was smart enough to realize that it was about time, and gave George the tools.

It should be a cause of celebration amongst all of us that Michelangelo has started another ceiling." While the horror aficionados didn't have the opportunity to participate directly in this film—with the exception of zombie cameos by Simon Pegg and Edgar Wright, co-creators of "Shaun of the Dead," the film's star actor and director, respectively—many of them got their chance to be a part of Romero's next film, "Diary of the Dead" (see my review of that movie in this book for more information about this).

In an interview with the news website Ain't It Cool, Romero mentioned that the film went through a few different titles before finally locking in "Land of the Dead." Alternate titles included the natural extension of the Night-Dawn-Day theme, "Twilight of the Dead" in addition to "Dead City" and "Dead Reckoning." 20th Century Fox, one of the first studios to express interest in producing the film, at one point wanted the film to simply be titled "Night of the Living Dead," which thank goodness didn't happen! Romero really wanted to call the film "Dead Reckoning," so Fox countered with the offer to have the movie's title be "Night of the Living Dead: Dead Reckoning."

Romero found out that if Fox distributed the film as "Night of the Living Dead," then they could make a move to permanently own the rights to that name, so he declined to do business with them, ultimately going with Universal Pictures as "Land's" movie studio of choice.

Some cuts had to be made to the film so that it could earn an "R" rating for American theaters, and these cuts were also made in many international markets to allow the film to be seen by a wider audience. Ukraine was apparently having none of it, and banned the film outright–oh, those crazy Ukrainians and their irrational fear of the living dead! Upon theatrical release, the film received fairly widespread positive response from both audiences and critics alike.

Roger Ebert gave the film three stars, stating in his review that, "It's good to see him back in the genre he invented with *Night of the Living Dead*, and still using zombies not simply for target practice but as a device for social satire." The New York Sun went as far as to call it, "The American movie of the year." High praise indeed, and these accolades coupled with the movie's profitability goes to show that zombie fans are not only a loyal bunch, but are ravenous for new, quality material from "The Master" himself.

PLAY-BY-PLAY

As the film begins with the standard movie opening of the production companies' logos, Universal chose to use their "retro" logo from the 1960s, which is a nice nod to Romero, as "Night" debuted in '68. The film itself opens with a recap via an overlay of radio broadcasts with the words, "Some time ago," shown on the screen. It's an effective way to help "catch-up" the viewer without over-doing it.

Our first exposure to the undead in "Land" comes outside of a diner with a dilapidated, old-style "Eats" sign overhead, showing us that Romero is still not afraid to throw a little playfulness in with his horror stories. There are some impressive and unique zombie effects right off the bat–I especially enjoy the undead cheerleader with part of her mouth ripped away and the zombified three-man band in the park gazebo.

"Big Daddy" is obviously this movie's Bub (the "learning" zombie from "Day"), and I find it interesting how Romero gives the smart zombies nicknames, possibly avoiding real names so they don't come across as *too* "humanized." Right away, when Bag Daddy "calls" to other zombies, you can tell that "Land" isn't going to be a story that sticks to "standard" zombie conventions.

This film features a significantly higher-profile cast than any of the previous movies in the series. With John Leguizamo, Simon Baker, Dennis Hopper, and Asia Argento, this is a tenured Hollywood group. Fortunately, they live up to their reputations very well, and they all deliver great performances, including signature character quirks from Leguizamo and Hopper. Additionally, many of them have the opportunity to act alongside an inanimate force in the film: the massive, steel-plated, firework-spouting, rocket-launching, zombie-killing über-machine known as "Dead Reckoning." It is, quite simply, one hell of an urban assault vehicle.

Before long, the zombie action is in full swing. We see a costly lesson about being careless and letting your guard down when Cholo and his men are attacked in a liquor store. One zombie is decapitated by the human raiders and left on the sidewalk, where "Big Daddy" finds the still-aware head and steps on it fiercely, squashing it to bits. Was this a "mercy kill" on his part?

Back in the city, the audience gets its first exposure to Fiddler's Green; luxury living replete with a commercial that plays on a loop on televisions inside of the tower. Life in the Green is obviously quite the contrast from street life, and it's insightful commentary about class segregation, plus a small shopping mall reference for "Dawn" fans also!

Crockett alert! Alan van Sprang appears in this film as "Brubaker," a low-level military grunt that quickly becomes zombie fodder and eventually one of the undead himself. Alan van Sprang has the distinction of being the only actor to portray characters with dialogue in three different "Dead" films, as he follows up his brief appearance here with his portrayal of Sergeant Nick "Nicotene" Crockett in both of the next films in the series, "Diary" and "Survival of the Dead." (See my reviews in this book on both of those movies for more information about van Sprang and Crockett.)

Only two other people have been seen on-screen in three "Dead" films: effects wizard Greg Nicotero playing various zombies, and Romero himself in a few different cameo roles.

Big Daddy has some serious power over the zombie brethren. After their initial attack on the outskirts of the human settlement, the undead actually stop their feeding frenzy in mid-bite and follow him when he "calls" them. Speaking of the "Z-word," this movie sports the first time a Romero character ever says it on screen, when Hopper utters the deadpan-hilarious line, "Zombies, man…they freak me out."

The undead ratchet up the action as the movie progresses, and Romero gets to show that he's still got some unique ideas for zombie kills rolling around in his head. Of particular note here is the zombie with its head still attached only by the spinal column and the zombie who catches fire and is shot by Big Daddy (another mercy kill?). Of course, there is also the return of the "Sav-ombie"–effects guru Tom Savini in a pseudo-reprise of his once-human, now-undead biker character from "Dawn of the Dead." It's a real treat for fans who are paying close attention and who are "in the know."

In the final climactic scene, there are lots of gruesome kills and zombie-eating effects to go along with some slow devouring, just like classic "Night" style. As a briefcase of money catches on fire and trickles down from the sky, we are reminded of the quote from earlier in the film, "money burns." Interesting to note that only the inhabitants of Fiddler's Green were eaten by the zombies, as after the undead are stopped, the "poor" community emerges from hiding safe and sound. Does this count as a happy ending for Romero and his penchant for social commentary?

TAKE TWO: A.G.

First let me start of by saying *Land of the Dead* is one of my favorite zombie movies. From the first time I saw the theatrical release, I was hooked. It seems there are two camps for this movie: those that love it and those that hate it.

As a fan of it, I never understood why others don't like it.

The first reason I consider it one of the best is the production values. With CGI and a large bankroll, the special effects are better made, the blood splatters brighter, and the gore is just a little redder.

And because of the larger budget, the cast of characters are exceptional. Dennis Hopper is outstanding as the evil dictator. John Leguizamo plays the everyman. He's not good but he's not really bad either. He's just out for himself as many people are.

Simon Baker plays the leading man perfectly, with strength and kindness and even mercy when it's needed. And if you are a fan of Dario Argento, to have his daughter Asia as part of the cast makes it the icing on the cake.

Joe Pilato and Simon Peg have cameos as zombies as well and even the unknowns do an excellent job.

With a well rounded cast, it's even easier to accept that the world has been overrun by the living dead.

When the movie first begins, it starts with a bang as the raiders ransack a town. Blood and guts galore, and it gives us a taste of what's to come. Here we meet Big Daddy and get our first look at what is basically a "thinking" zombie.

I believe Romero handled this well. It makes sense that over time even a zombie would learn to do basic skills. Though its never been established what an IQ of a zombie might be, even if it's in single digits, over years of exposure to menial tasks a zombie would learn to pick up a hammer or even squeeze the trigger on a gun. In the movie, the zombies basically mimic the humans and Big Daddy only figures out how to use a gun by accident.

Another thing to point out is like human beings, where some are more special than others, so too, is Big Daddy. For a zombie, he's special, and more intelligent than the rest.

This was also a good thing to add to the movie to keep it fresh. Romero likes to try new things and after doing three previous zombie movies, he didn't want to come back twenty years later and do the same old thing all over again. So he added a twist, and it was that the zombies were beginning to learn, taking a piece from *Day of the Dead* with Bub.

When Cholo gets screwed out of his apartment at the Fiddler's Green because he's not the right kind of "people," he goes on the warpath for vengeance and steals Dead Reckoning, an armored tank on wheels. Now even if he didn't do this, the zombies were still coming for Fiddler's Green and I have always wondered what would have happened if the whole Cholo thing hadn't happened? Riley would have been in jail as well as his crew so when the zombies arrived they would have been trapped in their cells.

But "what ifs" don't matter.

Either way, when Cholo steals Dead Reckoning, he starts a chain reaction of events. After all, when he was about to take Dead Reckoning and Pretty Boy wanted to shoot the stenches, he told her no. If he had, then the zombies never would have reached the city, but would have been massacred by the guns of Dead Reckoning.

So once more Romero shows us how by not working together, we're doomed to failure.

Meanwhile, the zombies are "working" together and so they manage to get the upper hand.

When the zombies take the city, it's quickly overwhelmed and here, Romero gives us gorehounds what we want; buckets of blood and intestines.

Some of the best special effects in a zombie movie are seen here. Whether it's a face being peeled off or a head separated from a body, the effects are outstanding. Arms chopped off, grenades exploding bodies, and zombies set on fire are just a few of the atrocities you'll see here. One of my favorites is when Riley and another soldier come across the armory and find the zombies feeding. One zombie sticks its hand into an open mouth and pulls out the victim's insides, then sloppily sucks and chews on them...priceless.

Where many zombie movies—even Romero's movies—slow down in places, I always found this film holding my attention. It moves fast and there's barely a chance to catch your breath.

At a running time of an hour and thirty-five minutes I have always thought it was a little short compared to Romero's previous movies, and that's why the pace is so fast. Another fifteen minutes would have let the movie slow down but then that might not necessarily be a good thing.

But with most things you love, you always want more and though the movie is short, on the DVD there are plenty of added features to feed the zombie fans needs.

As a fan of apocalyptic fiction, this movie hit the nail right on the end. Whether it was the downed airplane Riley's crew drives by or the dust-covered stores they raid at the beginning of the movie, it paints a picture of a society in ruins, a world where there's nothing but rubble.

Over time, *Land of the Dead* will hold up well, as the movie itself is not set in a specific time and the clothes the cast wears are rather generic. Twenty years from now the movie will hold up even better than it does now.

As for Romero's take on Rumsfeld with Dennis Hopper playing the heartless, money-grubbing leader, I choose to ignore all that. I don't watch zombie movies for political reasons and all that background stuff can only bother you if you let it. Kaufman is a dictator in the movie, plain and simple and throughout time there have been many such as him. And there will be again, I'm sorry to say.

So if by some crazy chance you have never seen this movie and have no idea what this review meant, then I hope I've peaked your interest and you now want to see it.

I promise you won't regret it.

THE LIVING DEAD AT THE MANCHESTER MORGUE

YEAR: 1974
COUNTRY: Italy/Spain
RUNNING TIME: 93 minutes
WRITERS: Sandro Continenza, Marcello Coscia, Juan Cobos, Miquel Rubio
DIRECTOR: Jorge Grau
PRODUCER: Edmondo Amati
EXECUTIVE PRODUCER: Manuel Perez Garcia
MUSIC: Giuliano Sorgini
LIGHTING CAMERAMAN: Francisco Bird
SPECIAL EFFECTS: Luciano Bird
DIRECTOR OF PHOTOGRAPHY:
MAKE-UP: Giannetto De Rossi
SPECIAL OPTICAL EFFECTS: Giannetto De Rossi
ART DIRECTOR: Rafael Ferri
PRODUCTION DESIGNER: Carlo Leva
COSTUME DESIGNER: Carmen De La Casa
CAST: Ray Lovelock (George), Cristine Galbo (Edna Simmons), Arthur Kennedy (The Inspector), Aldo Massasso (Kinsey) Giorgio TRestini (Craig), Roberto Posse (Benson), Jose Ruiz Lifante (Martin)

TAKE ONE: T.S

COMMENTARY

We've got to give credit where credit is due, and "The Living Dead at the Manchester Morgue" deserves kudos for being made significantly in advance of the popular wave of late '70s/early '80s zombie films.

The film, shot in Italy and Spain, was released in 1974, over five years before George Romero's "Dawn of the Dead" sparked heavy interest in stories about the living dead, which in turn led to a swell of domestic and international zombie films created between 1979 and 1986. "Manchester Morgue" was distributed in the United States under the far-goofier title "Let Sleeping Corpses Lie," one of many alternate titles the film acquired through international distribution (more on this below).

The plot of the film itself is quite unique, even more so when you remember the fact that this story came out far before many other films started to recycle ideas about how the dead might return to life. Antiques dealer George is traveling from his shop in Manchester to the surrounding countryside when he stops at a gas station and his motorcycle is accidentally hit by Edna as she's pulling away from the station. George demands she give him a ride, to which she agrees, but first she needs to stop at her sister's home. When they become lost on the country roads, George asks directions from men working with a strange, experimental agricultural machine; during this time Edna is attacked by a red-eyed zombie, and she manages to escape when he inexplicably disappears.

The movie soon spirals into a tense "predator versus prey" fight between the living dead and the duo, with local police becoming increasingly suspicious that the two travelers are actually to blame for the rash of violence.

The film, while a little dated both by the appearance and the mannerisms of the characters (the police Sergeant even goes so far as to insult George's "long hair and faggot clothes"), gives the viewer a surprisingly strong story and original approach to the living dead, both in the description of the genesis of reanimation and the rather interesting peripheral effects of the reanimation process. The final scenes draw immediate parallels to Romero's original "Night of the Living Dead," but give director Jorge Grau credit for taking the story one step further than Romero's conclusion did, even if it is a bit of a stretch in the believability department.

As mentioned above, this movie was apparently the trend-setter in the odd habit of foreign zombie films having multiple different titles when distributed in foreign markets. "Manchester Morgue" ended up with almost twenty different titles when it was all said and done, although the original title is still displayed in the film's opening credits regardless of where the film was released.

While the thought process behind the change of titles is vague and confusing at best, some of the alternate monikers are downright (unintentionally) entertaining. A few of the highlights are as follows:

- "*Non Profanare il Sonno Dei Morti* (Don't Disturb the Sleep of Dead Men)" and "Fin de Semana para los Muertos (Weekend for Deads)," Spain
- "*Das Liechenhaus der Lebenden Toten* (The Resting Place of the Living Dead)," Germany
- "*Levende Doden in het Lijkenhuis* (Live Killing in the Morgue)," Dutch-speaking countries
- "Don't Open the Window," "Breakfast with the Dead," "Brunch with the Dead," "Weekend with the Dead," and "The Living Dead," certain English-speaking territories
- "*Da Dove Vieni?* (Where Do You Come From?)," Italy

The Italian version was also re-released in the early 1980s after the success of Lucio Fulci's "*Zombi 2* (Zombie)" and was re-titled once again, this time as "Zombi 3: Da Dove Vieni? (*Zombie 3: Where Do You Come From?*)."

Through it all, "The Living Dead at the Manchester Morgue" is a great piece of zombie fiction, especially in the eyes of those who live near Manchester and throughout the United Kingdom. British director Charlie Brooker even name-checked the film during his 2008 television zombie-horror miniseries "Dead Set," when he has one of his characters describe another character as having "a face like a Manchester Morgue." With its eerily slow developing pace and spooky, atmospheric moments of undead carnage, this is a film full of images and ideas that are sure to stay with the viewer long after the movie is over.

PLAY-BY-PLAY

Right away, the viewer will realize that this is a film with a different feel to it, as we get a very trippy opening sequence with a hypnotizing close-up of what appears to be some sort of zombie portrait in George's antique shop. As he closes up shop, he takes an odd-looking statue with him, and right away this begs the question: will this item come into play later?

George has quite the interesting motorcycle ride into the countryside, including a blissfully random moment where a nude woman streaks across a crowded traffic intersection. Eventually, fate connects him with Edna, and the classic mid-'70s gender tropes come to the forefront in the duo's interaction with each other, most notably when George presumes to be the one to drive her car (Edna certainly doesn't try to stop him, even though they just met).

The first truly unique piece of the story is presented, as the British Agricultural Department is out in the fields using an "experimental" piece of equipment that uses "ultrasonic radiation…not a chemical involved," in an attempt to agitate pests into fighting with and killing one another. This is a key piece of information that will be used heavily throughout the rest of the story.

Our first zombie quickly appears and attacks Edna. Interesting to note here that the zombie features what I would call the "Rage" eyes—his pupils are bright red and quite beautifully rendered, just like the Infected in the films "28 Days Later" and "28 Weeks Later," both also reviewed in this book. The "28" movies were also set primarily in England, which begs the question of whether the folks who made those movies knew about "Manchester Morgue," possibly even paying homage to it. Nothing I've been able to discover gives any indication of this, but it's an intriguing thought nonetheless.

As mentioned above, the film settles into a very creepy, atmospheric vibe early on. The viewer quickly has more questions than answers, and it seems the filmmakers like it that way. The spooky vibe is highlighted with the very direct musical cues that indicate when a zombie or "evil" in general is about to come into play.

Another unintentional side effect of the ultrasonic radiation is that it agitates all "primitive" nervous systems, and it seems to affect babies as well. At the hospital we see three babies, all born in the last few days, that the doctor describes as "violent, almost homicidal." One baby even scratches a nurse's eye out!

The original zombie we meet puts an odd, reddish liquid on other dead people's eyelids, and they reanimate as well. While it's not immediately known exactly what the substance is, George speculates that it's blood of recently-killed people, which helps to motivate the dead to return to life. Creepy!

George continues with a lengthy but fascinating conjecture regarding the reanimation; he believes that the radiation brings back the nervous system of the recently dead, who in turn can bring others back through the blood of the living. It seems to make sense, but the theories are never *officially* proven.

The zombies presented in this film are super-slow and deliberate in their actions. The looks on the zombies' faces are truly scary, almost cognizant, and indeed they do seem to retain at least a base amount of knowledge. They use tools when the situation calls for it, and they seem to know that fire equals "bad," but by the time they figure this out, it's too late for them to save themselves from being incinerated.

The sheer stress of the situation soon overwhelms Edna, and she starts to see the zombie version of her dead brother-in-law everywhere and in everyone's face. She has officially checked out from reality, and I can't say I blame her too much for it. The police don't believe her and George's story about the dead returning to life, which makes it that much more difficult for them to find any help to stop it.

We're treated to the "classic" tragic ending to the zombie horde attack at the hospital when the police shoot George, still believing he's the cause of the carnage and not the zombies.

The Sergeant stands over George's body and says, "I wish the dead could come back to life, so I could kill you again." Well, be careful what you wish for, my friend, for the Agricultural Department has fixed their ultrasonic machine from George's previous attack, and you'll soon find one pissed-off zombie waiting in your hotel room to extract his revenge!

TAKE TWO: A.G.

Though made a few years before George Romero's *Dawn of the Dead* and Lucio Fulci's gorefest titled *Zombie*, comes a zombie movie that gives the audience a taste of true gore and the direction future zombie movies would be going in.

Whether a woman's breasts are being ripped off, an old woman is feasting on a dead cop's eye, or organs are being torn out of the same dead cop for the zombies to feast on, this movie doesn't hold back on the blood and guts.

Where *Night of the Living Dead* attested the rise of the dead loosely to radiation from space, Manchester gives the audience a straight answer.

It's the Ministry of Agriculture—those evil bastards.

It seems they have invented a way to use ultrasonic radiation to kill pests and insects so that farmers will have better crops. Completely safe, the ultrasonics only affects the nervous systems of the most primitive life on the planet: insects.

But what if when a person died, their nervous system was still active? Even if just for a short time? Could the ultrasonics affect those corpses and reanimate the dead?

You betcha.

And that's where George and Edna come in. After Edna accidentally backs up at a gas station and damages George's motorcycle, she volunteers to drive him to his destination. But George takes Edna to where she was going first, which was to her sister's house.

A homeless man who drowned a week earlier soon arrives and kills Martin, Edna's brother-in-law. When Edna's sister is blamed for the crime, it's up to George and Edna to get to the bottom of it.

The only thing is the pesky dead are walking and keep getting in the way. And each time they kill someone, its George and Edna who get the blame. These zombies aren't like Romero zombies. They can use tools and seem to actually be able to think. They work together and can reason, if only slightly. They don't die from a bullet to the head but fire does the job nicely.

One of the more interesting differences about the zombies in this film is they don't moan or groan. They rasp, as if an old man is taking his last breath, before dying in his bed. The "death rattle" as it were is haunting and adds a realistic feel to the ghouls.

The special effects are done well, with the gore exceptional. Just be patient if you start to get bored. The first half of the film is slow but the atmosphere should keep you interested. And while none of the cast will be nominated for an Oscar for their performance, I found all of them to be more than adequate, especially for a low budget zombie film.

Now like most Italian zombie films there are plot holes galore, and a host of inconsistencies and idiocies run throughout the movie, but for any true horror aficionado these can be overlooked.

And unlike many Italian zombie flicks, this one has a sense of humor. My favorite line of the movie is when George and Edna are talking about zombies as she tries to convince him they're real. He has brought her to the cemetery so they can see that the homeless man that attacked her is safe in his coffin. Before they head up the path to the cemetery, he stops and turns to her and says, "The dead don't walk around except in very bad paperback novels. They're dead and that's that!"

Like in most zombie movies from Italy, the characters make very bad decisions, but then if they didn't, there wouldn't be much of a story. When trapped in the cemetery, the policeman with Edna and George leaves the safety of the cottage to get his two-way radio. Why does he need it so bad? His sergeant knows he's there and will surely come to investigate soon enough. All they have to do is hold off the dead till that time. But he doesn't do that. Instead he opens the door and runs for it and makes it about ten feet if that. He is then abruptly killed and eaten.

Bitten by a zombie will not make you rise up as one, but it seems blood from a ghoul when touched to a corpse will animate it. Best not to think too hard on that one. Unlike many Italian zombie movies, this film actually has a message to share. Though it's subtle, it's not *too* subtle.

From the opening credits we see the city with its trash and pollution, then we see the rolling hills of the England countryside. Then we go back to the city as it's buried in garbage, then back to the majestic beauty of the country. And when the reason for the dead rising is mankind wanting to kill the insects to grow more food for its populace, a populace that is choking the planet, then it's easy to see why the dead rise up.

Depending on your point of view, you could say the dead are fighting to take back the planet from humanity.

By today's standards *The Living Dead at the Manchester Morgue* seems tame, but back when it was released, it was something of a first for a mass-market horror film. Many of the best scenes were removed back then and thanks to DVD releases, audiences can now enjoy the film the way it was meant to be seen, in true gut-munching horror.

NIGHT OF THE LIVING DEAD (1968)

YEAR: 1968
COUNTRY: USA
RUNNING TIME: 97 minutes B&W
SCREENPLAY: George A Romero, John Russo
DIRECTOR: George A Romero
PRODUCER: Russell W Streiner, Karl Harman
DIRECTOR OF PHOTOGRAPHY:
MAKE-UP: Harman Associates, Inc.
CAST: Duane Jones (Ben), Judith O'Dea (Barbara), Karl Harman (Harry Cooper), Marilyn Eastman (Helen Cooper, Bug-eating zombie), Keith Wayne (Tom), Judith Ridley (Judy), Kyra Schon (Karen Cooper), Bill "Chilly Billy" Cardille (Field Reporter), George Kosana (Sheriff McClelland)

TAKE ONE: T.S

COMMENTARY

George A. Romero is, quite simply, the man.

Now, don't get me wrong: no one is perfect, and George is far from without fault, as many of us can attest to from seeing several of his movies, both zombie-centric and otherwise. Yes, he does have many non-zom films under his belt, in case you weren't aware, he has directed fifteen feature films since his first, "Night of the Living Dead," in 1968, and only six of them have been about zombies (seven if you count "The Crazies," as some fans do).

But what the man dubbed as the "Grandfather of Zombies" does right as a director, writer, and producer of films focused on the undead far outweighs any shortcomings his stories may have. And it all started for him in the late 1960s with his first feature film, when he teamed up with John Russo to create the movie that would eventually become the template for all modern zombie films, "Night of the Living Dead."

Before I speak about my thoughts on the actual movie itself, I'd like to share with you, dear reader, some of the back-story surrounding this now-legend of a movie. The behind-the-scenes tales of "Night's" road through production and post-release tribulations feels somewhat akin to a soap opera. Tired of simply making commercials and segments for TV shows, Romero teamed up with Russo and eight other friends to form Image Ten Productions, with the intent of making the "next great horror film." Each member of the fledgling production company thought that, if they each pitched in $600, the $6,000 total would be enough for them to make the movie they wanted. They quickly discovered they would need more money and resources, so working together they raised $114,000, which was considered a small budget even by the standards of the time.

So the team cut corners where they could. There were no "professional" costumes; actors wore their own clothes or whatever they could buy at a local Goodwill store. The blood on the actors and the zombies (called "ghouls" at the time, more on this below) was simply chocolate syrup. The makeup applied to the monsters was basic, at best, and largely consisted of simply giving many of the extras "raccoon eyes." The flesh being eaten was simply roasted meat and entrails that were donated by one of the actors, who also happened to own a chain of butcher shops. Romero and company shot the movie using low-grade, 35mm black-and-white film, although this ended up being a blessing in disguise, as most critics and viewers hailed the gritty look as adding realism to the tale.

Once the movie was complete, the team had trouble securing a film studio to distribute the film, as it was termed too "dark" and "gruesome." Two different studios, Columbia and American International Pictures, asked that Image Ten re-edit the movie, including shooting a "happier" ending, requests to which the team stoutly refused. Finally, the Walter Reade Organization agreed to show the film, uncensored, but they had one small request regarding the title of the film. You see, "Night of the Living Dead" was originally titled "Night of the Flesh-Eaters" by Romero and his Image Ten crew. As the film was preparing for release, the distribution company went to copyright the name of the film, when they found out that there was (somehow!) already a copyrighted film by that name. So, a "big-wig" at the distribution company encouraged Romero and Russo to change the name to "Night of the Living Dead" to avoid copyright issues, and also because the big-wig thought it sounded scarier. So, change the name they did…except Walter-Reade forgot to copyright the title, making it a "public domain" movie upon its release. And that, boys and girls, is why seemingly anyone and everyone can remake "Night," and any old video company can put out a version on DVD, whether it's remastered, colorized, 2-D, 3-D, "collector's edition," and the like. At last count, there were 22 different versions of the original movie on DVD, according to IMDb.com. Heck, I'm thinking of putting my own version of the movie out, starring hand puppets! (Warning: the previous sentence is mostly fictitious, and entirely ridiculous.)

And so, on October 1, 1968, "Night of the Living Dead" was released to theaters. It was shown as a Saturday-afternoon matinee, as was the

NIGHT OF THE LIVING DEAD (1968)

custom for horror films at the time. Since the MPAA had not yet put any kind of movie ratings system in place, any person of any age could go and see the movie. On his website, Roger Ebert recalls seeing the movie on its opening weekend with people of all ages in the theater with him: "The kids in the audience were stunned. There was almost complete silence. The movie had stopped being delightfully scary about halfway through, and had become unexpectedly terrifying. There was a little girl across the aisle from me, maybe nine years old, who was sitting very still in her seat and crying... It's hard to remember what sort of effect this movie might have had on you when you were six or seven. But try to remember. At that age, kids take the events on the screen seriously, and they identify fiercely with the hero. When the hero is killed, that's not an unhappy ending but a tragic one: nobody got out alive. It's just over, that's all."

I know this is a lot of detailed background information, probably more than you'll get for any other movie in this book, but "Night of the Living Dead" holds a special place in my heart, as it does for many zombie fans. This is the first zombie movie I ever "seriously" watched: as a young man in my late teens, I obviously wasn't watching it as a new release, but I certainly was able to appreciate what the movie was trying to say to its audience on more than one level. I think that's why it resonated with so many other fans as well, and truly has inspired a whole genre of movies, books, games, and stories, all revolving around the reanimated corpses of dead humans who have risen from the grave and are "coming to get you, Barbara!"

PLAY-BY-PLAY

The movie sports a great opening sequence, with Johnny and Barbara's car ride really showing the isolation of the surrounding area and the remote nature of the cemetery they were headed to visit. Rusell Streiner and Judith O'Dea, the actors playing the brother and sister duo, have a fun (and believable) back-and-forth banter that makes the viewer feel like they are really hearing two adult siblings trading verbal spars. In Jason Paul Collum's book "Assault of the Killer B's," O'Dea recalls how much of the dialogue in the movie was actually improvised by the actors themselves: "I don't know if there was an actual working script! We would go over what basically had to be done, then just did it the way we each felt it *should* be done."

The viewer can quickly and easily see that Johnny is made out to be cold, uncaring, and agnostic. Is that why he was the first to be killed? I love the irony of the "they're coming to get you" scene, and I have to believe that the iconic phrase that Johnny speaks immediately before the first undead attack, "they're coming to get you, Barbara," is one of the most well-quoted lines in horror movie history.

As I mentioned before, no movie is perfect, and some of the inconsistencies of "Night of the Living Dead" begin to be seen in these opening scenes. Why doesn't the first zombie eat Johnny after he falls and hits his head? Instead of eating the flesh of the living as the zombies later in the movie do so ravenously, this reanimated corpse instead immediately goes after Barbara. Also, he does a fair amount of running while chasing after our girl and even uses a stone to break the window of Johnny's car in an attempt to reach Barbara. My only thought here is that, clearly, the definition of these creatures and they way they move and think (or lack of skills thereof) was still being established. Indeed, not only do other zombies use tools (rocks, wooden beams, etc.) to smash car headlights, the creatures also seem very afraid of fire, and later in the movie the undead are shown eating bugs! Clearly, Romero and company wanted to show the "ravenous" nature of the creatures, but were still working on exactly what kind of parameters their creations were going to operate under.

Throughout the entire film, we can see that there is a very "deliberate" style of camera work: watching minute details carefully, following where characters look, and just generally allowing the viewer to really pay attention to the "small things." I think what a lot of people took away from this movie after seeing it is that Romero is, at his core, simply a great filmmaker. There are a lot of these little details in the movie that, upon rewatching the film, the average viewer (myself included) finds himself or herself catching more and more. A prime example of this can be found when Romero uses the television and radio newscasts to relay information to the characters that may seem, at the time, fairly inconsequential. There are talks of the Explorer probe carrying radiation from Venus but the probe being destroyed before it returned to Earth, and the scientific community being torn on whether the reanimation of the dead bodies is related to the events of the probe; even the radio announcer dropping subtle lines talking about how the "Mayors of Pittsburgh, Philadelphia, and Miami" are concerned about the problem that has "seized the eastern portion of the nation" really help to give the viewer a sense of what might be happening in areas apart from the small farmhouse we are stuck in with the main characters. Even as the characters start to talk over the broadcast, viewers with keen hearing will pick up snippets relating to "scientists from NASA" in "Houston and Galveston," and "conspiracy theories, along similar lines of 'creatures from outer space.'" If, as it is said, the Devil is in the details, then Romero made sure he had one hell of a movie on his hands.

I could go on and on about the nuances of the movie, but the important piece of information for most zombie lovers is that, as the movie progresses, the carnage and mayhem increases exponentially. Starting with Ben retelling his first zombie encounter (a fairly large affair that Romero did well to save on budget by having Ben simply re-tell the story instead of trying to show it via flashback), things really start to get fast-paced. Barbara begins to lose it mentally, and when Ben tries to literally shake her out of it, she slaps him; what neither she nor the viewer expects to happen next, however, is that he retaliates by punching her! Obviously, this was done less in self-defense and more to knock her out as a means of protecting her from herself, since she said she wanted to go outside, but it's still a pretty shocking moment in the movie.

We get some amazing images of zombies shambling toward the farmhouse; these are very iconic images that have been often imitated in films and graphic novels since, but none of them will ever compare to the originality of the source material. "Night of the Living Dead" is actually so original that Romero and the makers of the movie didn't even realize they were creating a new type of movie monster! Never once are the creatures referred to as zombies, instead they are termed as "flesh-eating ghouls" by the news anchor, and the other characters call the creatures "ghouls" multiple times throughout the movie. This, in my opinion, is why Romero deserves all the credit he receives. He wasn't trying to come up with something new and flashy for a marketing scheme or anything like that, he simply wanted to tell a scary story that had never been told before.

The movie is incredibly character-driven, both with what you could term "good" and "bad" characters, although some fans may debate which side certain characters should fall on. Harry Cooper, the over-protective father and emotionally-aloof husband, is not necessarily a bad guy, Romero simply made him a character that is a little more self-centered than the rest. Ultimately this is his downfall, and it's pretty clear that's the point Romero was trying to convey with this character, and it's a common theme throughout the rest of his "Dead" series: people do better when they work together.

Throughout the movie, we get great social commentary to go hand-in-hand with the character development, and this is especially poignant in the scenes that involve fighting amongst the characters that ultimately leads to the survivors' downfall. By the time the zombies finally do break into the house, you just get the feeling that it's all over for most of the characters.

We get to see some really frenetic activity by the zombies at this point, the first time the viewers really see them all go crazy towards a single cause. The zombified daughter killing her mother with the spade is an incredibly creepy scene, even after all these years. Finally, we end up with Ben all alone in the basement. He was so adamant about not going down to the basement and ultimately that's the only place he can find that keeps him safe…how's that for irony?

I love that Romero and his team went out on a limb with their "anti-happy" ending of having none of the characters survive, and I'm even further impressed that they refused to change it even when multiple studios told the team that they would show the film if the ending was altered to be more "positive." It's that kind of creative integrity that should give hope and encouragement to any aspiring creators who have a specific idea to truly "stick to your guns."

Romero ended "Night of the Living Dead" with pictures during the credits of men with meat hooks tossing around bodies like slabs of meat. This may just be the perfect piece of symbolism for the movie that launched an entire sub-genre of entertainment whose sole focus is eating human beings.

NIGHT OF THE LIVING DEAD (1968)

TAKE TWO: A.G

Though this is one of my favorite movies, because of its status as a horror classic, there has been a lot of information written about it—from how it was created to the ins and outs of production.

And if you're like me, then you've no doubt read most of this stuff. So for me to now write a review for this cult film seems rather redundant as I am by no means a professional reviewer.

So I will keep this review very simplistic.

I like this movie a lot. Not as much as *Dawn of the Dead*, but still, as a fan of zombies, how couldn't you not love this movie?

The claustrophobia of a small group of survivors trapped in a small farmhouse as the flesh-eating dead try to break in and kill and eat them?

Perfect.

Or how about the typical attitude of the men in the movie (Harry and Ben) to fight one another instead of working together (something Romero would use again and again in his other horror movies, especially the *Dead* films.

And of course, the ending of the movie, which even by today's standards is shocking. In a world where it seems every film has to have a happy ending, NOTLD shatters that rule and buries it in the backyard.

Most zombie fans have seen it countless times, but can you imagine someone who has never seen it and how they would react to the ending?

And though color is a wonderful thing, especially for a zombie movie, the black and white of NOTLD gives it a more down to earth feel, as if you're watching a documentary instead of a movie.

So, if you have never seen NOTLD and are wondering just what the hell I'm talking about, then there are two things you can do to alleviate your crisis.

One, you can read the fantastic review by my co-author in this book, or you can go get this movie and watch it.

Just make sure to watch it at night and with the lights out.

PLANET TERROR

YEAR: 2007
COUNTRY: US
RUNNING TIME: 105 minutes international, 91 original release
WRITER: Robert Rodriguez
DIRECTOR: Robert Rodriguez
PRODUCERS: Elizabeth Avellan, Robert Rodriguez, Quentin Tarantino, Erica Steinberg (uncredited)
EXECUTIVE: Harvey Weinstein, Bob Weinstein, Sandra Condito
ASSOCIATE PRODUCERS: Tom Proper   (associate producer),
LINE PRODUCERS: Luz Maria Rojas Magnón, Bill Scott
MUSIC: Robert Rodriguez
FILM EDITING: Ethan Maniquis, Robert Rodriguez
CINEMATOGRAPHY: Robert Rodriguez
PRODUCTION DESIGNER: Steve Joyner
COSTUME DESIGN: Nina Proctor
SET DECORATION: Jeanette Scott
ART DIRECTION: Caylah Eddleblute
CSTING: Mary Vernieu
CAST: Rose McGowan (Cherry Darling), Freddy Rodríguez (Wray), Josh Brolin (Dr. William Block), Marley Shelton (Dr. Dakota Block), Jeff Fahey (J.T.), Michael Biehn (Sheriff Hague), Rebel Rodriguez (Tony Block), Bruce Willis (Lt. Muldoon), Naveen Andrews (Abby), Julio Oscar Mechoso (Romy), Stacy Ferguson (Tammy), Nicky Katt (Joe), Hung Nguyen (Dr. Crane), Cecilia Conti (Paramedic Cecil), Tommy Nix (Paramedic Nixer), Tom Savini (Deputy Tolo), Carlos Gallardo (Deputy Carlos), Skip Reissig (Skip), Electra Avellan (Babysitter Twin #1), Elise Avellan (Babysitter Twin #2), Quentin Tarantino (Rapist #1 / Zombie eating road kill), Greg Kelly (Rapist #2), Troy Robinson (Soldier #1), Derek Southers (Soldier #2), Jason Douglas (Lewis), Michael Parks (Earl McGraw), Jerili Romeo (Ramona McGraw), Felix Sabates (Dr. Felix)

TAKE ONE: T.S.

COMMENTARY

I think I was born in the wrong decade.

Although I grew up watching the great horror movies of the 1980s, I seem to have a special affinity for the "groovy," rough-and-gritty feel of the 1970s horror films. Maybe I just enjoy cinematic experiences from the times when the writing and characters had to drive a story and the special effects were a supporting player. Nowadays it seems to be the exact opposite, with each new CGI-tacular movie trying to outdo the last. But every so often, a current film will come along that breaks the trend and gives its viewers both a good-looking film and a great story as well. Throw in a healthy dose of retro feel with a homage to a bygone era of cinema, and you've got the makings of one amazing movie-watching experience, specifically known as "Planet Terror."

Half of the ambitious two-movie "Grindhouse" project put together by directors Quentin Tarantino and Robert Rodriguez (Tarantino's B-movie/exploitation homage "Death Proof" being the other half), "Planet Terror" is simply a good old-fashioned zombie movie made by people who know how to entertain. Rodriguez has actually said in multiple interviews that he came up for the idea of this movie while filming "The Faculty" way back in 1998. In fact, he even told "The Faculty" stars Elijah Wood and Josh Hartnett that he firmly believed zombie movies were going to "come back in a major way," and he started writing a zombie movie so he could be one of the first to ride the wave. Unfortunately, Rodriguez got caught up doing other projects and his zombie film fell by the wayside, but when Tarantino approached him about doing "Grindhouse," he knew the time for his zombie movie had finally arrived.

The cast is clearly having fun and know how to entertain: there is an eclectic mix of well-known stars (like Rose McGowan, Naveen Andrews, Josh Brolin, Marley Shelton, Fergie from the musical group The Black-Eyed Peas, and Bruce Willis) who really take the time to chew the scenery and make the most of their parts, and this makes the film feel like equal parts blockbuster and B-movie. The zombie kills are gory and plentiful, and it just seems like everyone involved knew exactly what kind of movie they were making—one to entertain and not worry about winning any awards—and had no problem executing.

Granted, the movie features your standard-fare "Romero-style" zombies, but I like the way the "plague" is presented—initial exposure to a top-secret army gas is what turns you into a zombie, but prolonged, regulated exposure to the gas can actually keep you normal, a tactic some of the military men in the movie attempt to use to keep themselves non-zombied. Also, super-mega-bonus points to a movie that is ballsy enough to amputate its leading lady's leg halfway through the movie—and then replace it with a fully functional machine gun!

Surprisingly, I felt that a lot of the reactions and responses of the characters in this movie were pretty realistic. There was such a broad spectrum of the types of characters in the story, and so many of them reacted to what was going on in different ways, but ways that were consistent with their characters' personalities, it definitely added a realistic feel to the film.

There's lots of great gore and grossness in the film, especially during the scenes that take place in the hospital during the initial phase of the mass outbreak. And the editing of the film takes this category's score "to the Max," especially with the addition of one of the iconic pieces of the '70s B-movies—the missing reel! Rodriguez purposefully omitted a key scene in the film and never explained how things in the story went from one condition (relatively calm) to the extreme (house on fire! Zombies everywhere!), and somehow missing this scene (replete with the kitschy "reel missing" logo and scratchy 16-mm film graphics) actually adds to the overall entertainment value of the film.

Make no mistake: "Planter Terror" is a singular viewing experience, a damn near perfect marriage of respect for what has come before, originality in its own right, fun story, good acting, and a plethora of bitchin' special effects. It's a great film that belongs firmly entrenched in any zombie lover's collection.

PLAY-BY-PLAY

Even though it's not specifically zombie-related, I love that the movie has its own "fake" preview, created by Rodriguez and Tarantino for a fictitious movie called "Machete." At least, the film was fictitious at the time of "Planet Terror's" release—Rodriguez loved the concept so much that he actually ended up making "Machete" a few years later!

After the preview and the oh-so-classy, retro-fabulous "Feature Presentation" graphic, the movie actually begins, and we are treated to the main credits playing over a scene of Rose McGowan's character, Cherry Darling, stripping–pardon me, "go-go dancing," as she corrects multiple characters throughout the film. Whatever it's called, it's fun to watch and a great way to open the film.

After she's done on stage, Cherry speaks with her manager backstage and says, "I need a dramatic change in my life," as she puts her thigh-high boot on her soon-to-be-amputated right leg. Rodriguez proves to be a master of the "ironic foreshadowing" throughout the story, and this is the first prime example of the tactic in action.

Through some smooth-flowing scene transitions, we are soon introduced to the origin of the soon-to-be-a-massive-problem zombie-making agent: a government venture, "Project Terror" (also the original name of the film), involving a souped-up nerve gas. Naveen Andrews plays Abby, a thoroughly unconvincing scientist with an odd infatuation with male genitalia (his jar of testicles…why, Rodriguez, why?), and even though he isn't terribly believable as a scholarly man of science, he does serve to give us enough of the back story of the military project so we can understand what's going on. This scene is also where the cameos kick it into full throttle with a brilliant one – Bruce Willis!

A quick word about Willis' cameo: it's actually a very sly homage to a favorite tactic of the old "grindhouse" style movies, which was to cast a well-known actor and have he/she come in only for one day of filming, doing frontal shots only, while the rest of the scenes that character was in was filmed from the back with a body double. This was a huge cost-saving measure for the filmmakers, and the actor's face would then feature prominently on the movie poster, leading potential viewers to believe he/she was a much greater part of the movie than they actually were. Now that you're "in the know" about this, check out Willis' scenes: his character, Lt. Muldoon, is never in the same frame with any other actor when shown from the front, only when shown from the back (when it may or may not actually be Willis himself). Whether or not Willis was actually isolated from the rest of the cast during filming is unknown to this reviewer.

Back to the film! The effects in the first military scene are gruesome and intense right away, which quite frankly, is awesome. This trend continues into the hospital scenes where the zombie virus truly breaks out, and we get lots of insanely gory and pustule-popping looks at a variety of patients making the transition from living to dead to undead. The gore parade continues through much of the remainder of the film, including the notable scene of El Wray and Cherry's automobile accident and the ensuing gruesome zombie attack that leaves Cherry minus one appendage.

Speaking of effects, it's nice to see Tom Savini get a role in this film, even if he is cast as the bumbling Sheriff with terrible aim. His character's name, Tolo, literally means "fool" in Spanish and Portuguese.

For a grindhouse/exploitation film, the presentation of the story throughout the film is actually quite sublime. The build is slow and the characters, which are quite the eclectic mix, are developed well in a relatively short amount of time. I also love how the characters "almost" cross paths many times throughout the film; it gives things the feeling of being nicely tied together on the whole.

As we progress through the story, the important and noteworthy moments come fast and furious. The zombified Dr. Block tries to kill his wife, coming at her slowly while saying, "I'm gonna eat your brains and gain your knowledge." Not only did their son utter this line while playing with his toys earlier in the film, but it is a direct reference and homage to the 1986 horror film "From Beyond." It's also fun to note that both that film and this one featured prominent characters named Dr. Block/Bloch, spelled differently but pronounced the same.

Here comes the Missing Reel! We go right from a tender moment between Cherry and El Wray to utter calamity with The Bone Shack ablaze and the zombie horde in full-on attack mode. Just when you think the blood and guts couldn't possibly get any more extreme, Rodriguez and crew always seem to find a way to out-disgust themselves. I think this movie may have been shooting for "Dead Alive's" unofficial record of goriest movie ever…and they certainly might have come close.

In the climactic final third of the film, we start to lose some characters through various types of demises. Quentin Tarantino even shows up as a horny military man who meets a rather asexual (and utterly gross) end. Before he dies, though, he ends up with a piece of Cherry's splintered leg in his eye—is this a homage to the splinter-in-eye scene in the classic undead film Zombie (also reviewed here in this book), or just a fortuitous coincidence?

The final charge out of the military installation is exactly what you would expect in a film like this—death and carnage to the extreme, ridiculous action stunts that require copious amounts of suspension of disbelief, and cheesy one-liners—but wow, it's an impressive and enjoyable ride. After the big escape, we're given a final scene that establishes quite an interesting ending. Rodriguez himself explains the final scene as his version of "an anti-'Army of Darkness" type ending.

Rodriguez says, "In "Army of Darkness," Ash is returned to normal suburbia and battles the undead. In my film, the characters are taken out of suburbia and now battle the undead in a more barren landscape."

It's a little at odds with the rest of the film, admittedly, but quite remarkable, very "1970s," and a fitting ending for a very unique film.

TAKE TWO: A.G

Filled with more gore, pus, action and bullets than any zombie movie should have, comes *Planet Terror*, written and produced by Robert Rodriguez.

Made to pay homage to the grindhouse movies of the 1970's, this movie is filled with big busted women and more gratuitous violence than you can shake a zombie at.

When a chemical agent is released into the air, a small town becomes ground zero for a zombie invasion. Explosions abound as gun-toting chicks blow the infected into a thousand pieces. And I do mean a thousand. A side effect of the infection is lots of pus. Shoot a zombie and it will probably explode like a water balloon filled with blood and pus. Hit one with a truck and watch it pop, spraying gore in all directions.

Cherry Darling was once a Go-Go dancer and now finds herself as the hero of the apocalypse. When she loses her leg, she gets a new limb, this one a machine gun.

Now there's one important thing to take with you when you watch this movie and that is, don't take it too seriously. It's a homage to an age of low budget movies where all they had going for them was naked women and shock value. If you want to pick the plot apart, there's plenty there, but if you are that kind of viewer, this movie isn't for you.

This movie is for the laid back viewer who is in it for the blood, gore and action. Though you don't have to be in your forties to appreciate this movie and what it was made for, let me tell you, it sure helps. I highly doubt an average seventeen year old can appreciate this film the same way older folks can. The grainy pixels (put there on purpose), the time when the film pretends to burn in the projector, all takes us old folks back to a different time.

Still, there's enough action and gore to please the most discerning zombie fan and if you're a fan of pus, well this movie is for you.

And unlike most zombie movies that have your typical ending, this one is made like a big budget summer blockbuster with massive explosions as the survivors make a mad dash for freedom.

Made with a Hollywood budget instead of a shoestring, the special effects are outstanding and done by Greg Nicotero, a man who has worked on most of George Romero's Dead films.

Tom Savini has a small role as a deputy and he's a blast to watch.

And these zombies aren't slow plodding ghouls. They move fast. Not as fast as *28 Days Later*, but still much faster than a Romero ghoul.

So if for some reason you have never seen this movie, you're missing out on a great popcorn flick.

Just don't sit too close to the screen or you may get covered in pus.

RE-ANIMATOR

YEAR: 1985
COUNTRY: USA
RUNNING TIME: 86 minutes
SCREENPLAY: Dennis Paoli, Stuart Gordon, William J Norris
DIRECTOR: Stuart Gordon
PRODUCER: Bran Yuzna
EXECUTIVE PRODUCERS: Michael Avery, Bruce Curtis
MUSIC: Richard Band
DIECTOR OF PHOTOGRAPHY: Mac Ahlberg, Robert Frederic Ebinger
MAKE-UP AND SPECIAL EFFECTS: Anthony Doublin, John Naulin, Mechanical and Makeup Imageries
PRODUCTION DESIGNER:
ART DIRECTOR: Robert A Burns
COSTUME DESIGNER: Robin Burton
CAST: Jeffrey Combs (Herbert West), Bruce Abbott (Dan Cain), Barbara Crampton (Megan Halsey), David Gale (Dr. Carl Hill), Robert Sampson (Dean Alan Halsey, Carolyn Purdy-Gordon (Dr. Harrod)

TAKE ONE: T.S

COMMENTARY

Straight out of the 1980s came "Re-Animator," an amazing film that somehow took zombies, gore, comedy, an unknown cast, threw it all together, and created a one-of-a-kind experience for zombie and horror lovers everywhere.

H.P. Lovecraft wrote the serialized story "Herbert West: Re-Animator" back in the early 1920s, proving to be stunningly ahead of his time in his descriptions and depictions of re-animating the dead. Even though the 1985 movie I'm reviewing here shares the same name and a few characters and locations, make no mistake: this movie is its own entity, brought to life by writer/director Stuart Gordon and the performances of its cast, most notably the over-the-top personification of the titular Dr. West played to perfection by Jeffrey Combs. "Re-Animator" is, quite simply, a unique movie-watching experience, not likely to be reproduced any time soon, if ever.

The genesis of the movie was simple enough: during a discussion with some friends in the early '80s, Gordon lamented the fact that there were so many Dracula movies, and that he wished there were more Frankenstein-type of films. Someone asked him if he had ever read Lovecraft's "Re-Animator" tale, and even though he had enjoyed much of the author's work, "Re-Animator" was out of print at the time and Gordon had never read it.

After a trip to the Chicago public Library allowed him to enjoy the tale, Gordon decided he wanted to adapt the story for a live-stage version. Soon, he and his collaborators, Dennis Paoli and William Norris (who actually both wind up with co-writing credits on the film), decided that the tale would work better as a half-hour television pilot, eventually updating the location and characters to present-day and expanding the story into thirteen episodes of a full-hour television series. Bob Greenberg, a special effects wizard who got wind of the project, advised Gordon and company that horror would not work on television, and instead encouraged them to take their story to Hollywood. Greenberg connected Gordon with producer Brian Yuzna, who loved the story and got Gordon a motion-picture deal with Empire Pictures. And so–at the risk of overloading my pun allowance–"Re-Animator" was officially re-born.

The movie had a solid following, and performed well from the get-go. It made over $2 million in its North American theatrical run, which is a decent return on the $900,000 it cost to make the film. In addition, it was well-received by critics, getting three stars from Roger Ebert and a slew of praise from newspaper columnists across the country. The film quickly went into "cult" status, and Entertainment Weekly magazine has it listed as #32 on their list of "The Top 50 Cult Films."

Plain and simple, as a movie-watching experience, at its core "Re-Animator" is good old-school fun. From the opening scene with its one random zombie through the "it's over…or is it?" ending, the movie keeps the viewer engaged and wanting more. Sure, the look of the film has gotten a little dated, but that's part of what makes it grand. Re-Animator is a great example of a "splatter film" made in the prime of splatter films, the '80s.

The movie scores bonus points for details that are pretty unique to zombie cinema, including a severed zombie head that can still control it's body, varying levels of the zombies' abilities based on the "freshness" of the body, a reanimated "zombie cat," and who can forget the synthesized, glowing "re-agent" that must be injected directly into the body's pituitary gland. The true "high mark" of the film is that so many of its ideas and concepts are so unique and specific to the story of this film that they haven't been replicated by other zombie movies.

The movie is well-paced, with the unrated cut actually clocking in at nine minutes shorter than the theatrical cut (95 mins theatrical, 86 mins unrated). The gore is astounding, plentiful, and looks great for an '80s film—according to the DVD commentary, the special effects supervisor used twenty-four gallons of fake blood throughout shooting!

I easily put this film in the "must-see" category for any true zombie fan. It's a unique spin on a fairly standard tale, and the performances of the cast coupled with the great effects really put this movie over the top. If you see this film and enjoy it, then you should definitely look forward to seeing the two sequels, "Bride of Re-Animator" and "Beyond Re-Animator," which are both surprisingly above-average as far as original-sequels go.

PLAY-BY-PLAY

The film opens with an attention-grabbing sequence at a medical school in Switzerland, which actually gives the viewer more questions than answers, but does introduce us to our first re-animated creature right off the bat. After this short scene, the opening credits are shown over medial sketches, which begs the question to the first-time viewer—will this be a cerebral film? Exactly how much actual medical science will come into play during the course of the movie?

The first scene at Miskatonic Medical School (a division of Miskatonic University, the fictitious school that Lovecraft created and featured in many of his stories) introduces us to Dan Cain—is the last name a biblical reference?—who is shown initially as a "good" doctor but also somewhat foolish, as he is admonished by his attending doctor for not "knowing when to stop," a theme that will play throughout the story.

Many viewers and critics alike have praised "Re-Animator" for its near-perfect blend of subtle comedy and horror, and this blend is evidenced very early in the film. The security guard at the morgue, who proves time and again throughout the film how woefully inappropriate for the job he truly is, waxes poetic with Dan on why they keep the doors to morgue locked: "Nobody wants in, and ain't nobody gettin' out!"

Even though we see him in the opening scene, we're now officially introduced to Lovecraft's title character, Herbert West. Jeffrey Combs brings to his portrayal of Herbert just the right amount of creepy: somewhat normal and a nice-ish kind of guy, but there's just something about him and his mannerisms that is inherently off-putting. In this scene there is also a confrontation between West and the pompous Dr. Carl Hill, which serves as a sign of things to come in the story.

I mentioned earlier that the first time viewer may wonder how much medically-related content will be included in the film, and things are indeed very med-centric early on, including the special effects, which are good and seem very realistic. Soon enough, though, we move from medical science into the more fantastical, highlighted by the reanimation of Rufus, Dan's dead cat. Here we are introduced to the unsung "character" of the film, the Re-Agent serum, which is what allows West to reanimate dead bodies. It's an interesting concept, especially when we see with Rufus that the Re-Agent lets one bring things back multiple times, not some one-and-done miracle drug or something along those lines. Again, the supposition seems very grounded in actual medicine, and it's a nice change of pace from many of the more fantastical zombie stories.

Dan initially seems repulsed by West's experiments, but his "curious doctor" side gets the better of him, and soon he's dragged into the dangerous experiments. As they try to reanimate their first human corpse, West deadpans the line, "Any reaction would be ideal." I think he gets the reaction he desires when the zombie literally hops off the gurney and starts flipping out! For all his smarts, the uncertainty of the dosage of the Re-agent shows that West's research is still very unproven and that, really, at this point he is just guessing.

West wants to continue experimenting on the just-killed medical school Dean, Dr. Halsey, but Dan is not so sure that's wise, especially because Halsey is the father of his girlfriend Megan. That's the key difference between the two characters, their primary motivating factor: where West's is pure scientific curiosity, Dan's is clearly emotion. In any case, Dr. Halsey does indeed reanimate, and this is where the heart of the story lies: just how *alive* is he? What are the ethical questions surrounding his rights as a person?

Soon we see the storyline take a turn for the fantastic. Hill tries to steal the Re-Agent from West, so he cuts of Hill's head—Hill was pretty power-hungry, in West's defense. Astute viewers may come to the realization that, even though it's never said out loud or addressed directly, the trio of Doctors (Cain, West, and Hill) have probably all gone insane at this point.

The final third of the film ends up serving as one drawn-out, insane sequence filled with death, reanimation, revenge, zombie drones under the control of Hill's decapitated head in a pan, and copious amounts of blood and guts. Oh, and a little bit of reanimated romance, as Hill uses his new-found power to satisfy his obsession with Megan by having his headless body strip her naked and feel her up! I don't know quite how to feel about that...

And make no mistake here: Hill doesn't have just one or two revenants doing his bidding, he has a decent-sized zombie horde that are not only under his command, but are ready for a sneak attack at a moment's notice. Hill is surprisingly well-prepared for a body-less head.

Just when you think things can't get any stranger, at the end, we are treated to West shouting, "Overdose!" as he pumps Hill's body full of Re-Agent, which sets in motion a delightfully goofy and gory sequence I like to call "The Attack of the Fightin' Intestine!" West's fate is left purposefully vague, which helps set up the storyline for the film's sequels.

We seem headed for the typical "guy and girl escape, get married" ending, when boom–Megan's killed, just like that. But wait...death really isn't the end when you've got some Re-agent left, eh? A great open-ended conclusion to a wonderfully entertaining film.

TAKE TWO: A.G.

The movie Re-Animator is basically one that most of us wish would happen. And that is to have a life after death.

At the Miskatonic University in Arkham, Massachusetts, things are about to get very weird. Meet Herbert West, an unstable yet genius of a man who is obsessed with life after death. With the theory of there being a twelve minute window limit on the life of the brain after death, West had created a serum which reactivates dead tissue.

Nothing escapes his experiments. Cats and humans alike are injected in the name of science.

When West becomes the border of Dan Cain, paying up front, Cain finds himself quickly embroiled in West's antics.

Dr. Carl Hill, a ruthless doctor not above stealing another man's life's work, quickly becomes the evil villain and he plays it perfectly.

West fights back and beheads the unfortunate doctor, but not able to leave a fresh corpse alone, he can't help himself and injects the severed head and the headless body with his serum. But Hill is a master of hypnotism and for some unknown reason is able to command his now headless body. After knocking West unconscious, he steals the formula for himself.

Cain has been dating Megan, Dean Halsey's daughter, and she too quickly becomes caught up in the madness. When her father is killed by one of West's experiments gone wrong, West reanimates him, turning the Dean into a gibbering idiot.

Hill quickly uses the reanimated Dean to his benefit and has him capture his own daughter for his sick pleasures. Infatuated to the point of stalking, Hill has what could only be called a fatal attraction to Megan.

When the undead Dean brings his daughter to Hill, one of the most titillating yet sickest scenes in horror movie history comes to pass. Seeing a severed head give well, head, to a strapped down Megan, has to be seen to be believed.

When West and Cain show up to save Megan, they're in for quite a surprise. Through lobotomies, Hill has learned how to adapt the reanimated dead to become his slaves. Like the zombie movies of old where the zombies are merely tools for the zombie master, Hill controls them and then sics them on West and Cain.

The zombies in *Re-Animator* aren't flesh-hungry ghouls and in fact have no interest in eating a person. Instead, they are gibbering vessels that cannot speak or articulate in any way. They yell a lot, due to the fact that coming back from the dead is obviously painful and they will seek to kill any who stand in their way. The plot is loosely based on H.P Lovecraft's six stories that were published in a small publication called Home Brew. Those stories revolved around Herbert West and are set at the turn of the century. Though the movie is nothing like the stories, most fans agree that the spirit has been preserved, the tone intact.

In the end, if you look past all the gore and dead bodies, this is a tale about a man, Dan Cain, who loses everything he cares about after running afoul of Herbert West. It goes to show how fragile our happiness is and at any second, it can all be taken away from us, most times before we realize it's even happening. Cain became too close to everything and if he even once took a step back, he would have seen how out of control things were.

(Spoiler Alert: Don't read if you haven't seen the movie.)

At the end of the film, Cain's girlfriend is dead in his arms and he struggles to revive her to no avail. As the staff leaves and he gazes down at her still form, he realizes he has nothing left to lose, so he reaches into his bag for the glowing green serum, pulls back her head, and injects it into her brainstem. As the screen goes dark and we hear Megan's anguished scream of rebirth, we can't help but wonder if in the same position, would each of us do the same thing to a loved one?

I believe most of us would.

And that's the scariest thing of all.

RESIDENT EVIL

YEAR: 2002
COUNTRY: UK/Germany/France/USA
RUNNING TIME: 101 minutes
WRITER: Paul S Anderson
DIRECTOR: Paul S Anderson
PRODUCERS: Bernd Eichinger, Samuel Hadida, Jeremy Bolt, Paul S Anderson
CO-PRODUCER: Chris Symes
EXECUTIVE PRODUCERS: Robert Kulzer, Victor Hadida, Daniel Kletzky, Yoshiki Okamato
MUSIC: Marco Beltrami, Marilyn Manson
DIRECTOR OF PHOTOGRAPHY: David Johnson BSC
MAKE-UP EFFECTS: Hasso Von Hugo, Animated Extra International
PRODUCTION/COSTUME DESIGNER: Richard Bridgland
ART DIRECTOR: Jorg Baumgarten
CAST: Milla Jovovich (Alice), Michelle Rodriquez (Rain), James Purefoy (Spence), Eric Mabius, (Matt), Ryan McCluskey (Mr. Gray), Oscar Pearce (Mr. Red), Indra Ove (Ms. Black), Anna Bolt (Dr. Green)

TAKE ONE: T.S

COMMENTARY

Movies based on video games don't always do so well. I guess it was good for "Resident Evil," then, that it was only *inspired by* the video game series of the same name, instead of its story being directly adapted from part of the game's story.

"Resident Evil" is a high-octane horror adventure ride from start to finish. The film tells the tale of an "accident" (read: sabotage) and the ensuing viral outbreak at "The Hive," an underground headquarters of the mega-conglomerate Umbrella Corporation. When The Hive's complex A.I.-computer system locks down the base and prohibits anyone from getting in or out, Umbrella sends in an elite military unit to override the computer and regain control of the situation.

The military unit is accompanied by Alice, a mysterious woman suffering from amnesia but who clearly has an association with Umbrella. Once they breach The Hive, however, the unit discovers they have much more to deal with than just an overzealous computer system. Zombies, mutants, and other nefarious things roam the complex with seemingly only one goal in mind: to feed on anyone that stands in their way.

In an odd twist of undead fate, the "Resident Evil" film began its life with the intent of being one of those "based-on" movies, and the story-writing duties were put in the hands of one of the great minds of horror cinema. In 1999, game publisher Capcom and movie distributor Sony worked together to green-light the film's production, and they landed what they felt was an absolute coup by signing the legendary George Romero to write and direct the film. Romero was familiar with Capcom from his stint directing an advertising campaign for "Biohazard 2" (the international title of the "Resident Evil" games) in Japan. The screenplay Romero created focused on the plot of the Arklay incident, a key piece of "Resident Evil" videogame lore, and the ending of the film was to be incredibly similar to the ending of the first game in the series.

Sony and Capcom balked at the idea, and production of the film ground to an abrupt halt. In an interview with DGA magazine, Romero had the following to say in retrospect about the experience: "I don't think they were into the spirit of the video game and wanted to make it more of a war movie, something heavier than I thought it should be. So I think they just never liked my script." While I have nothing but mad love for Romero, the studios most likely looked at the long, unsuccessful track record of films adapted straight from the plot lines of video games and simply decided they wanted to try something different. Enter Paul W.S. Anderson.

Anderson had previously directed multiple films with unique blends of action, sci-fi, and horror. Some of his work included "Event Horizon," "Soldier," and another video-game property, "Mortal Kombat." Sony hired him to write a new screenplay, and they liked what he delivered so much, they asked him to direct the film as well. In an interview with *News Spong* website, Anderson declared that "under-performing movie tie-ins are too common and 'Resident Evil,' of all games, deserves a good celluloid representation."

Though it utilized familiar characters and elements of the video game, Anderson's story stood apart from what had been previously been presented in the video game series, even though numerous elements from the film have been referenced in subsequent "Resident Evil" games since the film's release.

The movie was originally titled "Resident Evil: Ground Zero," but the subtitle was removed after the 9/11 attacks. The film contains numerous references to the classic story "Alice in Wonderland," and even though some of the allusions are very prominent (such as Milla Jovovich's character's name of Alice and the computer program being called the "Red Queen"), others are a little more well-hidden (like the use of a white rabbit for testing the T-Virus and the mirrored "looking-glass" wall that opens to the underground train station).

For the film's zombies, professional dancers were primarily hired, since the thought process of the creative team was that these folks would have better control in their body movements.

For dancer-zombies and non-dancer zombies alike, Anderson reportedly took a very laid-back approach in directing them, simply instructing them to move however they thought a zombie would move given the various physical maladies associated with each individual creature.

After shooting began, the crew discovered they actually didn't have enough extras to represent the large number of undead they wanted to portray, so a little bit of scrambling and "creative casting" was involved: some of Capcom's executives and the film crew, including producer Jeremy Bolt, agreed to appear as the undead. Now *that's* a job perk!

Despite mixed critical reaction to the film, "Resident Evil" quickly became financially successful, making $17 million on its American opening weekend and over $102 million in worldwide theatrical gross. For a film whose budget was "only" $32 million, a sequel was a no-brainer, and even though there have been three subsequent films in the franchise with varying degrees of critical and financial success, the original is such a unique viewing experience, it's the only film of the series truly deserving to make our list for this book.

PLAY-BY-PLAY

A computer-animated graphical introduction gives the viewer a brief history of the Umbrella Corporation, a company that seems so mired in secret dealings that it feels difficult to believe something like it could exist. In reality, however, it's not that much of a stretch; companies like Enron, Haliburton, and even General Electric have long had their hands in both consumer and military development, and corporate dealings have definitely never always been performed directly in the public eye.

I really dig the techno-style music that comprises "Resident Evil's" background music and soundtrack. It adds a very current/edgy vibe to the story. Speaking of edgy, it doesn't take long for the Red Queen to establish herself as a coldhearted piece of machinery, eh? While the viewer hasn't been officially introduced to her in the opening scene, we can immediately see that whoever is in control is very vicious with killing everyone in The Hive without a second thought. At times it seems almost as if she is toying with some of them; she locks doors right as people get to them, she floods airtight laboratories with water, and decapitates a woman in an elevator–is this another Alice in Wonderland reference? "Off with her head!"

We're soon given an introduction to Alice, who was also knocked out by the Red Queen and wakes up naked on the floor of the bathroom. Jovovich has never been afraid to "show it all" in the name of cinema, has she? Between this movie and "The Fifth Element," it seems she performs in her birthday suit quite often, but it's never gratuitous and always seems to make sense within the scope of the film's plot.

The cameras in all the rooms that are watching Alice tells us this is an Umbrella-controlled mansion, and as the military unit enters, we see why: it's the secret entrance to The Hive. The train ride into The Hive starts to give us the scope of how big this facility truly is. Soon the team arrives at their destination, and as they unlock the outer doors and enter, we see that it's the same spot where we previously saw dead bodies in the corridor. Now, however, they're all gone...

Giving the physical representation of the Red Queen a child's voice makes the scenes where characters interact with the system infinitely creepier. Clearly the computer was designed to not be bothered, as shown by the plethora of booby-traps that surround her control room. "Laser Hallway" sucks!

This is the first part of the film that feels like a full-blown video game, and it's just as intense for the viewers as it seems to be for the characters. Before the laser-killing begins, Kaplan tells the team there is, "Nothing to worry about." Doesn't anyone learn anything from the list of "Things Never to Say in a Horror Movie?"

The action ramps up even further after this, as soon the zombies show up, then the mutants get out of their containment units as well. All hell has officially broken loose. We are even treated to a team of undead dogs! The zombified Dobermans are intense and disgusting.

The fight scene is crazy, but when Alice surprises herself with her commando-style skills, she starts to get some of her memories back and realizes she's definitely someone not to be taken lightly. Furthermore, flashbacks show that things with her and the other characters are definitely not what they seem...everyone apparently has shadiness and hidden agendas, even her.

I'm not sure I can recall ever seeing a movie where Michelle Rodriguez plays a character that *doesn't* die before the end of the film. At least here she gets to come back as a zombie, albeit very briefly. The final appearance and attack by the genetic mutant is summed up nicely by Matt: "What the fuck is that?"

The film has, in my opinion, a great ending. I love how the audience is continually just as confused as Alice is; it adds an extra layer of character connection that isn't always present in some movies. Alice ventures outside and sees that Raccoon City–and quite possibly the rest of the world–is screwed! There's even a "Day of the Dead" homage newspaper, the headline proclaiming, "The Dead Walk!"

It's a very bleak ending that most filmmakers wouldn't dare to leave audiences with. Much like the rest of this movie, it's a welcome change from the usual action/horror and video game adaptation tropes.

TAKE TWO: A.G

Before talking about this movie, I have a confession to make. I'm not a fan of the video games of the same name. But despite this, Resident Evil—and the following four movies at press time for this book—are all in my top ten favorite zombie movies.

The first zombie doesn't appear in Resident Evil until thirty-eight minutes in, but despite this, I've always found myself riveted to the screen. The atmosphere of the movie has always pulled me in. The claustrophobicness of an underground military base, where each turn in a hallway could be your death, makes for quite a ride.

The acting is top notch as well. Milla Jovovich does a great job as the star of the movie and the rest of the cast is equally enjoyable.

But let's be real, we all watch zombie movies for the zombies, right?

Well, once the first one appears, you will get your fill and then some.

Infected with the T-Virus, (a virus so potent that all the infected have to do is scratch you, or worse, bite you) these zombies are similar to Romero zombies. They are slow and plodding, but do pick up a little speed when their prey is close. The only way to put them down is with a shot to the head or destroying the spinal column.

Buried deep underground, the Umbrella Corporation facility under Raccoon City did everything from genetic testing to biological warfare. When the virus is set free thanks to a saboteur, the computer seals off the facility and kills every single person inside in an attempt to stop the pathogen from escaping.

Meanwhile, on the surface, Alice awakens with amnesia, thanks to the nerve gas she's been exposed to. She meets up with a mysterious man before the mansion they're in is attacked by soldiers, complete with gas-masks and automatic weapons.

The soldiers take her and the man with them underground to a subterranean train which then brings them even deeper to the Hive, the name of the facility. The Hive is massive and is directly under Raccoon City, a fictional city in the United States.

Once the soldiers penetrate the facility, they have less than an hour to find out why the computer shut the place down and escape before the Hive is sealed forever behind massive blast doors.

But the Hive isn't empty. The soldiers and Alice will soon find themselves battling five hundred flesh-craving zombies (the Hive's personnel), a murderous computer, and a genetic monstrosity called the Licker.

A little tidbit of information. George Romero was actually hired to write the original screenplay and he managed to incorporate most of the icons of the video game, including Jill Valentine as the female lead.

But the studio execs didn't care for his script and he was let go and Paul Anderson picked up the mantle. Paul, a big fan of the game, delivered a more intense action movie that holds back on the icons until the very end. In this way, *Resident Evil* is more of a prologue to the video game.

While not a masterpiece in any way, the movie still delivers frolicking action and seat-of-your-pants moments such as Alice battling zombie dogs.

This is a film that only gets better with age and defies being placed in a specific time, thus over the years it will only become more appealing to older audiences as well as new fans of the genre.

As a zombie movie, this is one hell of a ride and an exciting slice of popcorn-eating adventure.

RETURN OF THE LIVING DEAD

YEAR: 1985
COUNTRY: USA
RUNNING TIME: 91 minutes
STORY: Rudy Ricci, John Russo, Russell Steiner
SCREENPLAY: Dan O'Bannon
DIRECTOR: Dan O'Bannon
PRODUCER: Tom Fox
EXECUTIVE PRODUCERS: John Daly, Derek Gibson
CO-PRODUCER: Graham Henderson
MUSIC: Matt Clifford, Robert Randles, Francis Haines
DIRECTOR OF PHOTOGRAPHY: Jules Brenner
MAKE-UP EFFECTS: Bill Munns, Kenny Myers, Tony Gardner
PRODUCTION DESIGNER: William Stout
CONSULTING MORTICIAN: Timothy R Waters
SPECIAL EFFECTS: Robert E McCarthy, Kevin P McCarthy, Leslie Huntley/Fantasy 2 Film Effects Inc., Gene Warren Jr., Peter Kleinow
COSTUME DESIGN: Raggs Inc, Beverly Valbrown, Leslely Levin
ART DIRECTOR: Robert Howland
CAST: Clu Gulager (Burt), James Karen (Frank), Don Calfa (Ernie), Thom Mathews (Freddy), Beverly Randolph (Tina), John Philibin (Chuck), Jewel Shepard (Casey), Miquel Nunez (Spider), Brian Peck (Scuz), Linnea Quigley (Trash), Mark Venturini (Suicide), Jonathan Terry (Colonel Glover), Cherry David (Half woman corpse)

TAKE ONE: T.S

COMMENTARY

For such a comedic film, "The Return of the Living Dead" has a really sad story behind its creation.

Okay, maybe "sad" is not the right word. Unfortunate? Ill-fated? Regrettable? As fans of the genre may know, George Romero and John Russo worked together to create "Night of the Living Dead," but only Romero's name is attached to the sequels "Dawn of the Dead" and "Day of the Dead," as well as the other sequels further down the line. Astute fans will also notice that the "-of the Living Dead" moniker was replaced with simply "-of the Dead" from the second film on. Fans with even greater eagle-eyes will notice that not only does the "-of the Living Dead" moniker live on in a series of lesser-known films made between 1985 and today, they will see that the films (primarily this one being reviewed) are "based on a story by John Russo."

I know what you may be thinking: what's the story? All of these "-of the Living Dead" and "-of the Dead" movies must be connected somehow, right? How do all of these zombified puzzle pieces fit together?

It is indeed a convoluted tale, one seemingly taken right out of a soap opera for the walking dead, but I'll do my best to give you the "quick and dirty" version to help decipher it. After "Night" was filmed, Romero and Russo came to have some major creative differences, and they would up in a legal battle to determine who had the right to continue creating the film's storyline in future artistic endeavors.

Much like the average divorce, there was no clear "right," "wrong," or "winner." The final ruling came down that Romero retained the rights to the series' canon, giving him the sole ability to make direct sequels, but Russo won the rights to the "-of the Living Dead" sur-title, meaning that Romero's future films could not use this phrase, hence the change to "-of the Dead."

Russo, meanwhile, wrote a novel titled "The Return of the Living Dead," which was his extrapolation of the storyline created in "Night." He quickly got connected with film producer Tom Fox, and they planned to adapt the book to the screen, to be directed by legendary horror great Tobe Hooper (and to be shot in 3-D, no less). The distributing company, Orion Pictures, brought in writer Dan O'Bannon to perform some edits and fine-tune the script.

Shortly after this, Hooper left the project to direct "Lifeforce" instead. O'Bannon was offered the opportunity to direct the movie, which he agreed to only on the condition that he was allowed to drastically rewrite the script for the film. Where Russo's design was to keep the story closely tied to "Night" and Romero's sequels, O'Bannon thought it best to separate the two franchises as much as possible. Orion agreed, and O'Bannon quickly reworked the story, so much so that the end result we see on screen actually bears very little resemblance to Russo's original novel.

Russo was eventually given the opportunity to film his own take on the "canon" of his and Romero's original story, releasing in 1998 a significantly altered and extended "Night of the Living Dead 30th Anniversary Edition" followed by its own sequel, "Children of the Living Dead." Even though his contribution beyond the title ended up being rather minimal, he still retains a story writing credit on "The Return of the Living Dead."

As for the finished product of the film version of "ROTLD," it was both a financial and critical success, both in theaters and today on home video. Filmed on a budget of $4 million, it grossed over $14 million in theaters domestically. It's one of the first zombie comedies ever made, and its plot and presentation are solid: after an accident at a medical supply company in Louisville, Kentucky, a top-secret army toxin (and the corpse that came with it) is accidentally released, getting into the atmosphere and causing dead bodies in the local cemetery to reanimate. These aren't your average living dead, however. In one of the genre's first alterations on how zombies act, these undead folks are fast, vocal, pretty sarcastic, and frighteningly clever.

The end result is a comedic romp with more than its fair share of scary moments, as the humans try their damndest to survive the night without having the zombies munch on their "Brraaiinnss!"

PLAY-BY-PLAY

The film opens with what I'd call an "anti-disclaimer," a sarcastic text screen that proclaims, "The events portrayed in this film are all true. The names are real names of real people and real organizations." Cut directly to a shot of the company sign for the Uneeda Medical Supply, and this moment quickly establishes for the audience that we've got a very tongue-in-cheek approach to the story coming our way.

"ROTLD" quickly establishes that not only will it be a very quotable film, but the characters use a lot of dialogue that is full of ironic foreshadowing. Some examples include Spider saying, "I'm not in the mood to die tonight," as the teens are walking the street, making their plans for the evening.

The characters reference "Night" within the first five minutes of the film. The supposition here is that the original movie was based on a "real case" and the "guy who made the film" was strong-armed by the government into changing some of the details of the story. I guess the disclaimer at the beginning of the film makes a little more sense now, eh? Later, as the characters are trying to kill the reanimated cadaver and lamenting the fact that decapitation doesn't stop the creature, Frank screams, "It worked in the movie!" and Freddy replies, "You mean the movie…lied?" A thinly-veiled barb at Romero, but hopefully it was good-natured in its intent.

The cause of reanimation, according to this movie's lore, is a chemical developed by the government, 245-Trioxin. Although Frank thinks the chemical started as "spray-on marijuana," we see that the government is taking it very seriously, with round-the-clock monitoring stations waiting to hear about any potential outbreaks. Little does the government know that the missing shipment of 245-Trioxin, along with the zombified humans in stasis, have been in Uneeda's basement for the last fourteen years. When Frank shows Freddy the containers, he asks the valid question, "These things don't leak do they?" Note to Frank: don't punch the barrels! You're just asking for trouble, and surprise surprise—you get it!

The Trioxin quickly reanimates every dead thing in the building. The audience obviously sees the cutaway dogs and the cadaver come back to life, but eagle-eyed viewers will also notice the butterflies pinned on the display board have been resuscitated as well and are flapping their wings. This is a nice attention to detail on the part of O'Bannon and his crew.

The scene with the soon-to-be-headless cadaver zombie is pure ridiculousness, but is also pure fun. I guess this is the perfect example of the phrase, "running around like a chicken with its head cut off." Soon after this, we're introduced to one of the most memorable individual zombies of all time: Tar-Man! He's quite the resourceful zombie, using a good amount of reasoning and tools around him to help him capture his prey. Also of note here: this may be the first time ever a zombie says it wants "brains," which has now become a staple of what many people incorporate into their definition of a "zombie."

The film carries a definite "rock and roll" feel to it, through both the soundtrack and the personification of the high school characters. The characters, not just the younger kids but all of them really, are quite a random assortment, and their actions and dialogue are very haphazard. It's actually a very realistic interpretation of what might happen in the actual zompocalypse—an assortment of random people thrown together and forced to work as a unit if they want to survive.

As for the zombies themselves, once they start to rise *en masse* from the cemetery, we see that even though they're somewhat slapstick, in many ways they are much scarier than the shambling variety of undead. These creatures can move fast *plus* think, trick the living, and work together towards their goals. In actuality, they may be the scariest zombies ever seen!

The characters' conversation with the "halved" zombie woman is odd, but enlightening. We discover that these zombies don't want to eat flesh, only brains, and their rationale is that it lessens the pain of being dead. It's almost like an addiction—once they have a taste for it, they want more and more. Brains: they're the new "gateway" drug.

The film wraps up with a fun, if open-ended, conclusion. In typical government fashion, they think they've got things under control…and couldn't be more wrong! To date, there are four subsequent movies after this one that share the "Return" title, but none of the sequels have come close to matching the high entertainment value or the originality of the first film.

TAKE TWO: A.G

While George Romero was releasing *Day of the Dead* into theatres, at the same exact time, another zombie movie hit movie theatres.

This one was a horror comedy, and where Romero's zombies were slow and stupid, in this movie, they were fast, nearly indestructible, and could talk! This is also the first movie to introduce zombies that want brains.

The name of the movie is *Return of the Living Dead* and it hit theaters hard and fast, leaving *Day of the Dead* behind. Audiences wanted to laugh and *Day of the Dead* was just too intense for them.

Return of the Living Dead, filled with a wild punk musical score, a naked Linnea Quigley, and laughs in just the right places, filled the bill.

One of the funniest things of the movie is that the people in the movie are actually aware of horror movies. Where most movies have a zombie uprising and it's like there was never a movie made about them, ROTLD talks about *Night of the Living Dead* and references it multiple times, even to the point of discussing how to kill a zombie.

But this isn't you father's zombie movie.

For one thing, the zombies here are fast, real fast, and are virtually indestructible. You can stun them with a blow to the head but even dismembered, the parts keep attacking.

It all starts when a chemical called Trioxin escapes one of the barrels stored in the cellar of Uneeda Medical Supplies. It seems the barrels were from the Army and were rerouted to the warehouse by accident. Inside them are the remains of the zombies from *Night of the Living Dead*.

When the chemical is released, a corpse in the freezer is reanimated as well as half dogs used for veterinarians. As the split dogs lie on the floor, barking, the zombie in the freezer bangs to be set free.

When it does, even a blow to the head won't put it down. So what do they do? To cover up their blunder, they chop up the pieces and bring them to the mortuary next door to have the parts cremated, thus destroying the evidence. But as the parts are burned to ash, the ash rises out of the chimney and into the sky. Mixing with rain, it falls back to earth where the runoff seeps into a local cemetery.

Where Romero's zombies are recently diseased only, in ROTLD, all corpses dig themselves free of their graves to feast on the living, no matter how long they have been interred.

And they love brains especially. For some reason, the zombies know that brains will cease the pain of being dead, quelling their suffering for a little while.

As the cemetery disgorges its occupants, the survivors hole up and fight for their lives.

Here, we meet talking zombies for the first time.

As paramedics arrive to help, they are taken down and one of the zombies calls in on the radio, "Send more paramedics." Later another says, "Send more cops," into the mic of a squad car after devouring the police that arrived to investigate.

Meanwhile, the zombie from the broken barrel, a tar-covered pile of goop, nicknamed the Tarman says, "Brains," and "more brains," as he chases the cast around the warehouse.

We also see that zombies feel pain in this movie, which is why they want brains so bad. And as they hide in the shadows and wait for prey, we find out that they can think and reason as well. They don't act like simple animals running on instinct.

What I have always enjoyed about this movie is once the action starts, it's a nonstop ride till the end. There are no slow spots. One thing after another happens, keeping the watcher riveted to the screen. And as we all like to laugh, there are plenty of moments to chuckle. Some of the humor is subtle, where we laugh at the antics, but to the cast, what's happening is far from humorous. That makes it even more fun.

And the makeup effects are fantastic. The severed half woman zombie who is captured and fills the cast in on why zombies want brains is a work of art. As she speaks, her spine twitches like a tail, dripping fluid onto the exam table.

The zombies themselves look great, too. Looking as if they just crawled from the grave, their skin is rotting and their clothes are filthy.

And this is the movie that put scream queen Linnea Quigley on the map, as she runs around half naked, the sexiest zombie ever on the silver screen—well, except for Mindy Clarke in *Return of the Living Dead Part 3*.

So if you love your zombies with a side order of humor, this movie will do the job and then some.

SHAUN OF THE DEAD

YEAR: 2004
COUNTRY: UK/France
RUNNING TIME: 100 minutes
WRITER: Simon Pegg, Edgar Wright
DIRECTOR: Edgar Wright
PRODUCER: Nira Park
EXECUTIVE PRODUCERS: Tim Bevan, Eric Fellner, Natascha Wharton, Alison Owen, James Wilson
MUSIC: Daniel Mudford, Pete Woodhead
DIGITAL EFFECTS: Double Negative/Jeremy Hattingh
DIRECTOR OF PHOTOGRAPHY: David M Dunlap
MAKE-UP: Stuart Conran
ART DIRECTOR: Karen Wakefield
PRODUCTION DESIGNER: Marcus Rowland
COSTUME DESIGNER: Annie Hardinge
CAST: Simon Pegg (Shaun), Kate Ashfield (Liz), Nick Frost (Ed), Lucy Davis (Dianne) Dylan Morgan (David), Bill Nighy (Philip)

TAKE ONE: T.S

COMMENTARY

Looking over the list of movies included in this book, we have more than a few zombie comedies or, at minimum, films with at least some light-hearted aspects to them. Which is great, in my opinion; for a long time, people really didn't think horror and comedy could exist in the same movie together, unless it was a satirical take on horror. But like Paula Abdul taught me via song back in the '80s, sometimes opposites attract, and when done correctly, a zombie comedy can be infinitely enjoyable. Of all the zom-coms out there, it is my professional opinion that no film has meshed the two together more perfectly than "Shaun of the Dead."

I'm going to go out on a limb and say that every "good" zombie fan has to have seen this movie already. The plot, revolving around "everyman" Shaun and his attempts to not only survive both his humdrum daily life and the zompocalypse, but also to see his friends, family, and (ex-)girlfriend to safety in the process, quickly became a cult favorite here in the United States, as well as being wildly popular in the United Kingdom upon its release.

There are more than a few reasons for this, and the list of how "Shaun's" creators managed to get things so right is an itemized register full of components: lots of money in the budget, a multitude of well-trained comedy actors, ideal timing of the movie's release, and so forth. Even with all this, I feel that the two most important factors for the film's success are key pieces of the puzzle: first, and most importantly, Wright and company didn't make fun of zombie stories, they had fun with the genre by paying both homage to it and highlighting some of the inherent parallels to the zombie-ness our everyday lives already have. Secondly, the humor (or rather, *humour*, since it is a British film and all) of the movie is not simply throw-away jokes and one-liners, like so many base-level comedies. Instead, co-writers Simon Pegg (who also stars in the film as the titular Shaun) and Edgar Wright (who directs the film as well) give us nuanced comedic bits that not only repeat themselves throughout the film, they work on multiple levels that the intelligent viewer can appreciate all the more.

Below, I have given multiple examples of both points illustrated to perfection in the movie's plot and dialogue, in an attempt to keep things as spoiler-free as possible here in the commentary, for those of you reading this that have somehow avoided seeing "Shaun of the Dead" up to this point (yes, I'm talking to you, Mom). There is one point I can tell you about in this section, however: Pegg and Wright's dedication to the classic-horror-film-homage approach went so deep that it actually extended beyond what was shown on the screen and into the movie-production process as well. As shooting on their film began, "Shaun's" creators decided that they were going to pay £1 (one pound) per day to all of the people who came out to be zombie extras in the movie. This is a clear reference to how George Romero infamously paid $1 per day to all of the zombie extras who worked on his film "Day of the Dead" (it's often reported that Romero paid $1 to his extras on "Dawn of the Dead" as well, but this is false: they were paid like princes in comparison, $20 and a box lunch). It's the subtle and loving little nods to those that came before them, like this and other moments in the film itself, that earned Pegg and Wright the invitation from Romero himself to portray zombie extras in "Land of the Dead." These guys, quite simply put, "get it."

PLAY-BY-PLAY

Right out of the gate, astute zombie fans can tell that "Shaun of the Dead" will be heavily-laden with in-jokes and references to other undead films. The music playing over the Universal Studios logo and the pre-credits is immediately recognizable as the same cut of synthesizer-heavy music that was used during the hangar scene in "Dawn of the Dead."

The actual opening scene itself does an incredibly impressive job of quickly and easily setting up the relationships and personality traits of all four main characters. It's a great use of minimal screen time and really highlights the writing savvy of Pegg and Wright. It also lays the foundation for the "multi-level" theme the movie will employ. Attentive viewers will easily pick up the multiple meanings when the characters say things about "getting out and living" and "wanting more to happen in life."

This all happens even before the opening credits roll! During the title and credits presentation, we get some fun social commentary on how humans are already "zombies" in the way we mundanely live our everyday lives, listlessly going through the motions at our jobs, robotically swaying to the same music we hear on the radio, and so forth.

Highlighted throughout the movie is Wright's signature "kinetic-style" camera shooting, which he also effectively employed not only in "Shaun's" predecessor, the British television show "Spaced," but also in subsequent films like comic-book-adaptation "Scott Pilgrim vs. The World." The purposeful, cinematic shots of only mundane things (brushing teeth, making breakfast) give the viewer another great commentary on what's truly "exciting" in our everyday lives.

The recurring jokes are omnipresent throughout the film, and really help give a sense of the movie being tightly tied together instead of just a random assortment of things happening on screen. I haven't met a zombie fan yet who doesn't chuckle when I say "you've got red on you" to them. Even more impressive is the subtle way certain scenes are sometimes tied together. Take, for instance, the segment in which Shaun and Ed are at The Winchester Pub immediately after Liz has broken up with Shaun. Ed tells Shaun what their plans should be for the next day, in an attempt to help Shaun feel better about and move on from the break-up, but in reality Ed is actually outlining what *will* happen tomorrow once the zompocalypse hits them full-throttle. Observe, if you will, Ed's dialogue about his ideas for plans, with what actually happens in parenthesis: "You know what we should do tomorrow? Keep drinking! We'll have a Bloody Mary first thing (their first zombie attack is, of course, Mary the Checkout Girl in their backyard, who is in fact terribly bloody), have a bite at the King's Head (the "king" is Phillip, Shaun's father-in-law, who was bitten), a couple at the Little Princess (referencing David, Di, and Liz, Shaun's girlfriend and her two friends who are a couple), we'll stagger back here (and they do, as they stagger around and impersonate zombies in an attempt to blend in), and bang! We're back at the bar for shots (and shoot they do, as they repeatedly fire the Winchester rifle hanging above the bar)." How's that for a slice of amazing two-level dialogue?

In addition to the dialogue, the film also features excellent use of the "double scene," where something happens in a similar manner to earlier in the story, only in an entirely different context. Some of the best examples include when Shaun walks from his flat (British-speak for "apartment") to the store, Shaun's meeting up with Yvonne (even includes duplicated dialogue!), Shaun climbing through the window into Liz's flat, the couple making out/eating each other outside the Winchester, the pub's jukebox and "it's on random," Pete telling Ed to "go live in a shed," and of course, the multiple instances of "the front door is open!"

As mentioned previously, the references and nods to other horror and zombie films are plentiful. I won't list them all here, but keep your eyes peeled and you might see many more than just the obvious tips of the hat to "The Evil Dead," "Night of the Living Dead," "Dead Alive," "An American Werewolf in London," and Fulci's Italian zombie flicks. Also worth noting is the highly-comical debate between Ed and Shaun on whether one should actually call a zombie "a zombie."

The movie isn't all fun and games, though: quick bursts of some pretty serious violence in between the "normal" scenes let you know early on that something sinister is definitely going on. Shaun and Ed's gruesome first zombie experience, once they come to grips with what it truly is, is actually quite terrifying. In the same vein, Phillip's death in the car is actually very touching—chalk this up to both the writing and Bill Nighy's great acting ability, even as a zombie.

The emotional impact of the reality of the rampant death and destruction isn't limited to just the one scene. The viewer is given another touching and realistic moment in the death of Barbara, Shaun's mom; Shaun's reluctance to kill her, even after she turns into one of the undead menace, is a deep theme in a lot of zombie stories, and the writing duo did a great job of touching on major themes like this while still keeping things fresh.

Could bumbling, irreverent Ed be the best sidekick ever captured on film? His final word after a particularly touching moment—"Gaaay!"—makes me seriously consider it. The film itself gets something most zombie movies don't: a fun ending that actually shows what happens after the undead menace is contained and brought back under control. Give the creative team credit for not only that, but for including a plethora of story-enhancing extras on the DVD release, including a segment called "Plot Holes," where animated comics narrated by the characters themselves help give us some closure to a few unanswered questions.

When it's all said and done, everything about the film combines to give the viewer an experience like none other, and "Shaun of the Dead" easily ranks high on the list of must-see zombie films.

TAKE TWO: A.G.

Shaun of the Dead is more than a horror comedy about zombies. Much like *Dawn of the Dead*, it's an insight into humanity and how self-absorbed the average man and woman is. If you haven't seen the movie yet, you might not want to read this review as it has a few small spoilers in it.

At the beginning of the movie, we find Shaun with his girlfriend Liz at the Winchester Bar. Shaun is on the verge of losing her which would be a terrible mistake. Liz is smart and beautiful and any man would love to have her as their girlfriend. But Shaun is a little of a screw up. With his deadbeat friend Ed, the ultimate slacker, Shaun repeatedly makes the wrong choices.

Shaun works in an appliance store, selling TVs and refrigerators, a dead end job to add to his going-nowhere life.

But Liz cares for him and gives him another chance. They agree to meet at a restaurant the next night, alone, just the two of them. But of course, Shaun messes up and doesn't book the reservation. Liz, angry at being disappointed by Shaun yet again, kicks him out of her flat, and thus, breaking up with him.

All this drama is nothing special in a romantic movie. Loser boy has great girl, loses her and then tries to get her back. But see, all this happens while a zombie outbreak begins.

As we watch Shaun living his life and dealing with these things, in the background, the outbreak is beginning. Shaun sees none of this, which is hilarious. When the news reports come on, he changes the channel, and when a zombie is feeding on someone in the street, he thinks it's a couple necking.

What's so amusing about this is that Shaun isn't too far from the truth on how most people would act in the same situation. Self absorbed, most people barely look left or right as they travel, only focusing on their destination.

Shaun and Ed go out and get drunk so Shaun can try to get over Liz. Here as well, we see the outbreak beginning, but once more, Shaun and Ed don't see it, too wrapped up in their lives to care about what's happening.

But the next morning, after Shaun has passed out in the kitchen, he wakes up to find a girl in the backyard. Ed and Shaun go out to see who she is and when they get a look at her, Shaun states that she's drunk. But she's not drunk, she's a zombie, only from a casual glance, yes, she looks drunk. She's sluggish, uncoordinated and her eyes are glassy, her mouth slack.

When she tries to bite Shaun and he pushes her away, she falls back on an old pipe protruding from the ground. She's impaled on it.

Shaun and Ed stare in disbelief, and as the girl slides off the pipe, she leaves a whole in her torso three inches round. It so clean you can see right through her.

Shaun and Ed have been introduced to their first zombie.

As Shaun takes a step away from the grisly sight, another zombie appears, this one big and fat with blood crusting its mouth.

Shaun and Ed go back inside to regroup, but when the two zombies break a window, they have no choice but to go out and deal with the unruly ghouls.

Here's where the fun starts as the two men grab anything in the house, such as the toaster and dishes, and throw them at the ridiculously slow zombies. They aim for the head (cause that's what you do in the movies, they figure) but almost always miss.

Then they start using records, also missing with the exception of one or two times. Finally, Shaun gets fed up and goes to the woodshed to get some real weapons, namely a shovel and a cricket bat.

With new weapons in hand, the two men take out the zombies easily.

With nothing else to do, they go back inside, have an ice cream cone and relax while watching television. Here they watch as the news plays out and explains what's happening.

After getting a call from Shaun's Mum and she explains that Shaun's step dad has been bitten, Shaun decides they need to go get her and probably take out Phil, his step dad. After saving Mum, they plan on going to get Liz, then all together, they will head to the Winchester Pub and wait out the zombie apocalypse in style.

Once more Shaun shows how utterly oblivious he is to the way the world works.

Note that during his montage of what he will do and how he will do it, the background music is taken from *Dawn of the Dead*, just like the music at the very first seconds of the film. These are wonderful homages to the movie that inspired *Shaun of the Dead*.

Before they leave, taking Pete's—Shaun's brother—car, Shaun goes to the bathroom to get cleaned up. This is where he finds Pete, who is in the shower and has turned into a zombie after receiving a bite to the hand the previous day.

Shaun, runs down the stairs leaving Pete in the bathroom, and he and Ed race to Pete's car. Jumping in, they speed off as all around them Shaun sees the world collapsing as the zombies attack.

Ed, of course, dense beyond dense, barely seems to care. He takes things in stride to the point of utter stupidity, but that also makes him funny.

After gathering Shaun's Mum and step dad, they head over to Liz's house. After Shaun convinces Liz and her two flat mates that it's not safe there, they all head to the Winchester Pub, where Shaun thinks they will be safe.

As Shaun leads the others outside, he wields the cricket bat like a warrior. And this is a major plot point in the movie. See, where in regular life, Shaun was a slacker and going nowhere in life, during a zombie apocalypse, he shines. He plans, strategizes and fights with bravery to save his loved ones. Where before he was a loser, in the new world of the walking dead, he excels and becomes the leader of their small group.

When they arrive at the Winchester, by of all things, walking slow and moaning, pretending to be zombies, they can't get in. Once more Shaun shows his heroics and quick thinking by attracting the entire zombie horde and leading them away from the pub so the others can get inside unseen.

When Shaun returns, they all get a small break to relax, but no sooner do they think they're safe than the zombies are back, no small part to Ed playing a video game that makes enough noise to attract them. And guess what? Shaun's Mum has been bitten. A touching death scene ensues, which makes this such a great movie. You really feel for Shaun and his loss.

When Mum comes back, she's put down in a glorious spray of blood and brain matter by a gunshot to the head by Shaun, who has done what he has to do. This once more proves he has it in him for greatness; to do what has to be done no matter what.

When the zombies attack from all sides, it's a great finish to a fantastic movie. Lots of zombie action here, and no one should be left unsatiated by the time it's over.

The end wraps up nicely on a good note, which many might say detracts from it. As we all know, many people want nihilistic endings on everything they watch.

If you follow the credits right to the end, you'll hear more music from *Dawn of the Dead*, this time the famous "Gonk."

SLITHER

YEAR: 2006
COUNTRY: USA
RUNNING TIME: 96 minutes
WRITER: James Gunn
DIRECTOR: James Gunn
PRODUCER: Paul Brooks, Eric Newman, Thomas Bliss
CO-PRODUCER: Jeff Levine
EXECUTIVE PRODUCERS: Norm Waitt Scott Niemeyer
MUSIC: Tyler Bates
CASTING: Eyde Belasco
ART DIRECTION: Michael N. Wong
EDITING BY: John Axelrad
CINEMATOGRAPHY: Gregory Middleton
STUDIO: Gold Circle Films Strike Entertainment
DISTRIBUTED BY: Universal Pictures
SPECIAL MAKE-UP EFFECTS SUPERVISOR: Eric Mussell
PRODUCTION DESIGNER: Andrew Neskoromny
COSTUME DESIGNER: Patricia Hargreaves
CAST: Elizabeth Banks (Starla Grant), Nathan Fillion (Bill Pardy), Michael Rooker (Grant Grant), Gregg Henry (Jack MacReady), Tania Saulnier (Kylie Strutemyer), Jenna Fischer (Shelby Cunningham), Brenda James (Brenda Gutierrez), Don Thompson (Wally), Whale Patrick McAreavy (McGregor)

TAKE ONE: T.S.

COMMENTARY

There's a fairly standard sci-fi/horror trope that a lot of stories use: semi-sentient alien organism visits Earth and takes over individual humans by entering our bodies through our mouths/ears/noses/butts/any other orifices they can wriggle into. Many times, the aliens "kill" the humans or incapacitate their brains when taking over the bodies, turning the infected folks into a creature most would call a zombie.

It's definitely not a new plot device, showing up as early as the 1930s in sci-fi serials, but if done correctly it can easily make for a story that is entertaining, suspenseful, and thought-provoking.

By plot line alone, "Slither" doesn't break any molds or cover any new ground: it's your fairly standard "alien slugs turn people into zombies and try to take over the world" scenario. However, it's the nuanced performances by the cast, the attention to detail on the part of its creators, and the broad humor mixed with tongue-in-cheek homage to former stories of this type that make "Slither," in my humble opinion, a must-see film for any fun-loving zombie enthusiast.

Now, take this review with a grain of salt if you're not a huge fan of the "classic" sci-fi/monster movies of the '70s and '80s, but I personally fall squarely in this movie's target demographic. "Slither" was directed by Troma Films vet and self-proclaimed long-time "schlocky sci-fi movie" lover James Gunn, who cites films like "Invasion of the Body Snatchers," "Shivers," and "The Brood" as direct influences on the movie he wanted to make. Even though "Slither" has been accused of being a "rip-off" of another great sci-fi/horror comedy film, "Night of the Creeps," having seen both movies I can definitively tell you that these are two different films with two very different "feels" to them.

Those of you who may be familiar with some of Troma's movies, including such classics as "The Toxic Avenger" and "Tromeo and Juliet," know that those folks like to put out over-the-top gross-out films with very lowbrow comedy liberally applied for good measure. Gunn is able to take what he learned during his Troma time and meld it with his knowledge of what the average moviegoer has come to know and expect, and the result is very positive. "Slither" takes place around the small community of Wheelsy, South Carolina, and the environment and mannerisms of the characters as the local population definitely play to the typical Southern stereotypes, but do so without going overboard.

The cast is superb, and Gunn really lucked out on hiring a few actors right before they truly "made it big." Starring as Starla, the unhappy wife of the first human to be infected, is Elizabeth Banks, who acted in this film directly after wrapping what would be her first major hit, "The 40-Year-Old Virgin;" cast as Bill Pardy, the take-no-prisoners yet oddly-goofball Sheriff who has had a major crush on Starla since high school, is Nathan Fillion, long before the TV show "Castle" brought him the recognition that "Firefly" and "Serenity" should have bestowed upon him.

Rounding out the cast of eclectic and highly-entertaining characters are Gregg Henry as eminently-quotable Mayor Jack MacReady (with possibly the best introductory scene of a public official ever captured on film), Jenna Fisher as a pre-"The Office" receptionist Shelby, Rob Zombie as the enigmatic (if short-scened) Dr. Karl, and Michael Rooker, long before he graced "The Walking Dead" television series with his presence, here starring as the first person to be infected, business owner-turned-alien monster Grant Grant (not a typo, that really is his character's name).

This movie was considered a box-office failure, with a production budget of around $15 million. The film's theatrical run in the United States only garnered $7.8 million, and with only another $5 million in theatrical revenue from the rest of the world, "Slither" still failed to make it into the green. The reasons for this subpar showing are unknown, of course, but I truly think audiences just didn't "get it."

This film was released shortly after "Shaun of the Dead" in theaters, and audiences probably just weren't ready for another horror-comedy at the time. That, coupled with minimal DVD promotion due to the aforementioned poor box office production, means that this movie went largely unnoticed by a vast amount of its target audience.

Which is a shame, because I don't think this movie could be much more enjoyable! Lots of action, good-looking zombies and aliens, and lots of jokes (of the subtle and not-so-subtle variety) make "Slither" one of the best movies, from a sheer-enjoyment standpoint, that I've seen in quite some time.

Being an homage-type of film that draws heavily from those that came before it, there's obviously not a great opportunity for a vast amount of original content.

But going directly for the comedic approach does garner some style points where other alien-possession movies don't go, and "Slither" does manage to make a few unique story marks of its own, including Grant Grant, the main protagonist that spends the movie morphing–both mentally and so-disgusting-it's-cool physically–from unlikeable regular-joe human to unlikeable giant-tentacled alien-thingy.

Criminally under-rated even to this day, "Slither" is a rockin' experience for those just looking to pop in a flick and have some good old-fashioned movie-watching fun.

Even though the critics didn't like it, I say let the true fans be the judge: Ebert and Roeper gave the film "two thumbs down" on their televised review show when the movie was first released, but in 2006 the film earned three Fangoria "Chainsaw Award" nominations (winning one, "Highest Body Count"), was listed as one of the "Top 25 DVDs of the Year" by Rolling Stone Magazine, and was named "Best Feature Film of the Year" by Rue Morgue in 2006. In the words of Fillion's, Sheriff Bill Pardy, "Now that is some fucked-up shit!"

PLAY-BY-PLAY

We are treated to a classic "virus from space" opening, replete with the alien-carrying meteor traveling through the cosmos to come crashing down in the backwoods of South Carolina. The small town it lands near, Wheelsy, has a billboard along its highway claiming it to be the "City of the Future," but in the introductory scenes we see the area isn't looking so hot these days, it's very run-down and economically challenged.

Director cameo! James Gunn pops on screen for a very brief scene with Starla as fellow teacher Hank, before Michael Rooker's character, Grant, comes and sweeps her away. Speaking of Rooker, it's hard to say that he steals the scenes he's in, since he's such a well-known actor, but he is at his true comedic best here, in his first zombie action film. Also be sure to note his dedication to the craft, as no matter how physically mutated his character becomes (up to and including the disturbing final scene of the film), you'd better believe it is always actually him inside of that getup.

So, Grant becomes the first human to get infected, and that makes him the *de facto* leader of the alien invasion. Let this scene be a lesson to everyone–repeat after me: "I promise to never follow behind an alien slug too closely or poke at it with a stick." Clearly, nothing good could come of this.

The scene where Starla gets intimate with Grant the morning after he's been infected is key to the plot development of the film. You have to understand, the alien has never been treated this way, with caring and affection, so this is why he emotionally attaches to her and continually spares her from death. The film really starts as a sci-fi story, then slowly transforms into zombie-horror. It just goes to show that the lines between these two genres really are quite blurred.

The characters really play well off of each other to create a sense of an environment that could truly exist in real life. It actually feels like this movie could take place in a small Southern town, and I give Gunn credit for not just throwing around a mish-mash of stereotyped characters just for the sake of advancing his story. Furthermore, when the characters respond to the situation they are dealing with (a hive-mind alien turning their friends and neighbors into bumbling zombie-types), their reactions, while written to be comical to the viewer, are reactions you could actually see–hmm, how can I say this politically correctly?–stupid people having. (Eh, not so P.C., but I think it gets the point across.)

In the "Effects and Editing" department, leave it to a Troma guy to get it right! I could tell watching the movie that Gunn and his team used a lot of physical models, apparatuses, makeup, and gore instead of going the CGI route, and my viewing of a few of the "behind-the-scenes" extras on the DVD confirmed my suspicions. While some folks may nitpick that so much physical effects work can actually detract from the realistic appearance of a film, I don't believe that's the case here.

And the effects look damn good! From the gruesome animal murders to the "Squid-Grant" cutting the hunter in half and having his guts literally spill out, to the giant amorphous blob that slug-mother Brenda becomes, it's an impressive mix of physical setup and some computer additions to augment the experience. Be sure and watch the DVD extras about the special effects to see how many of those little slugs the crew actually created and slapped up on various walls, people, sets, and other places.

Editing-wise, the movie goes along at a brisk clip, and I never once found myself bored or waiting for the next scene to come around. In fact, I was left with a feeling of wanting more of the story, especially when the credits began to roll, and I almost couldn't believe the movie was over. I think that's a good hallmark of an excellent editor.

Before we get to the end, though, the zombie mayhem finally gets in full swing. Things start to get intense when the little slugs start running amok through the town. One of the slugs infects a deer, which later gets into a rather comical fight with Fillion's character, Bill Pardy. The family of zombies is insanely disturbing, including the shiver-inducing twin daughters. Since these zombies are of a hive mind, they all have the exact same goal, and it's both creepy (especially when they are all yelling for "Starla!") and scary when they all get going full-throttle.

The climactic final sequence is something out of a disturbing-but-hilarious nightmare. The horror movie "The Human Centipede" doesn't have anything on the disgusting mish-mash of human bodies Grant has incorporated directly into his slug body. Fortunately, Pardy and Starla find a way to save the day and stop the alien threat for good...or do they? Make sure to stick around after the credits for a short final scene that you may love or hate, depending upon your preference for open-ended conclusions!

TAKE TWO: A.G.

The first thing to say about *Slither* is that it's a homage to 1980's B horror movies. *Night of the Creeps* is the best film to judge it by.

Nathan Fillion plays Bill Pardy, the new chief of Wheelsy, South Carolina. His childhood love, Darla, played by Elizabeth Banks, is the wife of Michael Rooker, who plays Grant Grant. Yes, he has the same first and last name.

When Grant goes out for a few drinks, he stumbles upon a strange cocoon-like pod in the woods. When he investigates, the pod shoots him with a quill-like dart that burrows into his body and then right to his brain.

Grant, now possessed by the alien creature, becomes obsessed with meat. This brings on some fun scenes where Grant stares at rows of meat in the supermarket. But like any species, this one needs to procreate, and Grant soon finds a woman to be his "womb," whether she likes it or not.

As Grant kills dogs, cats, cows and any other critter he can get his hands on, the town goes on a hunt to find him.

When they do, they end up in the middle of nowhere, in an old barn.

This is one of the best scenes of the movie, too. Grant's "womb" has swollen to the size of a small truck and inside her are Grant's "babies." The massively swollen woman is surrounded by the rotting carcasses of animals, the charnel house smell overwhelming.

When the babies are ready to be born, she explodes, releasing a deluge of foot long slugs that seek to enter a human host via the mouth. Once inside, they burrow to the brain and wallah, you get what is basically a zombie, only this host is still alive.

It takes an hour until the first zombie appears, but once it happens, it's a non-stop ride to the conclusion of the movie. The gore is outstanding but not over done. One scene, in which Grant is cornered, he whips his tentacle out and slices a man in two. As the man stands there, his eyes still moving, he slowly peels apart, his insides splashing to the ground as he splits in half.

Later, when Grant has set up shop and has the zombies bringing him bodies, the gore reaches yet another level. When the mayor becomes infected and the hunger for meat makes him begin gnawing on a human arm, he practically rolls his eyes in joy as blood shoots out and covers his face. Unlike many horror movies that fizzle out at the end, this one has a wonderful climax filled with spraying gore.

And this movie doesn't take itself too seriously. Lots of humor abounds, usually in just the right place to break up the tension and usually said by Bill

Pardy. One of my favorite scenes is just after Bill Pardy, Starla, the Mayor, and one more survivor all run from the zombies and jump into the sheriff's car. As they drive away, leaving the zombies behind, they all try to stay calm and wrap their heads around what's happening.

Bill looks into the rearview at the Mayor, then glances at Starla and says, "So, how's everyone's evening?"

Filled with energy, great production value and a fantastic cast, this movie should be on everyone's list of favorites if they love zombies.

STACY

YEAR: 2001
COUNTRY: Japan
RUNNING TIME: 81 minutes
SCREENPLAY: Chisato Ogawara
DIRECTOR: Naoyuki Tomomatsu
PRODUCER: Shinichi Umagami, Hiromitsu Suzuki, Naokatsu Ito
MUSIC: Tokusatsu
CINEMATOGRAPHER: Masahide Iioka
SPECIAL MAKE-UP EFFECTS: Setouchi Production
CAST: Natsuki Kato (Eiko), Toshinori Omi (Shibukawa), Chika Hayashi (Nozomi)

TAKE ONE: T.S.

COMMENTARY

"Stacy" is a very difficult movie to classify. Even with an extensive "critic-speak" vernacular at my disposal, the best word to classify the film may simply be to say that it is "different." Obviously I do not mean that in a bad way, as it made our list here, but the movie is a definite departure from what most audiences, including the average American viewer, is used to.

"Stacy" is a horror comedy film from Japan, released in 2001. It is the early-2000s predecessor of some of the best Japanese horror films, many of which have been "Americanized" for the US audiences to take to and understand better, like "The Grudge," "The Ring," and the like. Unlike these other films, "Stacy" infuses a healthy dose of comedic elements into its horror as well, which is never a bad thing if done correctly. Sometimes also referred to as "Stacy: Attack of the Schoolgirl Zombies," it is based on a novel by Kenji Otsuki. I have never read the novel, but if it is half as much of a mind-bending experience as the movie version is, I need to check it out! The plot of the film is convoluted, to say the least, but it starts out simply enough: in the not-too-distant future, the entire world is hit by a plague virus that only affects every girl between 15 and 17 years old. They die and reanimate as flesh-eating zombies, colloquially known as "Stacys," but that's only half the mystery. Before they die, each girl experiences a period of extreme giddiness, a period that can last for days or weeks, called "Near-Death Happiness," or NDH. Once NDH is complete, the girls die and come back, and the only way to stop them is rather gruesome–you have to chop them to pieces, and not just a few pieces, 165 different pieces, to be exact.

The film follows many characters in Japan, including young girls about to succumb to NDH and the police-esque group of men assigned by the government to "repeat kill" the Stacys, the Romero Repeat Kill Troops. That's right, the filmmakers (and possibly the original novelist as well) had the *chutzpah* to name their zombie-killing force directly after The Man Himself, George Romero. Personally, I think it's very funny, and a great nod to Romero's contributions to the genre. As you'll discover in the "Play-by-Play" section, this isn't the only comical direct reference to American horror movies this film makes.

The important thing to getting the maximum viewing entertainment out of "Stacy" is this: you *have* to watch this film with the knowledge that it is going to be a significantly different experience than the average American, Hollywood-style film. Japanese horror isn't always about giving the viewer an answer to every little question posed by the movie, it's more about the journey and experience the film gives you. You will get a lot of detailed information about the themes and sub-plots of "Stacy," but you have to be a diligent viewer in order to catch them. The movie is subtitled in English, with the actors speaking their lines in the original Japanese, so it can be a little bit of a challenge to read and watch at the same time, but the reward is definitely there for you: this is a fun story with some really big ideas, some very insightful commentary about sexuality and gender roles hidden in the goofiness of the action, and just a really cool and unique approach to telling a zombie story.

I hope this last paragraph hasn't scared you away from giving "Stacy" a chance. It's a "high-risk, high-reward" type of scenario, because there definitely is the possibility that you won't understand everything the movie throws at you (or at least, you may not get it all in the first viewing). But if you can make the commitment to putting a little more thought into your viewing experience than you might have to do with the "normal" films you watch, the reward will be great.

PLAY-BY-PLAY

The movie sports a very interesting beginning: the girl babysitting the younger children is dead, but how did she die? The children she was watching incorporate her death into their game, equating her to Sleeping Beauty in their innocence. This is a nice touch, and establishes early in the movie that we're in for a whimsical story in which nothing should be taken too seriously.

As mentioned, the references to other horror and zombie movies are plentiful. The longest-running reference in this film is easily the Romero Repeat Kill Troops, or RRKs as the badges on their shoulders identify them. In classic US propaganda style, the TV commercial for the recruitment of the RRKs uses bright graphics, peppy and upbeat vocals, and jocular phrases like "Kill your own daughters!" to entice men to join up.

Also of note early on in the movie are the rules establishing how exactly to kill a Stacy. It seems like a normal head shot usually doesn't do the trick. No, in order to perform a complete "repeat kill," one has to cut the Stacy up into 165 pieces. That's a lot of bone-cutting! Fortunately, some entrepreneurial folks have just the thing to help with this: a handy chainsaw that attaches via sheath directly to your hand, "The Bruce Campbell Right Hand 2!" The movie's creators are really letting the American-movie references fly! I wonder how many viewers in Japan actually get them? Anyhow, about the "Right Hand 2"—it comes in a variety of "designer colors"—and some saws even have artwork or patterns on them. Scenes like this really help to demonstrate that true comedy knows no borders, and that foreign film makers like to have just as much fun as the Hollywood-types do. A close-up of the actual "Right Hand 2" product in the film reveals that the saws actually say "Blues Campbell" on them instead of Bruce Campbell, which begs the question of why this was done: to avoid copyright infringement or just an example of "Engrish" in action?

The film does bounce around quite a bit, and the viewer—especially an American viewer who is not accustomed to this style of movie-making—has to pay attention closely, or else they will miss key elements of the film. This is evidenced in many of the scenes in the middle of the movie, specifically our introduction to the Drew Illegal Repeat Kill Troops, who explain who they are and why they are doing what they're doing, and when Nozomi searches for Momo, his pen-pal "sister," by trying to rescue her from the girl's school in the mountains. Important pieces of the puzzle are revealed, like further rationale and legal specifics of the RRKs as well as the connection between the girl's school, the RRK unit, and the Drew Illegal group.

When their time comes, the teenage girls are almost manic with their level of Near-Death Happiness. We are given a perfect example of this through Eiko, the girl who goes looking for someone to repeat-kill her. After an odd lull with a puppet-show dream sequence, Eiko confronts a group of RRKs with the interesting proclamation, "Thank you…we love you guys." This seems random, but is actually pretty important to figuring out some details of the genesis of the Stacy virus. It was at this point in the movie that I started to figure things out, that the Stacys actually *want* to be killed by people who love them.

Just in case you'd forgotten how much the creators of this movie like to reference other zombie flicks, the "mad" Doctor Sukekiyo makes sure to remind us when he says to the soldiers "Hell filled up, so the dead have come here. Is that from "Dawn of the Dead" or "Day of the Dead?""

During the final scenes at the girl's school, we get a twist on the classic "zombie horde" when a mass of reanimated young ladies in typical Japanese schoolgirl outfits attack the military unit, and it's quite a sight to behold! Even though during the scene it seems like some Stacys are put down with a gunshot to the head, severing a Stacy's head clearly doesn't stop them, as evidenced by Doctor Sukekiyo's experiments. We get to see some pretty gruesome stuff through his experimentation, like the Stacy whose head is removed with the entire spinal column still attached to it.

There is so much going on in this movie, and so many plot points and story lines floating around, that it takes what I call a "triple ending" on the movie's part in order to wrap everything up. Between the ultra-tragic ending for Eiko, the trippy ending of the dead-but-talking corpses of the Drew Illegal team, and the even trippier coda detailing how mankind not only survived the Stacy epidemic but also learned to breed with them to create a new race of beings, "Stacy" comes to a fitting conclusion for a movie of its ilk. A little confusing but infused with big ideas, and ultimately able to deliver a very enjoyable ride.

TAKE TWO: A.G.

Like many of the zombie movies in this book, the first thing is do not take Stacy seriously. If you do, you won't enjoy it.

The simple reason is that Japanese ideas don't always transfer well to U.S. ones. The best way to explain Stacy is by introducing you to a Japanese word. The word is "Moe" (pronounced moh-eh) and is a Japanese notion that will frankly, confuse the Western mind.

What Moe is, is a referral to an obsessive love to something imaginary, something that could never exist. One of these "somethings" is the school girl, complete with uniform, preferably Catholic.

Though someone adept at "Moe" would say that loving a school girl is a pure love I think we all know there is something more primal, more base at work here. Whether its animé or real life, in Japanese culture, the Japanese sailor suit has become an icon of sexuality.

And this is the theme for the movie *Stacy*.

The plot of the movie is this: All over the world, for some unknown reason, girls between the ages of fifteen to seventeen are dying only to revive as the walking dead. Dubbed "Stacys" for plural or "Stacy" for singular, these zombie girls return with a hunger for human flesh.

This of course means they need to be "repeat killed," something taken care of by the Romero Kill Squads. In this world, to join the Romero Repeat Kill squads is a sign of honor.

And there are more puns spread throughout the movie, my favorite being the chainsaw called "Bruce Campbell's Right Hand 2," a chainsaw you can slide your hand into the handle so the other hand is free. What's the chainsaw for? Why to cut up the Stacys when they come for you. See, they need to be cut up into a hundred and sixty-five pieces. And even then, the pieces keep wiggling and twitching.

And this is where the gore really goes all out. Barrels of thrashing human parts, heads severed from bodies, and one mad scientist who pulls a head off a Stacy, but keeps the spine intact. The head is then placed on the table and the spine curves across the surface like a snake, still connected to the body. As the head twitches and tries to bite, the legs kick up and down and the arms wiggle.

Other scenes of gore are just as over-the-top and hark back to scenes from *Dawn of the Dead* and *Day of the Dead*.

But despite all the gore and blood, in the end Stacy is a love story about a love that shouldn't be. If you can see past the gore and the often cheesy dialogue, you'll see a film that bares themes such as love, loss, death, and longing for something that cannot be. And if you don't get it or don't want to try, then sit back and enjoy the beheadings and blood spray. Just be sure not to sit too close to the screen if you don't want to get splattered.

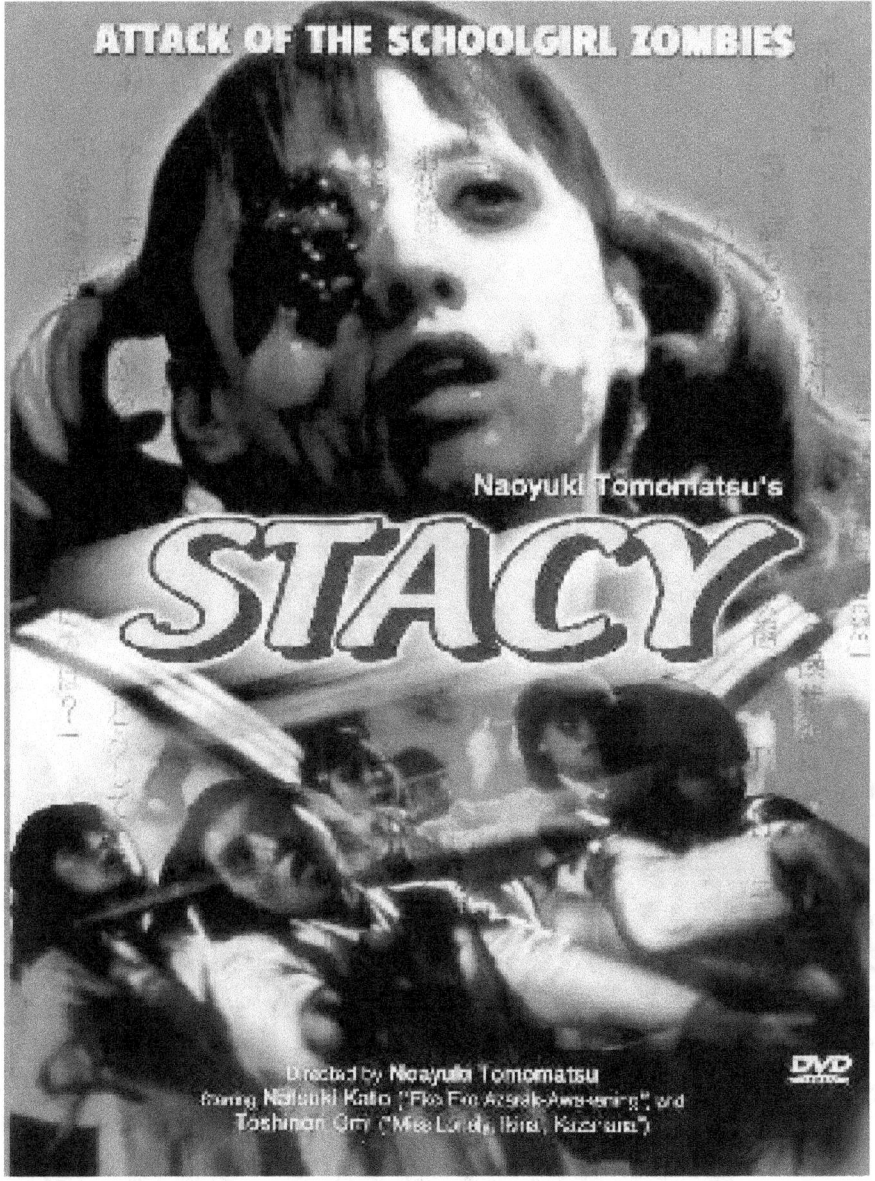

SURVIVAL OF THE DEAD

YEAR: 2009
COUNTRY: US/Canada
RUNNING TIME: 90 minutes
WRITER: George A. Romero
DIRECTOR: George A. Romero
PRODUCER: Paula Devonshire
EXECUTIVE PRODUCERS: D.J. Carson, Michael Doherty, Dan Fireman, Ara Katz, Peter Grunwald, George A. Romero, Art Spigel, Patrice Theroux
CO-PRODUCERS: Sam Englebardt, Jeff Glickman, Jesse D. Ikeman
MUSIC: Robert Carli
CINEMATOGRAPHY: Adam Swica
EDITING BY: Michael Doherty
ART DIRECTION: Joshu de Cartier
SPECIAL EFFECTS MAKE-UP CONSULTANT: Greg Nicotero
SPECIAL MAKE-UP EFFECTS ARTISTS: Patrick Baxter, Damon Bishop, Jason Detheridge
COSTUME DESIGNER: Alex Kavanagh
CAST: Alan van Sprang (Sarge "Nicotine" Crockett), Kenneth Welsh (Patrick O'Flynn), Kathleen Munroe (Janet O'Flynn and Jane O'Flynn), Devon Bostick as (Boy), Richard Fitzpatrick (Seamus Muldoon), Athena Karkanis (Tomboy), Stefano Collaciti (Francisco), Joris Jarsky (Chuck), Eric Woolfe (Kenny), Julian Richings (James O'Flynn), Wayne Robson (Tawdry O'Flynn), George Stroumboulopoulos (Talk Show Host)

TAKE ONE: T.S.

COMMENTARY

It's no secret that "Survival of the Dead" has met with some pretty heavy resistance from some members of the undead community. In many ways, this amount of criticism can be seen as a sideways compliment–it's a credit to George Romero's long-standing history of producing high-quality zombie films that people care enough to let him know when he's created a film they feel falls below the standards he's set so high with his previous works.

In creating this movie, Romero did something he rarely does: he re-uses characters from one of his other films. Stemming off of the continuity established in his previous film, "Diary of the Dead," "Survival" follows the exploits of a National Guard unit, led by Sergeant Nick "Nicotine" Crockett, after the unit members have gone rogue and struck out on their own. After the unit's run-in with the main characters from "Diary," they pick up a civilian traveler and, based on information he gives them, decide to head to the East Coast and Plum Island, a place where people are supposedly living a life free from the zombie threat. Upon their arrival to the island, however, the soldiers get far more than they bargained for. Not only are zombies very much present on the island, they seem to be retaining skills from their former lives and even learning new ones. As if this wasn't enough, the unit finds themselves between the two feuding clans that live on the island, the O'Flynns and the Muldoons, both with very different agendas and very different ideas about what to do with the zombies on the island.

As for the critical reception of the film, I have a different take than many other viewers, especially those in my "younger" age bracket. After my first viewing, I was left with some of the questions others who have seen the film have had: why did Romero make so many choices in the film's plot, editing, presentation, etc., that just seem so darn…odd? The pacing of the film is decidedly different than Romero's other films; there are significantly more comedic moments in this film, especially in the zombie kills, than in any of his previous "Dead" movies. Most notably, the classic "shamble" style of zombie that Romero practically single-handedly invented have been usurped by revenants that try to perform duties from their old careers, use guns, and even ride horses. Yes, we saw a hint of this with Bub from "Day of the Dead" and Big Daddy in "Land of the Dead," but nothing even remotely coming close to the scale of the high-functioning zombies we see here. Many people have asked, often times quite bluntly: why would Romero make these kinds of choices in this film?

The answer to these questions, and I apologize in advance for the gratuitous use of Caps Lock, is simple: BECAUSE HE IS GEORGE EFFING ROMERO. He has earned the right to do whatever he damn well pleases and to put out whatever kind of zombie film he wants to. YOU create a series of zombie movies that forever change the landscape of the genre, and then maybe you'll have the right to tell other people how to make their films.

Surely Romero was trying to do something else with "Survival" other than simply make a movie just for the hell of it, right? The answer to that question, I'm happy to report after multiple viewings of this film, is a resounding "yes." You see, on my second, third, and fourth times through the movie, I discovered something in "Survival" that not many people appear to have found: Romero is experimenting. Proposing new ideas in a genre that has largely started to do the same old things, over and over again. Pushing the limits of what the average viewer finds "acceptable" in his or her zombie stories. And after having this revelation, I have to admit, dear reader: I'm digging the vibe that Romero is laying down for us.

PLAY-BY-PLAY

The opening scene of the film shows us that even the military is having trouble doing things correctly these days, as a raid by the army unit has somehow gone awry. Here it is, forty-one years after "Night of the Living Dead" premiered, and Romero is still using the military as his spring board for social commentary.

We quickly get a brief recap on the story with usage of some footage from "Diary." This is a very different tactic for Romero, but it has to be, since as mentioned previously, this is the first time he's ever extended a storyline from a previous "Dead" movie.

Plum Island is introduced, and right away the division between the two families is imminently present, even though we don't immediately meet the other clan. Also of interest here is the fact that not only are both families prominently Irish, but they seem to be the only inhabitants of this fairly accessible island off the coast of Delaware...how does that happen, exactly?

So Patrick O'Flynn and his posse set out to eradicate all the undead on the island—seems like a noble enough cause, right? But when the posse enters the house with the zombie children and shoots the still-living wife in cold blood, we see that they may have a little more on their minds than just being out to kill the dead. The Muldoon posse shows up soon thereafter, under the leadership of Seamus, and it's the viewer's first real exposure to just how much these two clans don't get along. While the two patriarchs are talking at length, we get a lot of intriguing debate about whether zombies are truly past the point of "saving." Through all the quirkiness of the film, this is the heart and soul of the matter, one of the real questions surrounding the existence of zombies, and Romero puts it right up front like so many other creators have failed to do.

Muldoon goes on to make a big show out of saying "we take care of our own on this island," yet he is quick to evict O'Flynn and his posse–and his first preference was to shoot his counterpart! Soon we cut back to the now-rogue military unit. Tomboy is shown masturbating, which may initially seem crass, but remember that Romero has never shied away from exploring aspects of the zompocalypse that no one else dares to, and this situation is no exception.

When the group stumbles across the armored car with a million dollars inside, it gives a connection to the pre-zombie world, which in this storyline wasn't that long ago. When a viewer is engaged in a standard tale of undead terror, sometimes it's easy to forget how things "used" to be and how fresh this new world may be. Although, here in this story the world is almost four weeks into the siege with the walking dead, so I'm surprised the internet and cell phone services would still function.

Eventually the military group makes its way to Plum Island via ferry, with O'Flynn in tow. There are a lot of zombies that are still hiding on the ferry, and this gives Romero and crew the opportunity to present us with some fun zombie kills. Of special note are the undead that are terminated with the use of random objects like a fire extinguisher, a stick of dynamite, a hot dog on a stick, and even an emergency flare to the head. The viewer is also introduced to a zombie that is stuck in a car on the ferry, but has enough mental capacity to put the auto in both forward and reverse, and press the gas so the car actually moves. This car-driving zombie is the first indication that the zombies in this film will be smarter than your average undead-head.

Indeed, once we get to Plum, we see plenty more zombies trying to re-learn and re-live their pasts, including a postman, a field worker, and of course the female horse rider who is a daughter to O'Flynn. For all the fighting between the families, Muldoon really can't be seen as a "bad guy" until he starts killing the live visitors that O'Flynn was sending from the mainland to the island. This is when we get the reversal of good buy-bad guy roles in the eyes of the viewer, as O'Flynn becomes an increasingly sympathetic character and Muldoon assumes the role of the evil villain.

Of all of the original ideas Romero has explored in his "Dead" series, dating all the way back to 1968, there is one significant idea that he appears to have "changed his mind" on–that of zombies eating living things other than humans, at least initially in this film. The undead refuse to eat animals, and this plays a key role later in the film.

Many of the "domesticated" zombies don't seem overly interested in eating the humans that come near them. It's very "Bub-like" of them. As the action progresses, the two opposing human sides come to a full-on battle royale, and there's a lot of shooting at other people out in the wide open without hitting anyone, but that's to be expected (and forgiven) in a scene like this. Soon, however, the undead mount a "mega-horde," and the two sides have no choice but to fight the zombies instead of each other.

In the end, neither patriarch ends up being the outright "good guy," and there's plenty that occurs that could lend itself to an argument for them both to be pretty damn bad. Even after the "classic" tragic ending, Romero still has his undead doing strange things and trying to re-learn aspects of their old human lives. Leave it to George to finish things up in a film with almost more questions than answers.

In an interview conducted not long after "Survival's" release, Romero was asked what his plans were for the future of the "Dead" series. He told the interviewer he planned on making two more films stemming off of characters from "Diary:" one story about the action/coalition group of men seen gathering supplies in their makeshift warehouse, and another about the character Tracy Thurman, one of the few survivors from the college-aged group of main characters. Let's hope Romero finds enough in his bag of tricks to keep giving us "Dead" films for a long time.

Consider me first in line for them all.

TAKE TWO: A.G.

Okay, the first thing I need to remind you of, dear reader, is that I wasn't the biggest fan of *Diary of the Dead*. See my review in this book to see what I mean.

But where Diary fell a little flat for me, *Survival of the Dead* was a masterpiece.

I believe one of these reasons is that you need to be a certain age to appreciate *Survival* and its undertone and meaning. Where *Diary* was trying to relate to the teenage crowd, *Survival* goes back to the roots of Romero's dead films, by having a cast of all adults and only one teenager.

And the plot of the story is timeless. Two parties, neither wanting to concede to the other, both doomed to failure unless they work together.

After the first five minutes of *Survival*, I was hooked. The atmosphere was outstanding and the main character, Sarge, was perfect for a hero of the modern world. Neither altruistic nor entirely evil, he realizes it's every man for himself, and that he and his team would be better off on their own, rather than stay with the National Guard.

The plot is as follows. The dead have been walking for weeks and the world is falling apart. On a small island off the coast of Delaware, quaintly called Plum Island, two families are battling for control, the O'Flynns want to put down the zombies, no matter who becomes one, whether it's family or not, while the Muldoons want to save the zombies, hoping someone will find a solution to the undead plague.

Enter Sarge and his team, who are drawn to Plum Island in the hopes of safety and isolation. What they find instead is an age old war of the two families who refuse to cooperate even though it could mean the downfall of the entire island.

Where *Diary* fell flat to me on zombies and gore, *Survival* ups the ante ten fold. With the help of CGI, Romero gives us many tongue-in-cheek laughs as well as chilling moments of zombie dread.

The movie was based loosely on "The Big Country," and the western undertones will be apparent to all.

Still, in the end, *Survival of the Dead* is a more mature movie compared to *Diary* and thus spoke to me on many levels the other did not.

One of the main ones is that what Romero is trying to tell us silently isn't so heavy handed and is much more subtle, which is the polar opposite of *Diary*, where the director's opinions are practically forced down the viewers' throats.

Reminding me in feel and style to *Dawn of the Dead*, *Survival* takes Romero back to his roots, where tension and good characters are what make the movie great, and the zombies are just the icing on the cake.

ZOMBIE

YEAR: 1979
COUNTRY: Italy
RUNNING TIME: 92 minutes
WRITERS: Elisa Briganti, Dardano Sacchetti (uncredited)
DIRECTOR: Lucio Fulci
PRODUCERS: Ugo Tucci, Fabrizio De Angelis
MUSIC: Fabio Frizzi, Giorgio Tucci, Adriano Giordanella (uncredited), Maurizio Guarini (uncredited)
DIRECTOR OF PHOTOGRAPHY: Sergio Salvati
MAKE-UP AND SPECIAL EFFECTS: Giannetto De Rossi, Maurizio Trani, Rosario Prestopino (uncredited)
PRODUCTION/COSTUME/DESIGNER: Walter Patriarca
CAST: Tisa Farrow (Anne Bowles), Ian McCulloch (Peter West), Richard Johnson (Dr. David Menard), Al Cliver (Brian Hull), Auretta Gay (Susan Barrett), Olga Karlatos (Paola Menard)

TAKE ONE: T.S

COMMENTARY

Ah, the legalities of film distribution, what a tangled web you weave.

Witness, if you will, the story of the multi-titled horror film debut of Italian director Lucio Fulci. You see, when his film was released in Italy in 1979, Fulci intended the movie to have the simple title of "Zombie," or in Italian, "*Zombi*." Unfortunately for him, fellow Italian horror movie-maker Dario Argento had already used this title, and through a financing deal, Argento held the international distribution rights to George Romero's "Dawn of the Dead," and released that film in Italy in 1978 using the title—you guessed it—"*Zombi*." (See my review for "Dawn of the Dead" in this book for more information on this intriguing turn of events.) Since Fulci couldn't legally use the same title, he was advised by his producers to add a few scenes to his movie that would make it seem loosely connected to "Dawn," and the film was released with the title "*Zombi 2*" in an attempt to make it look like a direct sequel to "Dawn" (which it wasn't) and hopefully cash in on its success (which it did).

When the film made its way to American theaters, however, the international distributors changed the title back to "Zombie" for the US release. For reasons unbeknownst to me, the international distributors also changed the title a number of times for the film's release in other countries. The film that initially wanted a very simplistic title is now known in various markets as "Zombie," "*Zombi 2*," "Island of the Living Dead," "Zombie Flesh Eaters," and the tremendously-fun-to-say German title of "*Woodoo-Schreckensinsel der Zombies.*"

All of the legal titling aspects aside, the funny thing about the movie is this: it's a damn good zombie film in its own right. The story revolves around an American girl, whose father's yacht is founding drifting in New York Harbor with a zombie in it. In an attempt to solve the mystery of what the zombie is and where her father went, she joins forces with a journalist and travels to the remote island of Matool, where local voodoo curses appear to be coming to life in the form of the dead being reanimated. The pacing is slow and sinister, the storyline is very engaging, and there are multiple scenes in the film that are singularly memorable and easily move "Zombie" into must-see status.

Of these infamous on-camera moments, most agree that there are three different scenes that are of particularly unique note to zombie fans. First and foremost is, of course, the "zombie versus shark" scene, that really has to be seen to be believed. It comes relatively early in the film, and it delivers exactly what is advertised: a zombie attacks and fights a tiger shark underwater. Not only is it unique in terms of cinematic experience, it's also singular in its process of being captured on film, as it really did happen – no CGI, no mechanical animals; a living human being, dressed up as a zombie, got into the water and literally fought with a shark! An interesting side bit of trivia here is that the actor that was scheduled to fight the shark was "unable to perform" the day the scene was to be shot, so the shark's trainer, Ramon Bravo, was used instead. I've got no ill will to the actor who was "unable to perform" that day—I'm pretty sure that if I was scheduled to hop in the water and fight a shark, I might call in sick that day too.

The second infamous scene was actually named one of the "100 Scariest Movie Moments" by the Bravo TV Network. It revolves around Paola, the wife of Dr. Menard.

Menard is the island's resident physician who is investigating the phenomenon of the walking dead as well. Paola is attacked at home by a particularly aggressive and stalker-ish zombie, and the end to the iconic scene is incredibly suspenseful, as Paola is pulled through a shattered wood door by the zombie, her eye getting closer and closer to a particularly-vicious looking piece of splintered wood…

The third notorious scene involves the "Worm-Eyed Zombie" shown on many of the film's promotional posters. A rotting Spanish Conquistador, he gruesomely attacks and thoroughly rips out the throat of an unfortunate human woman. This revenant's appearance on the US theatrical poster, along with the brilliantly-simple-yet-effective tagline of "We are going to eat you!" and the film preview's humorous promise of providing "barf bags" to any viewer who requested them, directly contributed to the movie's success in US theaters and the massive cult following the movie gained upon its home-video release.

Even though it was banned in several countries due to its high content of gore, the film's impressive success in both the American and European markets helped rekindle Fulci's sagging career and reinvented him as a horror icon. Fulci went on to direct many more horror and zombie films, some other which are also included in this book, and "Zombie" introduced several "trademarks" that would become staples for the director in his subsequent films: the undead, an amazing amount of gore and blood dispensed in very realistic ways, and of course, a fixation on "eyeball gags." Even though "Zombie" spawned three sequels of its own ("*Zombi 3*," *Zombi 4*," and "*Zombi 5*"), none of them were directly related in plot to "Zombie," and none of them were released in American theaters.

Whichever title you chose to give it, "Zombie" was a singular experience for viewers and its director alike, and is a film that stands high above many others in the genre.

PLAY-BY-PLAY

The movie opens with an interesting prologue: a Doctor shoots a fully-bound Zombie wrapped in a sheet, then says to someone off-screen, "The boat can go now." It's utterly confusing as to what is going on at this point in the film, but it's very effective in drawing the viewer in to wanting to know more about the story.

After the main title of the film rolls, we are hit with some pretty tense moments right away. The abandoned sailboat in New York Harbor gives lots of clues as to what might be going on: there is rotting food everywhere, maggots and worms abound (there are even disgustingly-oversized centipedes present!), and the calm quiet of the boat's external appearance is in direct contrast to what the viewer can easily feel of something being wrong. As I previously mentioned, this scene, as well as the final scene of the film, were added by Fulci after principal shooting had wrapped, in an attempt to make the movie seem more "connected" to Romero's previously-released "Dawn of the Dead."

Fulci really seems to want to take the time to utilize slow-building suspense in this film, and it shows from start to finish. Many directors like to start slow but then let the action fly full-throttle towards the end of the movie. Even though things do get a little intense towards the climax of the film, Fulci still does a great job of maintaining the pace of the film. I think that since he intended this to be Italy's first major exposure to zombies, he truly wanted to take his time with introducing and explaining the creatures, and the viewer definitely benefits from this tense kind of pacing.

Anne Bowles, the daughter of the yacht-owner, who is bent on discovering the whereabouts of her father, seems awfully quick and eager to hop on a plane to St. Maarten's accompanied only by Peter West, the reporter who was assigned by his newspaper to investigate the yacht's appearance. As a fun side note here, though, keep your eyes peeled for Fulci cameo-ing in his own film, as the news editor who assigns West the story.

Paola, Dr. Menard's wife, says to him while they are fighting in their home, "You won't be happy until I'm one of your zombies!" As viewers well know, she is later attacked and killed by a zombie, but does she return as one herself? Also, in making the possession of the zombies Menard's, Fulci may be engaging in a little deception/redirection of his audience, which is not at all uncommon, and doesn't feel like any kind of a "cop-out" here.

Next the viewer is treated to the "zombie vs. shark" scene, which I cannot stress enough is well-deserving in the amount of praise and publicity it receives! It is definitely an amazing sight to watch. In addition to being oft-talked about amongst horror and cinema fans, the scene is referenced as a pop-culture trivia bit in multiple television shows, band names/album titles/songs, and even recently on a Microsoft Windows 7 commercial. As an extra "behind the scenes" nugget for you, the scene was filmed in an enormously-large saltwater tank, and the shark was fed an inordinate amount of horse meat and sedatives before filming, in an attempt to ensure that the animal would be as docile and non-aggressive as possible during the actual take.

The zombies in this film definitely seem a little more "predatory" than the average undead shamble. They are slow, yes, but are also made out to be very deliberate, almost thoughtful in their actions and their killings. It makes for a very chilling experience to watch.

I know I mentioned this previously, but it's so prevalent, I think it bears repeating: Fulci is incredibly "cinematic" in this film. A perfect example is one of the most memorable scenes, when the zombie is attacking Paola in the house. Aside from "eye meets splinter," the scene is also memorable for the way Fulci shot it: as Paola struggles to keep the door closed and keep the zombie out, instead of just showing her struggle the entire time, he swings the camera to the wall and shows the shadow of the door opening for 10-15 seconds. This is incredibly effective at building suspense and will actually make many viewers, myself included, crane their neck to the side in an attempt to try and see more! The actual poking out of the eye with the wood is hideously gruesome, slow, and painful—and it's important to note that throughout the entire scene, we never once see the actual zombie.

Through all of the suspense built up in the first part of the film, viewers finally get their first full-on horror of zombies doing what zombies do best when the quartet of travelers make their way to Menard's house. Here, the horde is slowly devouring—almost savoring—Paola, and the full horrific reality of the situation hits the characters *and* the viewers at the same time.

As the survivors flee the house, I have to admit that the graveyard of the Conquistadores may not have been the ideal rest stop for them to take a breather. Here again Fulci flexes his cinematic muscle in the "slow reveal" department. We are treated to some very impressive effects work on the actual zombies: lots of decaying flesh, live worms wriggling, and rotted-out eye sockets. It's all incredibly atmospheric, and any true horror fan will easily appreciate the look being given use here.

Viewers may wonder why so many of the characters stand around looking dumbfounded, even as the undead shamble right up to them. Well, I can't speak from experience, never having been in that situation, but I can only imagine how utterly shocking and traumatic it all would be. I'd probably be frozen with fear and at a complete loss as for what to do as well! This may be one of the more realistic depictions we're given of human reactions to the undead.

With the ending of the film, particularly the final scene where the survivors discover that the zombie plague has spread quickly through New York, Fulci is setting up a bleak outlook for the future, and it certainly does beg the question: is he looking to establish his own "zombieverse," or incorporate into Romero's? Fortunately, the Italian director took a cue from his American counterpart and decided that it was better to leave some questions unanswered, as all of his zombie films that followed this one never directly referenced the film or the ending. Which is fine by me; a nice, ambiguous ending makes for much more interesting debate among fans.

TAKE TWO: A.G.

An abandoned boat is discovered in the Hudson River. When the police investigate, they're attacked by a large, flesh-eating zombie. One policeman is killed and the zombie is shot, knocking it over the side where it sinks.

The boat belongs to Anne Bowles father who was last seen on a distant island where voodoo is still very much alive.

An intrepid reporter, Peter Wells, joins up with Anne and soon they are sailing off to the same island on a boat owned by Brian and Susan, two tourists who were about to sail away on vacation. After Susan is attacked by a shark and escapes, then an underwater scene where a zombie battles the same shark, the four escape only to find out the boat's driveshaft had been damaged. With no choice, they go onto the island where they meet Dr. Menard, who has been having some trouble with the living dead. It seems the dead won't stay that way and there's some kind of outbreak. Whether they are freshly dead or four hundred year old conquistadors, the dead are walking and seem to very much want to eat the flesh of the living.

Paola—Dr. Menard's wife—finds this out first hand in one of the best scenes of horror ever put to film. When she's attacked by a zombie in her home, she barricades herself in but the door is flimsy. A hand shoots through the door, splintering it, and grabs her hair. As she's slowly drawn to the shards of jagged wood jutting from the hole in the door, we see her eye is lined up with a particularly nasty splinter.

One thing director Lucio Fulci doesn't do is pull away when the gruesomeness begins. We the audience, get to see every gut-churning second as the wood slides into Paola's eye, then into her skull.

The zombies in this movie are particularly nasty. With eye sockets filled with worms and maggots, they most definitely look dead. They are slow beyond slow, some barely moving at a baby's crawl, and they keep their eyes closed, stumbling about as only an animated corpse could.

This is the movie that jump-started Italian horror and showed the world what the Italians could bring to the horror genre, specifically zombies.

Like in Romero's movies, a bullet to the head seems to be the only way to put the zombies down for good, though fire does equally well.

A bite by one of the zombies will have the victim dead in either hours or days. Headshots are seen in glorious blood spray and feeding zombies tearing at organs is right up there with *Dawn of the Dead*.

Unfortunately, there are some flaws. This is a low budget movie and sometimes the makeup is lacking, merely being mud. And the dialog and plot can sometimes wan. But compared to many zombie movies to follow, this is most definitely one of the best. The Italians always know how to get the most out of a shoestring budget and *Zombie* is no different. At the end of the film, when the zombies are stumbling over the Brooklyn Bridge into New York, the entire scene was filmed "rogue." The film crew had no permits, but snuck in early in the morning. If you look below, you can see the morning traffic going on as normal, despite the fact that the city is supposed to be under a state of national emergency.

But no matter how you look at it, *Zombie* is a landmark zombie movie that provides one of the best preludes to a zombie apocalypse.

With its over the top gore, a great musical score, and shock value to make even a hardened fan cringe, long time fans remember it fondly and the film should be in any true walking dead connoisseur's library.

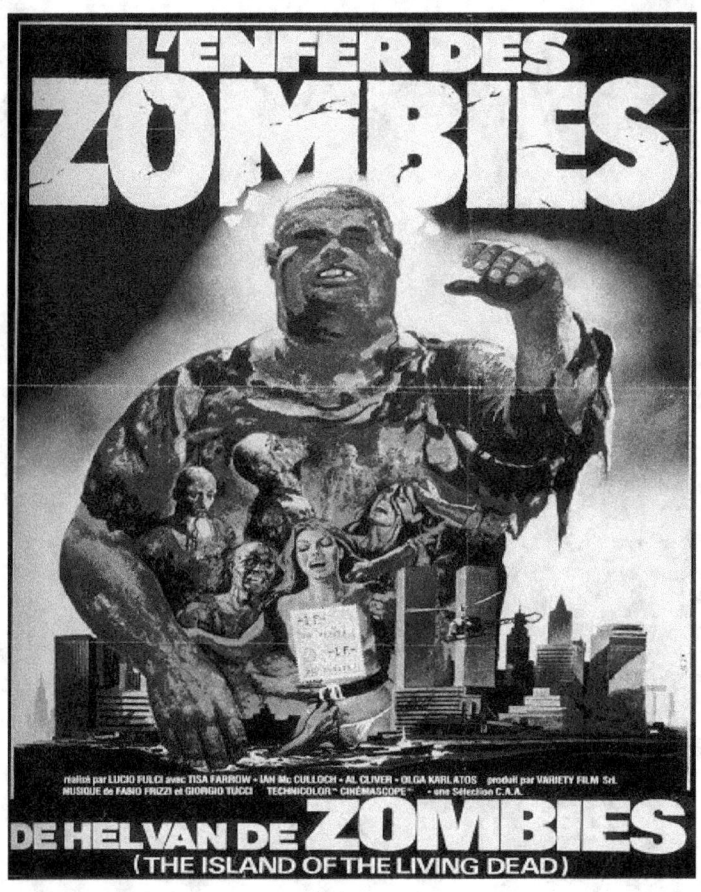

ZOMBIELAND

YEAR: 2009
COUNTRY: US
RUNNING TIME: 87 minutes
WRITERS: Rhett Reese, Paul Wernick
DIRECTOR: Ruben Fleischer
PRODUCER: Gavin Polone
EXECUTIVE PRODUCERS: Ryan Kavanaugh, Rhett Reese, Ezra Swerdlow, Paul Wernick
ORIGINAL MUSIC: David Sardy
CINEMATOGRAPHY: Michael Bonvillain (director of photography)
FILM EDITING: Alan Baumgarten
CASTING: John Papsidera
SPECIAL MAKE-UP AND EFFECTS: André Freitas, Leo Corey Castellano, Gabriel De Cunto, Tony Gardner, Lee Grimes
PRODUCTION DESIGN: Maher Ahmad
COSTUME DESIGN: Magali Guidasci
SET DECORATION: Gene Serdena
EDITING: Peter Amundson, Alan Baumgarten
ART DERECTION: Austin Gorg
CAST: Jesse Eisenberg (Columbus), Woody Harrelson (Tallahassee), Emma Stone (Wichita), Abigail Breslin (Little Rock), Amber Heard (406), Bill Murray (Himself), Derek Graf (Clown Zombie)

TAKE ONE: T.S.

COMMENTARY

Anyone who has been a zombie fan for the last few years is most likely keenly aware of the hype that surrounded "Zombieland" leading up to its theatrical release. It had grown to fairly epic proportions, but with good reason for the excitement from fans—can you think of the last time a zombie movie received a major national marketing campaign and a coast-to-coast wide theatrical release? 2008's "Quarantine" had a few commercials on TV here and there, but 2004's "Dawn of the Dead" remake and Romero's 2005 "Land of the Dead" are the most recent movies that spring into my head in terms of big-time national exposure, and that was half a decade before "Zombieland's" release.

In any case, after having been one of the lucky few to see "Zombieland" at a sneak preview screening before its national release (with free swag! I will wear my "Zombieland" T-shirt and hat with pride!), I am proud to say that the movie definitely lived up to the hype for the vast majority of people that have seen it, both theatrically and on home video.

"Zombieland" does a surprisingly good job of mixing action, horror, comedy, and even a dash of romance for good measure. The inevitable comparisons to "Shaun of the Dead" will surely arise, but believe me when I say that these are two *very* different films. They just happen to be two of the most prominent examples of zombie comedies–the only people who will compare the two are people who are too unimaginative to think of anything else to say.

The casting is pretty much spot-on. All four of the main characters seem totally believable and engulfed in their roles. Jesse Eisenberg as the twitchy, better-safe-than-sorry Columbus keeps a written list of the rules that have kept him alive through the zombie apocalypse, and the film does a great job of "presenting" these rules throughout the entire movie. Emma Stone and Abigail Breslin play Wichita and Little Rock, sisters who have issues trusting everyone on the planet but each other. Breslin, in particular, feels very natural and believable in the role–I honestly never once during the movie looked at her and thought "Hey, there's Little Miss Sunshine." She really made this role her own and I think viewers appreciate that. Woody Harrelson is definitely a scene-stealer as the enigmatic Tallahassee.

He shows a surprising range of emotions throughout the film, from begrudgingly taking Columbus under his wing to his one-man hunt for a very specific desert treat to showing some of the pain from his pre-apocalypse personal life, and he definitely gets to show the audience why he is a continually under-rated actor. The extras do a great job of being very believable and focused "fast zombies," and there is a cameo in the movie that is simply, pardon the pun, to die for! A brilliant turn by a brilliant actor, and the best part is that this person's scenes don't feel forced at all, they fit perfectly into the zany plot line.

My qualms with the movie were few and far between. A couple of noticeable visual goofs, with actors and objects being in one place or position and in a different spot when the camera shifts angles.

The liberal use of the phrase "Zombieland" by pretty much all of the main characters throughout the movie–we get it, you like to call your new world Zombieland. And, as is the case in many zombie films, the undead are conveniently not around when it's time to have the characters talk to each other to progress the plot or when they have something else important to the movie going on, but when the zombies do attack–surprise!–they come in droves out of nowhere.

Other than these few nitpicks, though, the movie is tremendously entertaining and easily one of the best zombie films I've seen in quite some time. The comedy is sharp and well-delivered, and kept many of us in the audience laughing continuously. The effects are great, very believable and very gory without going overboard.

The plot and pacing of the movie is fantastic, and kudos to director Ruben Fleischer and the creative team for not feeling like they have to spell out where the zombie virus came from and how it's taken over the world and what can be done to stop it. This is simply a great story about normal people living in a suddenly abnormal world and trying to make the best of it (i.e., survive).

I was fully entertained and engrossed by the movie the entire time. Granted, the film is a scant eighty minutes long, but I've got to think that Fleischer and his team knew that by adding more scenes, they may detract from the frenetic flow of the film. As it stands now, there are enough laughs, scares, and real moments to make this movie a tremendously engaging watch.

While the setting is your standard post-apocalyptic one, and the zombies are your basic "fast" ones, the movie gets unique kudos in two important areas. The climactic scenes are shot with our characters inside of an amusement park, so there are a lot of unique zombie kills and interactions based on what you find inside amusement parks, which I'm not sure has been featured prominently in a zombie movie before, if featured before at all. Second is the way Columbus' "rules" are displayed, literally–they pop up on screen in text when they are relevant to the scene, often in funny or ironic screen positions or animations. Good stuff, and very original!

As mentioned above, the characters are all very believable and "real," and their reactions to the world they are living in seem very on-par with their varied personality traits.

The state of the country as the characters travel through is very believable as well, with just a few suspensions of belief asked from the audience: why do the zombies attack in hordes sometimes but are nowhere to be found other times? How are the electrical grids still on and functional everywhere our characters go, even though this story takes place "months" after the onslaught of the apocalypse? No movie is perfect, and these very few details definitely do not detract from the highly-entertaining, movie-watching experience that is "Zombieland."

PLAY-BY-PLAY

The viewer is treated to great graphic representations early—and I mean "graphic"—as in art and stylized moments, not the gore, although the latter definitely comes in this movie. Shots like the "industrialized" view of the Earth and Columbus' rules popping up on screen indicate to us that we're getting a very "hip" film.

Hey, remember what I said about how the gore will come later? Surprise, it's here, and even before the credits to boot! The scene revolving around the lady not wearing her seatbelt shows the viewer that Fleischer and company may be making a comedy, but they're not going to pull any punches when it comes to showing us the viscera.

The opening credits of the film are easily one of the best credits sequences I have ever seen. They really set the tone for the unique experience of watching this movie, and I can't give enough kudos to the creative team for coming up with these. The opening credits show exactly the opposite of what you expect to see in a zombie movie. Normally you have people running away at full speed from the zombies, and maybe some "quick cuts" of zombie mayhem, but for the "Zombieland" opening credits we see, in super-slow-motion, tidbits of people trying to escape various zombies in various scenes of mayhem. The super-slow-motion of these scenes is what takes the cake: a zombie throwing someone off a railing, a zombie bride attacking her husband in mid-toast, a zombie attacking firefighters, even a zombie stripper chasing down frightened johns. Just hilarious stuff, and the fact that it's all in slow motion makes it seem even more surreal than normal.

I love that there is no big attempted explanation for the genesis of the virus—just "an infected burger at the Gas & Gulp" that takes Mad Cow disease to a whole new level. Instead, we are given some immediate character development, as Eisenberg's Columbus and Harrelson's Tallahassee meet for the first time in a humorous "hitching a ride while having a gun standoff" scene.

The use of the character's hometowns as their names is a great idea that highlights a concern for a lot of characters in zompocalypses: letting their guard down to strangers far too easily. As Tallahassee himself says, "No names…keeps us from getting too familiar." As a side note, the deserted highway they drive on with a plethora of abandoned cars (and even a downed passenger jet) is an awesome scene of post-apocalyptic carnage.

Columbus' "origin" story is really fun, and one of the most believable pieces in the entire film. I love that he changed the music he was listening to from hard rock while playing World of Warcraft to smooth, romantic music when his hot neighbor "406" comes in. It's also a well-filmed transition for her going to sleep human and waking up a zombie, replete with Columbus' ridiculous question of: "Are you okay?" The scene is a great blend of the two genres that zom-coms aspire to, as it's very humorous but at the same time very scary!

If, as it's said, "the devil is in the details," than this is one hell of a movie, because it's very clear throughout that Fleischer and his crew paid close attention to the little things as well as the big. The town Columbus and Tallahassee walk through after their car is stolen actually feels like a not-too-long-deserted town, with the attention to detail in the storefronts, cars, signs, trash, and so on. There is, however, an odd lack of zombies in town, though…where did they all go?

The quartet's road trip is filled with some very touching, comedic, and real moments, and this gives the audience much more opportunity to connect with these characters than in your average film. It all cumulates with the group deciding to hole up for a bit in the Hollywood mega-mansion of BILL MURRAY, in quite possibly the greatest cameo ever captured on film. He's clearly having a great amount of fun, he hasn't lost one iota of his impeccable comedic timing, and he looks damn good as a zombie!

Once Murray is dispensed with, things shift from comedy to tragedy, as we get a heart-wrenching moment with Tallahassee and the revelation of his lost son, "Buck" (whether that is his real name or not, we are never actually told). Not only does this moment serve to remind of the great pain that comes with an undead invasion, it once again confirms that Harrelson and his emotive range was a magnificent choice for this role.

Even though it's an absolutely terrible idea, there's a fun innocence to the sisters' desire to just mentally check out and spend what will probably be their final moments in the Pacific Playland amusement park. While the younger sister probably just wanted to visit to have a good time and didn't know any better, I have to think that her older sister—Emma Stone—knew that this could easily be the end of the road for them, but decided to go anyway, in an attempt to make her sister happy. Couple this with Harrelson's previous scene and the moment earlier in the film when Columbus comes to the realization that his family is most likely dead and gone, and we've been subtly given very effective connections to these characters, a key factor in elevating this funny, gory movie easily into "must-see" status.

TAKE TWO: A.G.

Welcome to *Zombieland*, a world overrun by fast zombies, a world where if you're overweight, you were probably one of the first to go. A world where if you don't follow a few simple rules of survival, you'll probably end up as a Happy Meal.

Zombieland is a comedy, but there's more than enough gore and chills for the most discerning horror buff. There's just one thing to remember as you watch this movie. And that's to not take it too seriously. Why should you? The movie sure doesn't. As far as being a standard zombie movie, there are plot holes galore and the characters do things that would make a zombie aficionado scream in anger.

But you see, that's not what this movie is about. It's not a serious film. It's a popcorn movie; you're there to have fun and if you look at it like that, then fun is what you'll get. In this film, the zombies aren't actually dead. Tainted hamburger meat is the culprit and the result is a virus that turns people into raging killer cannibals. Hey, close enough to a zombie for my needs. And they are fast, like Olympic sprinter fast. Serious bodily harm will put them down and though a head shot is best, it's not necessarily the only way to stop them. The movie starts out strong and we are introduced to Columbus, a germaphobe, neurotic shut-in, scared college student who has managed to survive by following some simple rules. These rules are smart and at the same time funny to see them enacted.

Next we meet Tallahassee, an over-the-top redneck who loves killing zombies and tolerates Columbus for some unknown reason.

As you can see, there are no actual names to the characters, instead, Tallahassee names them by where they're headed. Tallahassee has a thing for Twinkies which adds yet more comedy to the film.

The two become traveling companions and the first thing they do is search for Twinkies. In a supermarket, they meet up with two sisters, Wichita and Little Rock. These two young ladies have been hustling people long before the apocalypse and do so now. After tricking Tallahassee into giving up his guns, the two girls steal the boys' SUV and leave them to fend for themselves.

And where are they going? To Pacific Playland, an amusement park where Wichita says it's "zombie free."

But the boys catch up to them when the girls' stolen SUV breaks down and once more, they catch the boys unawares and take their new Hummer. Though this time they let the boys stay.

Soon, an uneasy alliance is formed and they travel together. They drive across the country, for some reason not seeing any zombies, and reach Hollywood. Here, they come across about ten zombies, and as they need to rest, Tallahassee says he knows where they can stay for the night.

They drive to where all the famous actors live and where do they go? Why, Bill Murray's house, of course.

But Bill's not dead, and he welcomes them with open arms. Only Bill isn't so good at playing jokes, and—dressed up as a zombie, with makeup on his face—he tries to scare Columbus who promptly shoots him with his shotgun…Ouch!

Oh well, it was a cameo anyway. With Bill dead, they stay the night in his house and by morning, the girls are gone. See, Wichita doesn't trust anyone, though the previous night, she did show signs that her hard exterior was crumbling with Columbus.

Tallahassee wants to go to Mexico on his hunt for more Twinkies but Columbus wants to go to the amusement park to find the girls. See, he's developed a crush on Wichita.

Tallahassee has a change of heart and the boys go together to see the girls. Meanwhile, the girls make it to Pacific Playland, and the first thing they do is put on the power. As the amusement park lights up, it's like a beacon to the zombies in the surrounding area.

Sorry to say but this drove me absolutely crazy. If the world has collapsed months ago, why would there still be power? And in a world where zombies are everywhere, wouldn't you want to be low key? To not want to attract attention to yourselves? So the last thing you would ever want to do is put on every light in an amusement park, lighting it up to the point it can be seen for miles around. Like I said, a few plot holes for the real zombie fan, but like I also said before, overlook these items, it's not that kind of movie where all the details need to be perfect.

So of course, as soon as the park is lit up, the zombies come and before you know it, the girls are trapped on a ride as the zombies try to get them.

This is the strongest part of the movie for any true zombie fan. Where the movie seemed to be on a budget to how many zombies they could use, here, at the amusement park, they pull out all the stops and there are enough zombies to make you feel that yes, this is what would happen if this was real life and a virus turned people into raging killers.

In the end, this film is more of a road trip movie, about four unlucky people who become a family. Some may not like this but others will understand what the movie is really about and let me say, I can't wait for the next installment in the franchise as a second movie is even now being made.

Just remember those rules and you'll be fine.

ABOUT THE WRITERS

Anthony Giangregorio is the author of 35 novels, almost all of them about zombies and has edited over 20 anthologies.

His work has appeared in Dead Science by Coscomentertainment, Dead Worlds: Un-dead Stories Volumes 1-7, and Wolves of War by Library of the Living Dead Press. He also has stories in End of Days: An Apocalyptic Anthology Vol. 1-5, the Book of the Dead series Vol. 1-6 by LDP, Zombie Zoology by Severed Press, and two anthologies with Pill Hill Press. He is also the creator of the popular action/zombie series titled Deadwater and his action/ horror novel Dead Rage is being optioned for a movie.

Check out his website at www.undeadpress.com.

Tony Schaab is a thirty-something writer, currently living in Indianapolis with his wife, dog, and daughter. In addition to having stories and articles published in multiple humor, horror, and sci-fi magazines and anthologies, Tony has a special affinity for zombies: he runs a zombie-centric review site, www.TheGOREScore.com, the content of which is also now available in two volumes of full-length printed books. He is currently working on authoring his next projects: the third installation of "The G.O.R.E. Score" series, and his first full-length fiction novel, "Zombies Can't Dance." In his free time, Tony works as a DJ, is an alumni member of the improvisational comedy troupe "IndyProv," and volunteers at his local Humane Society. Read more of his work at www.TonySchaab.com.

PLAYING GOD: A ZOMBIE NOVEL
by Jeffery Dye

It was supposed to be a regeneration virus to help soldiers on the battlefield—regrowing limbs and healing wounds— but a simple act of carelessness unleashed it on an unsuspecting world.

For the virus was not perfected, and once exposed, the host quickly dies, only to rise again as one of the undead.

As countries are quickly overrun, scientists and military teams battle to contain the outbreak.

There is no other option.

If the infection continues to spread, soon the entire globe will be consumed. And perhaps that will be a just punishment for a mankind that dared to try to play God.

DEAD HOUSE: A ZOMBIE GHOST STORY
by Keith Adam Luethke

The old mansion on the edge of town, aptly named Dead House, has a history of blood, pain, and death, but what Victor Leeds knows of this past only scratches the surface of the true horrors within.

But when his girlfriend is attacked by a shadowy figure one rainy night, he soon finds himself caught up in a world where the dead walk and ghostly wraiths abound. And to make matters worse, a pair of serial killers are fulfilling carefully made plans, and when they are done, the small town of Stormville, New York will run red. The last ingredient to open the gates of Hell, and plunge this small upstate town into madness, is rain.

And in Stormville, it pours by the gallons.

The Lazarus Culture
by Pasquale J. Morrone

Secret Service Agent Christopher Kearns had no idea what he was up against. Assigned on a temporary basis to the Center for Disease Control, he only knew that somehow it was connected to the lives of those the agency protected...namely, the President of the United States. If there were possible terrorist activities in the making, he could only guess it was at a red alert basis.

When Kearns meets and befriends Doctor Marlene Peterson of the Breezy Point Medical Center in Maryland, he soon finds that science fiction can indeed become a reality. In a solitary room walked a man with no vital signs: dead. The explanation he received came from Doctor Lee Fret, a man assigned to the case from the CDC. Something was attached to the brain stem. Something alive that was quickly spreading rapidly through Maryland and other states.

Kearns and his ragtag army of agents and medical personnel soon find themselves in a world of meaningless slaughter and mayhem. The armies of the walking dead were far more than mere zombies. Some began to change into whatever it was they ate. The government had found a way to reanimate the dead by implanting a parasite found on the tongue of the Red Snapper to the human brain. It looked good on paper, but it was a project straight from Hell. The dead now walked, but it wasn't a mystery.

It was The Lazarus Culture.

RISE OF THE DEAD
by Anthony Giangregorio

DEATH IS ONLY THE BEGINNING!

In less than forty-eight hours, more than half the globe was infected.
In another forty-eight, the rest would be enveloped.
The reason?

A science experiment gone horribly wrong which enabled the dead to walk, their flesh rotting on their bones even as they seek human prey.

Jeremy was an ordinary nineteen year old slacker. He partied too much and had done poorly in high school. After a night of drinking and drugs, he awoke to find the world a very different place from the one he'd left the night before.

The dead were walking and feeding on the living, and as Jeremy stepped out into a world gone mad, the dead spotting him alone and unarmed in the middle of the street,
he had to wonder if he would live long enough to see his twentieth birthday.

THE CHRONICLES OF JACK PRIMUS
BOOK ONE
by Michael D. Griffiths

Beneath the world of normalcy we all live in lies another world, one where supernatural beings exist.

These creatures of the night hunt us; want to feed on our very souls, though only a few know of their existence.

One such man is Jack Primus, who accidentally pierces the veil between this world and the next. With no other choice if he wants to live, he finds himself on the run, hunted by beings called the Xemmoni, an ancient race that sees humans as nothing but cattle. They want his soul, to feed on his very essence, and they will kill all who stand in their way. But if they thought Jack would just lie down and accept his fate, they were sorely mistaken. He didn't ask for this battle, but he knew he would fight them with everything at his disposal, for to lose is a fate worse than death.

He would win this war, and he would take down anyone who got in his way.

MONSTER PARTY
Edited by Anthony Giangregorio

Zombies, vampires, werewolves and ghosts are just a few of the monsters in this anthology.

But this isn't any anthology, you see, this is a party.

Or to be more to the point…a *Monster Party*.

Ever wonder what would happen if a werewolf and a zombie squared off? Or perhaps a vampire and a Frankenstein monster? Or better yet, how about a world where every conceivable monster is real and humans are their prey?

If those burning questions have been driving you mad, then look no further than this book.

So go on over to the buffet table, grab yourself a plate (the shrimp looks good) and get yourself a drink, and enjoy the fun ride that is the *Monster Party*.

THE WAR AGAINST THEM: A ZOMBIE NOVEL
by Jose Alfredo Vazquez

Mankind wasn't prepared for the onslaught.

An ancient organism is reanimating the dead bodies of its victims, creating worldwide chaos and panic as the disease spreads to every corner of the globe. As governments struggle to contain the disease, courageous individuals across the planet learn what it truly means to make choices as they struggle to survive.

Geopolitics meet technology in a race to save mankind from the worst threat it has ever faced. Doctors, military and soldiers from all walks of life battle to find a cure. For the dead walk, and if not stopped, they will wipe out all life on Earth. Humanity is fighting a war they cannot win, for who can overcome Death itself? Man versus the walking dead with the winner ruling the planet. Welcome to *The War Against Them*.

DEADTOWN: A DEADWATER STORY
BOOK 8

by Anthony Giangregorio

The world is a very different place now. The dead walk the land and humans hide in small towns with walls of stone and debris for protection, constantly keeping the living dead at bay.

Social law is gone and right and wrong is defined by the size of your gun.

UNWELCOME VISITORS

Henry Watson and his band of warrior survivalists become guests in a fortified town in Michigan. But when the kidnapping of one of the companions goes bad and men die, the group finds themselves on the wrong side of the law, and a town out for blood.

Trapped in a hotel, surrounded on all sides, it will be up to Henry to save the day with a gamble that may not only take his life, but that of his friends as well.

In a dead world, when justice is not enough, there is always vengeance.

END OF DAYS: AN APOCALYPTIC ANTHOLOGY
VOLUMES 1-3

Edited by Anthony Giangregorio

Our world is a fragile place.

Meteors, famine, floods, nuclear war, solar flares, and hundreds of other calamities can plunge our small blue planet into turmoil in an instant.

What would you do if tomorrow the sun went super nova or the world was swallowed by water, submerging the world into the cold darkness of the ocean? This anthology explores some of those scenarios and plunges you into total annihilation.

But remember, it's only a book, and tomorrow will come as it always does.

Or will it?

THE PLACE TO GO FOR ZOMBIE AND APOCALYPTIC FICTION

LIVING DEAD PRESS
WHERE THE DEAD WALK
www.livingdeadpress.com

www.ingramcontent.com/pod-product-compliance
Lightning Source LLC
Chambersburg PA
CBHW052023070526
44584CB00016B/1871